Controversy

the Humanist / Christian
Encounter

Controversy

the Humanist / Christian
Encounter

HECTOR HAWTON

℞ Prometheus Books

an ethical humanist press

923 Kensington Ave.
Buffalo, New York 14215

PEMBERTON BOOKS

First published 1971 by Pemberton Books
(Pemberton Publishing Co Ltd), 88 Islington
High Street, London N1 8 EN

ISBN 0 301 71021 7 *cloth*
      0 301 71022 5 *paper*

Printed in Great Britain by
Richard Clay (The Chaucer Press) Ltd,
Bungay, Suffolk

CONTENTS

ONE

THE CHANGING CLIMATE OF OPINION

In 1963 the Bishop of Woolwich raised a storm by writing in a popular paperback what had been said about atheism more discreetly and allusively in learned journals for some time. He wrote: 'Suppose that all such atheism does is to destroy an idol, and that we can and must get on without a God "out there" at all? Have we seriously faced the possibility that to abandon such an idol may in future be the only way of making Christianity meaningful, except to the few remaining equivalents of flat-earthers (just as to have clung earlier to the God "up there" would have made it impossible in the modern world for any but primitive peoples to believe in the Gospel)? Perhaps, after all, the Freudians are right, that such a God—the God of traditional popular theology—*is* a projection, and perhaps we are being called to live without that projection in any form.' (*Honest to God* p 17)

If this is no more than a forceful way of denying an anthropomorphic idea of God—the Old Man in the sky—it says nothing very new. It certainly did not merit the alarm and abuse it aroused. But it was taken more seriously by traditionalists like T. E Utley, and agnostics like Alisdair MacIntyre. The former said that it raised 'a question of discipline which cannot be shirked without the gravest repercussions on the whole Anglican Communion.... It is not always clear, indeed, whether the Bishop's aim is to convince agnostics that they can conscientiously go to church or to persuade Christians that there is no real need to do so. At the lowest, he seems to me to be violating the principles of honest commerce by trying to sell as Christian a commodity that bears no relation to the historical and accepted meaning of that word.' (*Sunday Telegraph*, March 24, 1963)

These are harsh words, but Alisdair MacIntyre went farther still. 'What is striking about Dr Robinson's book is first and foremost that he is an atheist' (*Encounter* September 1963)

As Dr Robinson bluntly advocated 'Non-theistic Christianity' this interpretation is not surprising, though a closer scrutiny suggests that it is mistaken. There are many degrees between pure atheism and pure theism. A similar confusion once led to Spinoza's being regarded simultaneously as a notorious atheist and 'a God-intoxicated man'. Dr Robinson has explicitly rejected the pantheism of Spinoza, and he is certainly not an atheist in the sense that Hume was.

The furore has died down, but it had the merit of bringing to light very vividly the revolution in Protestant theology associated with the names of Paul Tillich, Rudolph Bultmann and Dietrich Bonhoeffer. Their concern was with the obvious fact that Christianity, as presented by the main churches, no longer appeals to the majority of educated people in this secular age. The liberal theologians in the recent past had tried desperately to close the credibility gap and they failed. Modernism, as it was inappropriately called, is already out-of-date. Protestants have largely abandoned it, though the movement is stirring once more into uneasy life in the Roman Catholic Church. The mantle of Modernism has fallen upon the Humanists who try to present a clearer and more acceptable outlook to modern man than is afforded by an emasculated Christianity.

THE RISE OF HUMANISM

The rise of contemporary Humanism is one consequence of the decline of religion. Humanism, of course, long antedates the organizations that have sprung up as vehicles of its public expression. At different times Humanists have worn different labels—Freethinkers, Secularists, Rationalists

—but the substance of their beliefs was the same. Throughout this book I shall use Humanist and Rationalist as interchangeable terms. There are differences of emphasis between the respective organizations but their main principles, and above all their scale of values, are substantially the same. What they believe is restricted by the available evidence. In that sense they use reason as a scientist does, namely as a tool for correlating our experiences. Consequently they reject any appeal to an oracle—eg an infallible Church or sacred Scriptures. This could equally well be described as Naturalism in contrast to Supernaturalism. It follows that man is not in any way regarded as being apart from the rest of nature.

What makes man unique is the possession of a more complex brain which gives him the power of conceptual thought and the means of communication through language. Man is a social animal, therefore he must devise rules to enable social life to be carried on with the maximum of satisfaction and the minimum of friction. He must solve his problems with his own unaided human resources. We are gaining sufficient knowledge of natural processes to ameliorate the conditions of life on this planet for the entire human race. But progress cannot be measured solely by the increase of power. What matters most is the extension of the area of human concern—the moral decision to use knowledge to decrease misery and create a society in which all members can reach the ceiling of their capacities.

Rationalists, Humanists, Secularists are sometimes lumped together under the generic term 'unbelievers'. This is obviously a loaded word. The Humanist believes as much, if not more, than the orthodox Christian; but he believes different things. To the Moslem, all Christians are unbelievers. The more drastic epithet 'infidel' is seldom used today. Religious controversy has become more polite. Even the Roman Catholic Church has ceased to castigate Protestants as 'heretics'. They are now described as 'separated brethren'.

Machinery has been set up for dialogues with atheists. The preference given to 'dialogue' rather than 'debate' is another symptom of the remarkable change in the climate of opinion. In a dialogue you do not seek to score off your opponent; you try to understand his point of view and discover what common ground, if any, exists.

FLOGGING A DEAD HORSE

If the Church no longer hurls anathemas and consigns its opponents to the flames, neither do those who reject its message echo Voltaire's passionate indignation. Religion seemed evil to Lucretius because such monstrous things as human sacrifice were done in its name. It seemed infamous to Voltaire because men were broken on the wheel for refusal to conform.

No such dreadful deeds are excused by contemporary religion. Indeed the genocide and torture which have been practised in our own time had no connection with religion. It is tempting to think that the decline of religious influence makes it unnecessary even to take the claims of institutional religion seriously enough to dispute them. A generation has grown up without any interest in the old doctrines, and unfortunately lacking a sense of history. They feel that the issues have been settled. The Humanist who takes part in religious controversy is accused of flogging a dead horse.

But is the horse really dead? I have no doubt that when the history of our time comes to be written one of the most significant features will be seen to be the decline of religion. Throughout vast areas of the world—eg Russia and China —there is now an atheistic Establishment. Elsewhere, church-going has catastrophically declined. The ecumenical movement, with its hopes of closer co-operation if not formal reunion of the churches, is a recognition of the need to close the ranks. The real enemy is not seen as militant atheism but apathy and indifference, and this is because the lines of communication between the Christian churches and the mass of the people have gone dead. In an attempt to restore them the creeds and the Bible are being rewritten in modern language. The Catholic liturgies are being translated from Latin into the vernacular. The religious horse is not dead, but it is very sick.

Nevertheless, in comparison with organized Humanism, the churches are still in an immensely strong position. Whereas the churches count their members and income in millions, Humanists count theirs in thousands. In Great Britain the Church is still entrenched in the corridors of power. The Church of England is 'by law established'. Corporate worship is enforced in schools by law at the moment of writing. The Churches have privileged access to broadcasting.

It would be rash to suppose that empty pews necessarily imply a total lack of interest in religion itself. Newspapers understand this very well, as can be judged by the coverage given to the pronouncements of religious leaders, the dissensions within the Catholic Church, the controversy over birth control. National newspapers do not give space to topics that bore their readers; nor do television producers. What plainly emerges from a survey of religious publicity is that the interest has shifted from obscure points of doctrine to questions of practical conduct. The conflict a hundred years ago was centred on matters of belief; today it is focused on morals. The activities of powerful religious pressure groups in the lobbies of Parliament when reform of the laws on abortion and divorce was proposed leave no doubt that these are forces still to be reckoned with.

MORALS WITHOUT RELIGION

Humanism, however, is not just a negative attitude concerned only with criticizing religious beliefs. It has a positive contribution to make as an alternative way of life. In a phrase, it is 'morality without religion'. But conduct and belief cannot be completely disjoined. Traditional Christianity teaches that the moral law was revealed by God and must be obeyed. Whether right and wrong are known through the pronouncements of a church, or by the action of some Inner Light on the individual conscience, is secondary. The Christian acts as he does because of certain beliefs. This becomes clear in any dialogue between Christians and Humanists. Sooner or later they come to this insuperable obstacle and fall silent.

The reason why Humanists reject Christianity is quite simple: they do not believe it is true. They may, or may not, be able to give a coherent account of why they cannot accept ideas that seem so certain to many of their fellows— some of the highest intellectual capacity. They may feel the puzzlement once voiced by that fine Humanist, Gilbert Murray: 'I confess it seems strange to me as I write here, to reflect that at this moment many of my friends and most of my fellow creatures are, as far as one can judge, quite confident that they possess supernatural knowledge. As a rule, each individual belongs to some body which has received in writing the results of a divine revelation. I cannot share in any such feeling.' (*Five Stages of Greek Religion* p 171)

In the half century that has passed since Murray made that confession far fewer people share the confidence of which he speaks. Yet the puzzle remains and the Humanist must come to terms with it. To utterly ignore the impact of one of the most formative influences in human history is a crippling posture for anyone who sets out on the adventurous journey of thinking for himself and passing judgement on received opinions.

The object of this book is to examine some of the controversies in which such an independent thinker can hardly fail to become involved. By listening attentively to the best case that can be presented on both sides we cannot fail to clarify our own ideas and, if necessary, revise them.

I make no apology for approaching many of these problems historically. None is needed. Those who hold with Henry Ford that 'History is bunk', need read no further. I do not believe, for example, that the existence of God, or the immortality of the soul, can be usefully discussed without reference to how mankind came to form such extraordinary ideas. Similarly the persistence of Christianity and the failure of its high ideals in practice cannot be understood if we simply look on it as a doctrine in a book. The paradox is resolved when we realize that as a social force Christianity has been changed by the world in the two thousand years of its existence far more than it has changed the world.

IS HUMANISM ENOUGH?

More and more people seek a new outlook that will coordinate the great advances of knowledge and provide a more credible frame of reference than religion; but they sometimes complain that a purely scientific philosophy does not satisfy their inner demands. It is important to try to understand the attitude of those who have lost the old faith and cannot find anything better than 'a dusty answer'. A strictly rational attitude strikes a chill. They feel, with Wordsworth, that 'we murder to dissect'. It seems to lead to a 'brave new world', a cold, inhuman utopia, colourless and unfeeling.

Victorian literature is haunted by the pathos of vanished simplicities. The crumbling of the citadels of orthodoxy was viewed by Tennyson with helpless dismay, by Browning with uneasy defiance, by Matthew Arnold with wistful melancholy.

> *And here we are as on a darkling plain,*
> *Swept with confused alarm of struggle and fight,*
> *Where ignorant armies clash by night.*

Nor has the poetic vision become brighter since. The mood of disillusion was rhetorically expressed by the young Bertrand Russell in a well-known passage from *The Free Man's Worship*—though he later looked back on it rather apologetically.

'A strange mystery it is that Nature, omnipotent but

blind, in the revolutions of her secular hurryings through the abysses of space, has brought forth at last a child, subject still to her power, but gifted with sight, with knowledge of good and evil, with the capacity of judging all the works of his unthinking mother.'

For T. S. Eliot the darkling plain became the desert of man's hopes.

> *This is the dead land,*
> *This is the cactus land.*
> *Here the stone images*
> *Are raised, here they receive*
> *The supplication of a dead man's hand*
> *Under the twinkle of a fading star.*

Without the hope of immortality, or the safety of the belief in God, the individual seems at first to be disorientated. The vogue of Existentialism after the last war expressed this sense of abandonment. *Angst* became a fashionable word, but the anxiety was real and only the way of voicing it was new. It was the panic of a lost child too immature to stand alone.

> *I a stranger and afraid*
> *In a world I never made ...*

Science was seen as the destroyer of security leaving man without illusions. We must learn to live without opium, said George Eliot. Life, said the Existentialists, is a journey into Nothingness. We are victims of a cosmic shipwreck, thrown into the world only to be annihilated. 'Man is a useless passion.' (Sartre)

In less flamboyant language many people undoubtedly react in this way. The Humanist must try to enter into this unhappy state of mind with imaginative sympathy. It arises from a feeling that without religion no purpose can be discerned in the cosmic process, no meaning in our brief lives. We therefore seem to be thrown back either on a tight-lipped stoicism or sheer despair.

There are two ways of dealing with this predicament. In the first place what is the sense of asking whether the physical universe has a purpose? We might as well ask if an earthquake has a purpose. The idea that the great Lisbon earthquake was due to the inscrutable purpose of God infuriated Voltaire. Postulating the existence of divine Providence to account for natural catastrophies is no way of consoling the victims.

Secondly, it is simply not true that religion necessarily reduces anxiety. It is a sheer travesty to suggest that a scientific philosophy leads to unyielding despair by robbing us of a fairy tale as joyous and innocent as Father Christmas.

LESSONS OF HISTORY

The history of religion shows that it often drives men to despair and impels them to commit acts of violence and cruelty.

How un-Greek, for example, was the note struck by Augustine. The pursuit of virtue had been regarded by Aristotle as a rational endeavour, and he believed that if men were prepared to discuss the problem calmly and sensibly they could arrive at some agreement about the Good Life.

For Augustine, however, what was formerly regarded as 'unwise' became 'a foul and accursed joy'. He gives one of the most moving accounts ever written of the anguish of a mind divided against itself:

'But I wretched, most wretched, in the very commencement of my early youth, begged chastity of Thee, and said "Give me chastity and continence, only not yet!"' He cries out in despair: 'Whence is this monstrousness? and to what end?' And yet again: 'Thus soul-sick was I, and tormented, accusing myself much more severely than my wont, rolling and turning me in my chain, till that were wholly broken, whereby I now was but just, but still was, held.'

The 'dry light' of the clear, Hellenic sky had gone. Something had entered the consciousness of Western man, like opium from the East, but it brought no dreams of delight. In a mass-hysteria, which Gibbon described with such fine irony, many Christians clamoured for martyrdom. They found their ecstasy under the flagellating rod, and if no one would whip them they lashed themselves. They went out in droves to live as hermits in the Egyptian desert. Some of them, like Origen, castrated themselves.

Scientific learning was abhorred. Twice the great library of Alexandria was looted by religious fanatics, first by Christians, then by Mahommedans. Darkness settled over Europe and lasted for seven centuries. The distinctively Christian culture that emerged was distorted by the 'soul-sickness' that afflicted Augustine. There are few more preposterous legends than that which describes the Middle Ages as a sort of Golden Age. Modern scholarship has surely disposed once and for all of this fantasy; but it is only necessary to look at the carvings in the great cathedrals to see in what a demon-haunted world medieval man cowered.

The Inquisition, the public burning of heretics and witches by Catholics and Protestants alike, the massacres and the ferocity of the religious wars—are these delightful dreams which the dour Humanist forbids?

At the present time it would be difficult to think of a more anti-social and fundamentally immoral document than Pope Paul's encyclical banning the use of contraception although we are faced with a population explosion which must doom millions as yet unborn to misery and starvation. Many loyal Catholics, struggling to observe the ban, are plunged into a conflict compared with which loss of faith would be liberation.

TWO

THE GOD OF RELIGION

'I BELIEVE in God the Father, maker of heaven and earth...'
This affirmation is central to Christianity, although recently
some Christians have considerably qualified the meaning of
the words. They are, however, still recited in the services
of the main Christian denominations and the majority of
churchgoers accept them in a plain, straightforward sense.
Whatever may be doubtful in the recorded sayings of Jesus,
we cannot deny that he believed in such a God, not the God
of the philosophers but the God of Abraham, Isaac and
Jacob. Indeed, all world-religions with the possible exception of Buddhism, are theistic. That is why churches, synagogues, temples and mosques have been endured for thousands of years. They exist primarily for worship.

The meaning of 'religion' can be so broadened that it
embraces mere morality without reference to God or worship, but what is gained in breadth is lost in definiteness. A
category which includes both atheism and theism is so
comprehensive that it serves no useful purpose. It is little
more than a device to remove the vague discomfort felt
by those who have been conditioned to believe that there
is something discreditable if not dangerous in outright
denial.

Some, though not all of those who declare themselves
agnostics, are too queasy to say frankly that they are
atheists, though they behave like atheists in every way. It is
possible to answer the question 'Do you believe in God?'
with an honest 'Don't know'; but it is also possible that by
doing so we may yield to a sneaking desire to play safe.
This is what Engels meant when he described agnosticism
as 'shamefaced materialism'.

Why people believe, or half-believe, in God is a psychological question. It could still be true that God exists even if the reasons we give for believing it are the result of indoctrination. Conceivably, there could be a proof of God's existence too abstruse for most people to grasp. They would then be believing what was true on faith and their version of the truth would be limited and distorted. Thus most people believe that a material object is composed of atoms, but their idea of what an atom is like is as crude as that of Democritus. So it is not enough to say that the Heavenly Father is no more than a projection made in childhood of the human father, or a social projection of the tribal chief or king into the Divine King. On the other hand unless we have some good reason to suppose that these projections are more than shadows cast by the human mind we must surely assume that they are purely subjective. It is a sound rule not to multiply hypotheses unnecessarily.

RELIGIOUS EXPERIENCE

A number of defences are adopted by theists. They claim to have had personal experience of the presence of God and that this is so convincing it is beyond argument. Alternatively, or additionally, some claim that the existence of God can be demonstrated by logic. Finally, it is contended that even though the logical proofs may not be conclusive they at least provide a strong presumption in favour of theism. God can be postulated as the hypothesis that best fits the facts both of personal experience and of the law and order in the universe.

If there are rational grounds for believing that God exists we need not be disturbed by the admittedly subjective imagery in which he has been conceived down through the ages, it is said. Behind the Indian Brahma, the Greek Zeus, the tribal Yaweh, there may be a real Being who can be apprehended imperfectly by the analogies of King, Lawgiver, Father.

Let us look at the argument from religious experience. William James made the first serious psychological study of the subject in *Varieties of Religious Experience*. He defined religion as 'the feelings, acts, and experiences of individual men in their solitude, so far as they apprehend themselves to stand in relation to whatever they may consider divine'. This, however, presupposes that they already believe in *something* that is divine, whether or not they call it 'God'. The supposed unanimity of mystical experience, James tells us, has been exaggerated:

'It has been both ascetic and antinomianly self-indulgent within the Christian Church. It is dualistic in Samkhya, and monistic in Vedanta philosophy. I called it pantheistic, but the great Spanish mystics are anything but pantheists. ... The fact is that the mystical feeling of enlargement, union and emancipation has no specific intellectual content of its own. It is capable of forming matrimonial alliances with material furnished by the most diverse philosophies and theologies, provided only they can find a place in their framework for its peculiar emotional mood.'

The point is an important one. The claim that religious experience gives us information about a spiritual reality must meet the objection that it gives us too much information. The various types of entities of which different individuals claim to have privileged insight denied to ordinary vision is conflicting. The lives of the saints even within the framework of Christianity are full of accounts of visionary experiences that are contradictory and sometimes obviously pathological. Were the voices that St Joan heard more objective than the daemon of Socrates? Was it truly the voice of the risen Christ that spoke to St Paul on the road to Damascus?

The objection of Hobbes has never been satisfactorily answered: 'For if any man pretend to me that God hath spoken to him ... immediately, and I make doubt of it, I cannot easily perceive what argument he can produce to oblige me to believe it. ... To say he hath spoken to him in a dream is no more than to say that he dreamed that God spoke to him.' (*Leviathan* Chapter 32)

The Bacchic dancers in their frenzy undoubtedly believed that they were possessed by Dionysus; similarly the devotees of Voodoo today believe they are in communion in their trances with their own dark god. The peasant girl who saw an apparition of the Virgin Mary on the foothills of the Pyrenees was convinced of its reality, and millions still believe her testimony. But in all these cases belief in the existence of the object preceded the experience. Mystics who believe that God, or Dionysus, or the Virgin Mary has spoken to them had already believed in the real existence of God, Dionysus or the Virgin Mary.

We cannot doubt the reality of the experience itself; what is questioned is the interpretation. Apart from the above exceptional cases, the ordinary devout Christian, for example, is convinced that God is like an invisible companion with whom he can engage in colloquy. He has at times such a vivid awareness of the presence of God that no argument can shake it. It is as though he is in radio contact with a supernatural world. He can switch on and talk to God. This gives him great comfort and is one source of the immense strength of religious feeling. But it is not because of this feeling that he believes in God; he gets the feeling *because* he already believes in God.

In that case, it may be asked, how did he come to believe in God in the first place? Why should he start to believe in something wholly outside his ordinary experience? There could be a variety of reasons. The western world may be witnessing a decline of religious practice but the idea of God is part of our heritage. It is not something that people deliberately choose; it is part of the ideological world into which they are born.

The belief was much firmer in the ancient world, yet with slight modification what Robertson Smith wrote in *The Religion of the Ancient Semites* was as true of Europe until the beginning of the twentieth century: 'You could not be absolutely irreligious. It was a social obligation. You were born into a circle of divine beings as well as kinsfolk. Society was made up of gods and men.'

PHENOMENA OF CONVERSION

Obviously there was no need of faith before it occurred to men to doubt. But even now the doubt does not extend usually to the bare existence of God. 'I can worship just as well in the open air as in church' is often given as an excuse for Sunday golf. When the idea of God has been firmly imprinted on the mind of a child it lurks in the subconscious even if he subsequently becomes an agnostic. In sudden, unaccountable conversions the repressed idea comes to the surface.

In his autobiographical *Surprised by Joy*, C. S. Lewis describes his own religious conversion. 'I was driven to Whipsnade one sunny morning. When we set out I did not believe that Jesus Christ is the Son of God, and when we reached the Zoo I did.'

Canon Hugh Montefiore was brought up as a Jew. At the age of seventeen he had a sudden religious experience: 'In the morning I was a Jew: in the evening a Christian as well. If I said Christ appeared to me I might be using the conventional language of piety, but I would not be strictly honest. I saw in my soul One whom instinctively I knew to be Jesus Christ, full of light and power, and I knew that thereafter my life could never be the same.' (*Journeys in Belief* ed. Bernard Dixon p 180)

The intensity of religious experience can be no guarantee of its objectivity. We might as well suppose that the vividness of visions induced by hallucinogens proves that they reveal a new dimension of reality. Indeed, the claim has been made that lysergic acid 'expands consciousness'. It was advanced in all seriousness by Aldous Huxley who drew the conclusion that the austerities practised in the past by mystics could now be by-passed by this more painless method of penetrating behind the world of mere appearance.

'For an aspiring mystic to revert, in the present state of knowledge, to prolonged fasting and violent self-flagellation would be as senseless as it would for an aspiring cook to behave like Charles Lamb's Chinaman, who burned down the house in order to roast a pig. Knowing as he does (or at least as he can know, if he so desires) what are the chemical conditions of transcendental experience, the aspiring mystic should turn for technical help to the specialist—in pharmacology, in biochemistry, in physiology and neurology, in psychology and psychiatry and parapsychology.' (*Heaven and Hell* p 64)

Mystical experiences cannot be self-validating. If they are so regarded it would be impossible to distinguish between reality and illusion. Yet the higher forms of mysticism are not vulnerable to criticism because no verbal interpretation is attempted. There is no reason to dismiss all of these admittedly rare experiences as pathological. Those who have had them cannot communicate what they have felt in words. Unfortunately they sometimes write books to explain the futility of writing books.

EASTERN AND WESTERN MYSTICISM

Eastern mysticism is not concerned so much with intellectual formulations as with the quest for a unique experience, a sense of illumination and oneness with the cosmic process. The western scientist describes the situation of man as part of Nature—essentially an intellectual exercise; the eastern mystic seeks to *feel* what it is like to be part of Nature.

Commentators on the experience which Patanjali calls *samadhi* and Zen *satori* and Buddhists *nirvana* are compelled to resort to metaphysical and allegorical language because there is no other way of referring to what they regard as essentially incommunicable. But 'God' is not an essential part of their vocabulary. It is true that the original teaching was vulgarized and distorted by the very scholasticism and superstition which it rejected. The great difference between eastern and western mysticism, however, is that whereas the Christian seeks union with a divine Being wholly other than himself, the eastern mystic—to put it in simple terms at the expense of strict accuracy—seeks to *become* God. This is obviously to use the word in a very different sense, though some doubtfully orthodox Christians have used similar language and been rebuked by the ecclesiastical authorities. For example, Eckhart wrote: 'As the Godhead is nameless, and all naming is alien to Him, so also the soul is nameless; for it is here the same as God.'

'Those who know do not tell, and those who tell do not know,' said Lao Tzu. We cannot dispute with a man who says nothing. We cannot argue about the ineffable, the nameless. The position of the mystic is impregnable as long as he does not expose himself to debate. But this type of experience, like any other, is open to scientific scrutiny. It is not only in religious ecstasy that an individual feels the hard boundaries of the ego dissolve. The lover at the climax of sexual congress may sometimes feel such a oneness with his beloved that ordinary consciousness is lost without becoming totally unaware.

> *Oh night that joined the lover*
> *To the beloved bride*
> *Transfiguring them each unto the other.*

This is not, as might be thought, a poem of earthly love. It is entitled *Songs of the soul in rapture at having arrived at the height of perfection, which is union with God by the road of spiritual negation.* And the author is the Spanish mystic, St John of the Cross. The translations by Roy Campbell in the Penguin edition are introduced by Father M. G. D'Arcy SJ, who writes: 'There are those who will refuse to believe that this mystical verse is anything more than concealed human passion, and such critics persuade themselves that saints, like St John of the Cross, are victims of some pathological disorder.... To those who have ears to

hear, the accents of a genuine experience are unmistake-
able, and the unprejudiced reader must, I think, become
conscious of an unearthly glow in the verse, a strange quality which invades the images and persuades him that there
must be a love which is a secret between God and the soul.'

THE OCEANIC FEELING

Not many mystics are poets, but if erotic imagery is not
to be taken at its face value we would have to treat with the
same seriousness the outpourings of canonized nuns about
the embraces of the divine Bridegroom, and their visions of
nursing the Holy Child. Yet it is just a fact that similar
experiences can be induced by drugs and are found in certain types of mental illness. Some epileptics have described
a sense of 'oneness' with the universe immediately before a
seizure. Yogic deep-breathing exercises are known to lead
to high concentrations of carbon dioxide in the blood, and
this too can give rise to visionary experiences. So can fasting, combined with severe self-flagellation and reinforced
by solitude. Many ascetics have used these techniques by
withdrawing to a cave or to the desert, and they have been
rewarded by visions. The Catholic Church employs a
spiritual director to guard against false visions inspired, it is
said, by demonic agencies, though how to tell the false from
the genuine is not clear.

In more primitive civilizations mescalin and other drugs
have been deliberately used to produce hallucinations. Self-
hypnotism or the flashing of a stroboscopic lamp can open
the gates of psychedelic illusion and result in a trance. So
far from 'expanding consciousness' these techniques narrow
it down to a fantasy realm which excludes the larger
and richer world of human love, friendship and social
life.

Freud attempted to provide a psychoanalytical explanation of some of the phenomena. He termed the mystic sense
of union with 'the All' the 'oceanic feeling'. When the
Hindu seeks to merge his identity with 'Atman', the Abso-

lute, the One Reality behind the veil of illusory diversity, he is regressing, according to Freud to an infantile state of mind. But Freud doubted whether it inspired the need for religion, despite its obvious presence in certain varieties of religious experience.

'I cannot discover this "oceanic" feeling in myself...' he wrote. 'Thus we are entirely willing to acknowledge that the "oceanic" feeling exists in many people, and we are disposed to relate it to an early stage in ego-feeling; the further question then arises what claim this feeling has to be regarded as the source of the need for religion. To me this claim does not seem very forcible. Surely a feeling can only be a source of energy when it is itself the expression of a strong need.... I could not point to any need in childhood so strong as that for a father's protection. Thus the part played by the "oceanic" feeling, which I suppose seeks to reinstate limitless narcissism cannot possibly take the first place. The derivation of the religious attitude can be followed back in clear outline as far as the child's feeling of helplessness. There may be something else behind this, but for the present it is wrapped in obscurity.' (*Civilization and its Discontents* pp 20–1)

Be that as it may, the problem of religious experience raises the question of two opposed concepts of God. For the pantheist he is wholly immanent—ie identical with the cosmic process. Spinoza regarded God and Nature as synonymous. When Einstein was questioned about his religion he said he believed in the God of Spinoza; and this has sometimes been construed unwarrantably as an admission of theism.

VARIETIES OF THEISM

The God of theism is transcendent. He existed before the beginning of the world and would go on existing if the world ended. As theologians find it necessary to pay every conceivable metaphysical compliment to the object of their worship, they solve the apparent contradiction by asserting

that God is *both* immanent and transcendent. This is the
source of the confused talk about 'the death of God' and
'non-theistic Christianity'.

Bonhoeffer seemed very daring when he said that
modern, secular man must live as though God did not exist
and that Christianity today must be 'religionless'. All he
was attacking was the popular idea of God as *deus ex
machina*. The only novelty is the paradoxical language in
which this is expressed. 'The God who makes us live in this
world without using him as a working hypothesis is the
God before whom we are ever standing. Before God and
with him we live without God. God allows himself to be
edged out of the world and that is exactly the way in which
he can be with us and help us.'

Those who imagine that Bonhoeffer is saying something
revolutionary about man not needing God any longer now
that he has 'come of age' should read on: 'To this extent
we may say that the process we have described by which the
world came of age was an abandonment of a false conception of God, and a clearing of the decks for the God of the
Bible, who conquers power and space in the world by his
weakness. This must be the starting point for our "worldly"
interpretation.' (Letters and Papers from Prison p 164)

So it is back to the Bible after a tortuous, circular tour.
This is characteristic of the double-talk of fashionable
theology. Another example is to be found in Paul Tillich's
The Shaking of the Foundations in which Dr Robinson
found inspiration for his own recasting of popular religion.
Tillich contended that God is not a projection 'out there' of
whose existence we have to convince ourselves, but the
Ground of our very being. 'The name of this infinite and
inexhaustible depth and ground of all being is *God*. That
depth is what the word God means. If that word has not
much meaning for you, translate it, and speak of the depths
of your life, of the source of your being, of your ultimate
concern, of what you take seriously without any reservation.
Perhaps in order to do so, you must forget everything

traditional that you have learned about God, perhaps even that word itself.' (p 63)

RELIGIOUS EXISTENTIALISM

What theologians of this school appear to be saying is that God is not *a* Being but Being itself, and that Being—the Ground of the world—has certain characteristics. This metaphysical language makes little appeal to British empiricists though it is still in vogue on the continent. It derives from the German philosopher, Martin Heidegger who has influenced both Christian and atheistic Existentialism.

An exposition of these terms is given by Dr John Macquarrie in *Studies in Christian Existentialism*. He objects to the question 'Does God exist?' because it implies the idea of God as a possible existent entity, just as to ask whether a planet beyond Pluto exists implies that there might be such a planet. A scientific question is of a different logical order from a religious question. To be religious the question should be about the character, not of God—as one might expect—but of Being:

'God is the religious word for Being, understood as gracious. The words "God" and "Being" are not synonymous, for Being may have the character of indifference, and in that case would not be called "God" nor would any religious attitude to it be appropriate. "Being" can be equated with "God" only if Being has the character of grace and is responsive to man's existential predicament. Now Being cannot itself be regarded as an entity, for it is manifestly absurd to say "Being exists" or "Being is". Being does not itself belong within the category of particular beings—or "entities" as they may be called to avoid confusion—of which one can assert that they either exist or do not exist.' (p 12)

This highly abstruse formulation, however, turns out to be little more than a new, esoteric label on very old wine. For if we ask how we can know that Being is gracious—assuming that the question is meaningful—we are told that we know it by faith in a revelation. 'The impossibility of demonstration in these matters is simply a consequence of what we have learned from the analysis of man himself—that he is finite, that his is not the godlike but rather the worm's-eye view, that so long as he is *homo viator* he lacks the unclouded clarity of vision and must go forward in the attitude of faith, or in the risk of faith. . . . When challenged to produce the credentials of his subject, the theologian cannot in the nature of the case offer a proof, but he can describe this area of experience in which his discourse about God is meaningful, he can ask his questioner whether he recognizes his own existence in the Christian doctrine of man as finite, responsible and sinful, and whether he finds hidden in himself the question of God.' (pp 15–16)

The Humanist will admit that he is both finite and responsible, but he does not recognize man as innately sinful, nor can he understand the meaning of God 'hidden in himself'. Instead of this flight into metaphysics most Humanists would probably prefer Karl Barth's forthright statement: 'Belief cannot argue with unbelief; it can only preach to it.' For it comes to the same thing in the end.

THREE

THE GOD OF THE PHILOSOPHERS

MUCH less is heard nowadays of alleged logical proofs of the existence of God, although it is still the official doctrine of the Roman Catholic Church that a logical demonstration is possible. No particular proof is singled out as authoritative; you take your choice. What the Church condemns, however, is Fideism: namely, the view that God's existence can be known only by faith.

Thomism—the system constructed by St Thomas Aquinas in the thirteenth century—was pronounced the official philosophy of the Church by Leo XIII in 1879, and its status was reaffirmed by Pius XII in *Humani Generis*, when he denounced the type of Fideism implied by the religious Existentialism derived from Kierkegaard. Such a ruling is not an infallible pronouncement but it is—or was until recently—considered dangerous to express disagreement with it. The seriousness of disputing such a pronouncement of the *magisterium*—the supreme voice of the Church's teaching authority—is shown by the revolt of a substantial minority of both clergy and laymen against the ban on contraception in Pope Paul's encyclical *Humanae Vitae*.

Certainly in many seminaries throughout the Catholic world the five proofs of God's existence advanced by Aquinas are still received as though they were as certain as Euclid. The parallel is interesting and fatal to Thomist claims for the simple reason that geometry is a closed, deductive system. It tells us what follows from its axioms and postulates, but it does not tell us whether *real* space is Euclidean or non-Euclidean. Logic alone cannot be used to prove that something *exists*, hence the whole attempt to prove the existence of God, or of anything else, by purely logical means is bound to fail.

Nevertheless, those Christians who reject the possibility of proving God's existence throw away a useful weapon. (At least it would be invaluable if it were valid.) They are then obliged to rest their faith either on the shaky foundations of subjective experience or on the still more dubious blind leap of faith. Pascal and Kierkegaard are the outstanding opponents of metaphysical rationalism. For them an impassable gulf is fixed between God and man. It cannot be bridged by reason. God is 'the absolutely Other'.

It is surely to the credit of the medieval Scholastics and their modern successors that they had the utmost respect for reason. If you knew by incontrovertible arguments that God existed you had solid grounds, they held, for thinking that religious experience is not an illusion. Otherwise, how can you be sure?

Alas, the 'proofs' have not stood up to critical examination. The joint attacks of Hume and Kant were so devastating that there is little to add in spite of recent efforts to reformulate them in more sophisticated terms.

THE COSMOLOGICAL ARGUMENT

It would be tedious to analyse in detail the various proofs offered. They are mostly closely connected, and with the exception of the purely logical 'ontological Argument' they are based on appearances of the universe in which we find ourselves. They do not derive from narrowly personal experience but from the common experience, of a common world.

The arguments run as follows: We can observe, for example, that every effect is preceded by a cause, therefore unless we admit an infinite regress, there must be a First Cause. Similarly, we find order in Nature, and this cannot have arisen by chance; there must be an Orderer. Again, Nature seems to be constructed on a plan, therefore there must be an intelligent Planner or Designer.

Many people vaguely feel that there *must* be an explanation on these lines and 'God' seems to fill the gap. It is because of this inarticulate feeling that explicit atheism is confined to a small minority, though religion is in decline and people who shrink from denying that God exists, carry on as though he did not. Bryan Wilson, an Oxford sociologist, summed up this odd situation: 'Long ago Nietzsche mistakenly announced: God is dead; in fact, of course, he, too, is just one of the retired.' (*The Twentieth Century* Autumn 1961)

Something must have started it all, people feel, when they look up at the stars. This 'something' is at the heart of the Cosmological Argument. It is stated with his usual clarity and conciseness by Aquinas:

'We discover in phenomena an order of efficient causes. But we do not find, what is not possible, anything which is the efficient cause of itself, which is impossible. It is also impossible to go on to infinity with efficient causes; because in an ordered series of efficient causes the first is the cause of the one in the middle and the one in the middle is the cause of the last, whether or not these intermediates are one or many. Take away the cause and you take away the effect. Therefore, if there were not a first there would not be a last or any in the middle which is plainly not the case. Therefore we must postulate a First Efficient Cause, which all men name God.' (*Summa Theologica* i (ii) 3)

It looks highly plausible, but before scrutinizing the logic take a look at the typography. The conclusion does not make quite the same impression if we write: 'Therefore we must postulate a first efficient cause which all men name god.' Too little attention has been paid to the emotive effect of capital letters in religious debate. If you write God or Being or Ground instead of god or being or ground some curious psychological mechanism comes into play and an extra significance is insinuated into otherwise ordinary words. One reason for the misty profundity that infects so much German metaphysics is that in German, nouns are written with an initial capital.

THE CONCEPT OF CAUSALITY

Then consider the tricky word 'cause' which looks innocent enough because we use it continually in everyday speech. It is an extremely useful word for practical purposes: even so it is very hard to fix *the* cause of a particular happening. To a coroner the verdict on a car smash may be given as 'accidental'. But the cause of the accident may just as well be the carelessness of a motorist. The cause of his carelessness may be due to drunkenness, and so on. The slippery condition of the road may be another factor.

To isolate *the* cause, unless we have some special purpose in view, such as fixing legal guilt, is virtually impossible. And this was well understood by Aristotle—whose language was copied by Aquinas—when he distinguished four different kinds of causes: efficient, final, material and formal. Thus when a sculptor carves a statue, the sculptor is the *efficient cause* of the statue. The *final cause* is the end of his activity, possibly to exhibit his work for sale, or merely his own enjoyment. The *material cause* is the marble out of which the statue is fashioned. The *formal cause* is the shape given to the statue, a mythical being, an abstract pattern. Not any single one of these factors is *the* cause, they are all necessary to bring about the concrete result.

The cosmological argument is stated in terms of efficient causes, but it obviously leads us on to other types of cause. As the creator of the universe God is the first term in the series of efficient causes; he is the sculptor and the world is his work of art. But he is also the designer as well as maker —the work of art is something he planned. He must have had some end in view in making the world, and this is the final cause. It answers such questions as: What is the meaning of it all?

In a sense all the classical proofs hang together—or fall together. To the unphilosophical they may sound reasonable. The great puzzle seems to be neatly tidied up. Indeed, we must acknowledge that even to some contemporary philosophers there is nothing seriously wrong with the arguments. P. T. Geach in *Three Philosophers* (p 117) boldly speaks of Aquinas as 'having thus established the existence of a God who is the cause of the world and of the processes of it'.

The modern atheist could make a somewhat cavalier rejoinder. He could deny that we can be absolutely certain that no uncaused events ever occur. In an early essay, *Mysticism and Logic,* Bertrand Russell said flatly: 'All philosophers, of every school, imagine that causation is one of the fundamental axioms or postulates of science; yet, oddly enough, in advanced sciences, such as gravitational astronomy, the word, "cause" never occurs.... The law of causality, I believe, like very much that passes muster among philosophers, is a relic of a bygone age, surviving like the monarchy, only because it is erroneously supposed to do no harm.'

Since then other philosophers have begun to catch up with science. According to F. Waismann: 'The year 1927 is a landmark in the evolution of physics—the year which saw the obsequies of the notion of causality. To avoid misconceptions, it should not be thought that the concept fell a victim to the unbridled antipathy of certain physicists or their indulgence in fancies. The truth is that men of science came, very reluctantly and almost against their will, to recognize the impossibility of giving a coherent, causal description of the happenings on the atomic scale, though some of them—curiously enough among them Planck, Einstein, de Broglie. Schrodinger—could never bring themselves to accept wholeheartedly so drastic a renunciation of classical ideals.' (*How I See Philosophy* F. Waismann p 208)

THE ARGUMENT FROM MOTION

This is not the place to go into the technical reasons for

substituting the term 'functional dependence' for 'cause'. It could still be argued that if the world had a beginning, as some scientists believe, it could not have started itself. Something must have set the process in motion. So the concept of a First Cause leads us to another of Aquinas's proofs, that which seeks an explanation of the fact that things *move*. He accepted, of course, the erroneous view that nothing moves by itself. Newton, however, rejected the commonsense view by his proposition that what has to be accounted for is not that a body is moving, but that it changes its momentum or course. He does not start with the idea of an immobile planet which would remain stationary unless acted on in some way. On the contrary the planet would continue to go straight on unless deflected by gravity or some other force.

Nevertheless the supposed necessity of a Prime Mover cannot be so easily dismissed as a mere mistake about dynamics. In justice to both Aquinas and Aristotle we must acknowledge that they had a more comprehensive idea of motion. Their followers stress that the proof is not so much based on change of position and velocity as on *change* itself.

That things change and yet in a sense, remain the same, baffled philosophers from ancient times. Some went so far as to say that this must be an illusion, for how could a thing possibly change and yet remain the same thing? 'No man can cross the same river twice'—yet, surely, it is crossed and it is the same river. An acorn is not an oak tree, yet it becomes an oak. The child is the father of the man, yet both child and man are the same individual person. A new word is needed to describe the phenomenon; we speak of 'becoming'. Nothing in Nature is unchanging, all is in flux, all is in a state of becoming, or process.

But what is meant by *becoming*? A problem is not solved by inventing a new word. Aquinas thought the solution was to regard the passage from the acorn to the oak, or the child to the man, as being the development of what exists potentially into what exists in actuality. Change is the transition from the potential to the actual. It is doubtful whether this way of talking does more than rephrase the original question and we may still ask what causes this mysterious change. There must be something permanent behind the perpetual flux, something changeless behind change; and so the First Cause is described as the Prime Mover itself unmoved.

The objection that immediately suggests itself is that if *everything* has a cause, why should the First Cause be exempt? The orthodox answer is that God is self-caused, whatever that may mean. Similarly if all movement requires a mover, how can the Prime Mover effect change and yet remain unmoved? The fact is that all forms of the Cosmological Argument amount to saying that the world is what it is because of some agency outside it. And this runs counter to the whole of modern scientific thinking, which is an endeavour to find all explanations of natural phenomena *within* Nature.

Kepler required angels to keep the planets on a steady course; Newton rejected this extrinsic supernatural agency and explained the orbits of the planets by gravitation. Science today has no more need of the hypothesis of God than of angels.

THE COSMOLOGICAL FALLACY

David Hume put his finger on the essential fallacy in this type of reasoning. 'In such a (causal) chain of a succession of objects, each part is caused by that which preceded it, and causes that which succeeds it. Where then is the difficulty? But the Whole, you say, wants a cause.... Did I show you the particular causes of each individual in a collection of twenty particles of matter, I should think it very unreasonable should you ask me, what was the cause of the whole twenty.' (*Dialogues concerning Natural Religion* Part IX)

The same point is amusingly illustrated by Paul Edwards.

On the corner of Sixth Avenue and 50th St, suppose there are five Eskimos. If we can give independent reasons to explain why each of them happens to be standing there it is not necessary for any further explanation of the presence of the five considered as a group. (*The Rationalist Annual* 1958)

This is also the burden of Antony Flew's criticism of all the arguments which seek an explanation of what we find in the universe in an agency outside it. The onus of proof, he emphasizes, is not on those who do not look outside. 'Quite the reverse: the presumption, defeasible of course, by adverse argument, must be that all qualities observed in things are qualities belonging by natural right to those things themselves; and hence that whatever characteristics we think ourselves able to discern in the universe as a whole are the underivative characteristics of the universe itself. This, for us, is atheism; atheism as we have seen, has always to be interpreted by the reaction to the sense of *God* in question in the particular context. It is none the less atheism for being sometimes decked out in theistic clothes, as in the words of Einstein inscribed over a fireplace in Fine Hall, Princeton: "God who creates and is Nature is very difficult to understand, but he is not arbitrary or malicious." The present presumption was apparently first clearly formulated as such by Strato, next but one in succession to Aristotle as head of the Lyceum. It can be seen as the fulfilment of the naturalistic tendency in the founder's own thinking. It was "Stratonician atheism" which was received by the young Hume as an emancipating revelation.' (*God and Philosophy* p 69)

Whether we postulate God as the source of order in Nature, or as the designer and architect of the universe we still assume the existence of an agency *outside*—or, in a more technical term, transcendent. The God of Spinoza, Einstein and some Eastern religions is wholly within the universe, identified with it. The Judaeo–Christian tradition is a strange amalgam of the Unmoved Mover—detached from the world process—of Aristotle, and the dynamic Yaweh who constantly intervenes from outside, performs miracles, wins battles, punishes with pestilence and answers petitions.

THE SEVENTEENTH-CENTURY REVOLUTION

A great authority on the history of ideas sums up as follows:

'The truly revolutionary theses in cosmography which gained ground in the sixteenth and came to be pretty generally accepted before the end of the seventeenth century were five in number, none of them entailed by the purely astronomical systems of Copernicus or Kepler. In any study of the history of the modern conception of the world, and in any account of the position of any individual writer, it is essential to keep these distinctions between issues constantly in view.

'The five more significant innovations were:

1. the assumption that other planets of our solar system are inhabited by living, sentient and rational creatures;
2. the shattering of the outer walls of the medieval universe whether these were identified with the outermost crystalline sphere or with a definite "region" of the fixed stars, and the dispersal of these stars through vast, irregular distances;
3. the conception of the fixed stars as suns similar to ours, all or most of them surrounded by planetary systems of their own;
4. the supposition that the planets in these other worlds also have conscious inhabitants;
5. the assertion of the actual infinity of the physical universe in space and of the number of solar systems contained in it.

'The first of these—and, of course, still more the fourth— deprived human life and terrestrial history of the unique importance and momentousness which the medieval scheme of ideas had attributed to them, and Copernicanism had left to them. The theory of the plurality of inhabited worlds tended to raise difficulties, not merely about minor details of the history included in the Christian belief, but about its central dogmas. The entire moving drama of the Incarnation and Redemption had seemed manifestly to presuppose a single inhabited world. If that presupposition were to be given up, how were these dogmas to be construed, if, indeed, they could be retained at all? Were we, as Thomas Paine afterwards asked, "to suppose that every world in the boundless creation had an Eve, an apple, a serpent and a Redeemer"? Had the Second Person of the Trinity been incarnate on innumerable planets in turn, or was this the only portion of the universe in which moral agents had any need of redemption?' (*The Great Chain of Being* A. O. Lovejoy 1936)

The specific Christian beliefs here referred to lie outside the Cosmological Argument. No theologian suggests that they are capable of proof. All that logical argument can do is to point to a First Cause, Prime Mover or Designer. This is the starting point shared by all monotheistic religions. We cannot conclude that a Cause or Mover or even Orderer has the attributes which religion assigns to God. Nor can we strictly demonstrate that there is only one Cause, or only one Mover. There may be any number of chains of cause and effect leading back from individual occurrences to separate first terms.

Again, the fact that Nature is orderly does not entail an intelligent Orderer. There are an infinite number of possible systems of Nature, but some type of order could always be abstracted by an observing intelligence; *some* common features in the constituents could be selected by the observer. So there is no need to look outside the universe for the source of order.

CHANCE OR DESIGN?

Design, however, is another matter. A Supreme Designer must necessarily be intelligent. The blind action of the elements can fashion rocks into aesthetically satisfying patterns but there would be no sense in calling them beautiful

unless there were conscious beings whom they could satisfy
—ie before man had been evolved. The Argument from
Design is therefore somewhat different from the Argument
from Order, though the two are often confused.

Does the world *look* as though it were designed? Could it
have arisen from 'the fortuitous concurrence of atoms'? Are
two thousand million years long enough for the intricate
multiplicity of living organisms to have evolved by chance?
These are some of the questions which have led men of
powerful intelligence, and often of considerable scientific
achievements, to believe that the world did not make itself
but was created according to a divine blue-print.

Newton, for example, explained the movements of
heavenly bodies by natural causes, but he felt obliged to
assume a supernatural Cause of the universe as a whole.
'This most beautiful system of the sun, planets and comets,
could only proceed from the counsel and dominion of an
intelligent and powerful Being.... Blind, metaphysical necessity, which is certainly the same always and everywhere,
could produce no variety of things. All that diversity of
natural things which we find suited to different times and
places could arise from nothing but the ideas and will of a
Being necessarily existing.' (*Principia* General Scholium,
Book III)

Whereas the luckless Galileo was regarded by the Roman
Church as a danger to orthodoxy, Newton was hailed by
Anglican divines as defender of theism, even though his
version of Christianity was tinged with Arianism. It was
long before science came to be feared as the enemy of religion. The mood of the eighteenth century was expressed
by Pope:

> *Nature and Nature's Laws lay hid by night,*
> *God said 'Let Newton be' and all was light.*

To which J. C. Squire has added:

> *It could not last; the Devil howling 'Ho,*
> *Let Einstein be' restored the* status quo

However, the *status quo* before Newton was a refusal to accept that things behave according to their natures, that a thing is what it does and not what it is made to do by a transcendental agency. The changes that occur throughout Nature are to be explained by natural laws. The medieval view formulated by Aquinas was gradually superseded by the discovery of these laws: 'When diverse things are co-ordinated the scheme depends on their directed unification, as the order of battle of a whole army hangs on the plan of the Commander-in-Chief. The arrangements of diverse things cannot be dictated by their own private and divergent natures; of themselves they are diverse and exhibit no tendency to form a pattern. It follows that the order of many among themselves is either a matter of chance or must be attributed to one first planner who has a purpose in mind. What comes about always, or in the great majority of cases, is not the result of accident.' (*Summa contra Gentiles* 1. 42)

As long as the main scientific advance lay in astronomy the Argument from Design seemed to be corroborated. The movements of the stars gave the impression of a celestial clock that must have been fashioned by a Cosmic Clock-maker. Mechanical materialism seemed compatible with Deism and even to require it. Thomas Paine, militant critic of Christianity though he was, embraced Deism rather than atheism.

The change came with the progress of biology. Early theories of evolution could be made consistent with Design. It need only be said that the world was not created complete, but that it unfolded in accordance with a pre-determined plan. Why else should it unfold at all? But the theory of Natural Selection made the assumption of a plan superfluous.

Darwin may have been somewhat uneasy about the tremendous significance of his discovery, but he saw no alternative. In his *Autobiography* he wrote: 'The old argument of design in Nature as given by Paley, which formerly seemed to me so conclusive, fails, now that the law of Natural Selection has been discovered. We can no longer argue that, for instance, the beautiful hinge of a bivalve shell must have been made by an intelligent being, like the hinge of a door by man.'

There was a time when there was no life on the earth. In very different atmospheric conditions from those which prevail today, chemical changes were brought about in material molecules which started the long and complex evolutionary chain which led from the amoeba to man. The details of the way the various species of living organisms were diversified do not now concern us. The point is that the distinction between living and non-living matter is not so hard and fast as the ordinary usage of the terms suggest. It is a question of bio-chemical organization. There is no need to look for some agency outside the physical world. The conditions in which life emerged on this planet are a certain range of temperature, and certain chemical combinations which, it is widely believed today—though it was not some thirty or forty years ago—are probably found on numerous planets throughout this vast universe. The variations which gave rise to a multiplicity of species are due to mutations in the genetic material.

It might be said of course that God is responsible for these mutations and created all living things in this extraordinarily roundabout way. It is a last ditch argument. The objection is that the majority of mutations are harmful. They result in some species, like the giant reptiles which failed to adapt and became extinct after a run of millions of years. Some of them became so weighted down with protective armour that they could not defend themselves. *Homo sapiens* is running a similar risk today and could well meet the fate of the dinosaurs through the burden of nuclear armament. No Providence will intervene to save the last product of evolution on this planet.

The feeling that the world around us *looks* as though it had been deliberately designed is very deep, but it will not bear critical examination. Basically it is a feeling that there *must* be a design, because the planets move on time and a genetic code governs the marvellous stages of embryonic growth, and so on; consequently it is wildly improbable that blind, material forces should bring all this about. Chance seems no explanation at all, and the only alternative seems to be design.

But what do we mean by probability when we apply it to the universe as a whole? We can compare events within the universe and measure their relative probability, but we cannot compare the universe with some other cosmos distinct from it. Things are what they are, they happen as they happen. 'A rose is a rose is a rose' as Gertrude Stein said.

EVIL AND SUFFERING

There is a final difficulty about design. Suppose we infer from the observed regularities of Nature that it is, after all, the working out of a Plan. We can then infer some of the characteristics of the Designer from what he has made. Are there no blunders, no cruelty in the struggle for existence, no waste in the elimination of the unfit in the evolutionary scheme? Blake, contemplating the tiger, at once a symbol of beauty and savagery, compared it in wonder with the lamb: 'Did He who made the lamb make *thee*?'

It would be a semantic confusion to describe the viruses and bacteria which cause such indiscriminate suffering as 'evil'. They arose inevitably in the course of the evolution of life. But if we ascribe them to other than physical causes, if we say that they are part of a deliberate design, it is impossible to think of the Author of such a creation as both omnipotent and all-loving. The God inferred from the Argument of Design is certainly not the God of a religion which proclaims infinite compassion and providential care.

William Paley (1743–1805) is, perhaps, the best known Protestant advocate of the Design Argument, and though few modern theologians would express it in the same form it has a clarity which contemporary apologetics conspicuously lack.

Paley imagined that if a savage picked up a watch he would conclude that it had been designed. He went on to argue that animals showed even more design than watches, and so he was led to postulate a Supreme Designer.

J. B. S. Haldane commented in *The Rationalist Annual*, 1944: 'If then, animals were designed, they were designed for mutual destruction. If there was a designer, he is, or was, a being with a passion for slaughter, like that of the ancient Romans, and the world is his Coliseum. A much more reasonable consequence of the hypothesis of design is Polytheism. If each of the million or so animal species were the product of a different god their mutual struggle would be intelligible. One must particularly admire the ingenuity of the creators of some of the parasites, particularly those with several hosts. For example, the digenetic tremotode worms, such as bilharzia, which pass one generation in a water snail and another in human beings, causing an extremely painful chronic disease, often terminating in cancer, are an amazing piece of work. So are the malaria parasites, which live alternately in mosquitoes and human blood.... Wherever Paley's argument leads it does not lead to Christianity. If pushed to its logical conclusion it forces us to believe in a malignant creator, or, more probably, in a number of malignant creators. Certainly this creator, or these creators, are not wholly malignant. The world of life contains a great deal of beauty and pleasure; but one can admire the beauty only by closing one's consciousness to the pain and injustice which are bound up with it. A biologist who has spent his life in the study of parasitic animals must inevitably smother his feelings of pity to some extent and tend to take human misery and injustice for granted.'

THE HUMANIST CHOICE

We must take our choice between rival answers to a

question that has troubled the mind of man for thousands of years and still does so. However formidable the objections made by the atheist an obstinate feeling lurks in most people that the physical universe is not the whole of reality. On this it is prudent to be agnostic.

The universe we can observe is the only one of which we have any knowledge. It may, or may not be, everything that there is; it is all we know about, and we cannot infer a Designer from a hypothetical universe. The feeling that there *must* be a Supreme Mind in the background can be explained naturalistically as a projection of our own con- sciousness on inanimate Nature.

If we are still dissatisfied we must try another approach. When we say that something *must* be the case we are usually making an *a priori* judgment; that is, we are mak- ing an assertion that is independent of evidence. The Cos- mological Argument certainly appeals to evidence, but there is another type of argument which still exerts a powerful fascination and is not concerned with cause and effect, the order of Nature, or the appearance of design. Let us next consider what is known as the Ontological Argu- ment. If it is valid it could satisfy the craving which gives rise to religion by providing an answer that is absolutely certain.

FOUR

IS GOD NECESSARY?

THE inconclusiveness of the numerous 'proofs' of God's existence is shown by the fact that there are so many of them. Even such great philosophers as Descartes and Leibniz were so dissatisfied with earlier efforts that they tried to do better. They thought they had succeeded, oddly enough, by attempting a variant of the very proof that Aquinas felt obliged to reject. This is known as the Ontological Argument and it was formulated by St Anselm (1033–1109). If it is valid it is just what theologians had been hoping to find— a logical conclusion which cannot be denied without self-contradiction.

As a young man Bertrand Russell was delighted with the ontological proof. In *My Mental Development* he described his jubilation at the discovery. 'I remember the precise moment one day in 1894, as I was walking along Trinity Lane, when I saw in a flash (or thought I saw) that the ontological argument is valid. I had gone out to buy a tin of tobacco; on my way back I suddenly threw it up in the air and exclaimed as I caught it "Great Scot, the ontological argument is sound".'

Anselm's reasoning went as follows: Whatever is understood exists in the understanding. Even the atheist *understands* the meaning of the assertion that God exists and that 'God' means a Being than which nothing greater can be conceived. But if such a conception merely exists in the mind, the very Being than which nothing greater can be conceived is one than which a greater *can* be conceived, which is impossible. There is no doubt, then, that there exists a Being than which nothing greater can be conceived,

and it exists both in the understanding and in reality, in the
mind and outside it.

To put it more simply: 'God' is by definition 'the Perfect
Being'. Such a Being cannot lack reality or he would not be
perfect, no matter what other attributes he possessed. It
would be like saying the perfectly real is not real, which is a
contradiction. Therefore the proposition that God exists is
necessarily true.

Both Hume and Kant pointed out what is such a glaring
fallacy that it is astonishing that it should have intrigued
eminent philosophers and mathematicians. They sought a
better formulation because the prospect of being able to
demonstrate existence by logic alone is alluring. Yet the
goal is now generally recognized to have been as illusory as
the Philosopher's Stone.

The fatal flaw is to treat 'existence' as a property or
characteristic of a thing. To say that God is good or omnipotent is to name certain attributes. But 'existence' is not an
attribute or a predicate. It makes grammatical sense to say
that Hera was the wife of Zeus, but to assert that Hera
exists is a very different sort of statement. Mr Pickwick was
minutely described by Dickens, but to ascribe reality to him
—as the novelist only pretends to do—does not make him
other than fictitious. As Kant said, 'A hundred imaginary
thalers have all the predicates of a hundred real thalers.'

It may be objected, of course, that a Perfect Being is not a
'thing' in the ordinary sense. It is not like Hera or Mr Pickwick or a thaler. None of these, as defined, include reality as
a necessary characteristic. What Anselm claimed was that a
Being than which nothing greater can be conceived *must* be
a perfectly Real Being, and that to deny this is a self-contradiction. The short answer is that he is playing with
words. You cannot argue from the mere definition of a
word that something for which the word is said to refer
actually exists. You can set up a hypothesis, deduce what
would be the case if it were true, and then take steps to
confirm or falsify it. You can describe a unicorn, but until

somebody finds one it cannot be claimed that unicorns exist. The Loch Ness Monster and the Abominable Snowman are conceivable, but so far they are mere ideas in the mind. As long as a Perfect Being is only a definition we cannot certify that it is real.

THE MISTAKE OF LEIBNIZ

Yet although all this seems so obvious there may still be an uneasy suspicion that what is wrong with the Argument is merely the way it has been stated. Are not monsters or unicorns a false analogy? Plainly they need not be real; the world can get along very well without them. They might or might not exist. The same could be said of everything that we take to be real—trees, mountains, man, the earth itself. They are not *necessary,* in the logical sense; they are *contingent,* to use a technical term.

We cannot say of anything in Nature that it could not conceivably have been otherwise than it is. The universe as a whole is one among an infinitude of possible universes. If we had enough knowledge we could give a sufficient reason why everything in our universe behaves in just the way it does, but we are still left with the question: why is there a universe at all? Why should anything exist? On the other hand, if Nature is rational and therefore intelligible and we come to the end of our search for sufficient reasons for its multifarious activities, we are confronted, according to Leibniz, by the ultimate Sufficient Reason of the whole process, and this is God. No further reason can be given because God is the source of reason. We pass beyond contingent being to Necessary Being.

This is a blend of the Cosmological Argument—from the world to God—and the Ontological Argument, which states that God is logically necessary. He is not dependent on anything else for his existence, and so there cannot be any reason why He should not exist. In the words of Leibniz: 'The sufficient reason which has no need of any other reason must be outside the sequence of contingent things, and must be a necessary being, else we should not have a sufficient reason with which we could stop.'

The objection to this version, according to Antony Flew, is that it misconstrues the nature of explanation, since 'however much may ultimately be explained in successive stages of inquiry, there must always be some facts which have simply to be accepted with what Samuel Alexander used to call "natural piety".' The theist, like those who adopt a naturalistic explanation, must reach a point at which further explanation is impossible. He tries to explain the universe by something which cannot be explained. 'The ultimate facts about God would have to be, for precisely the same reason, equally inexplicable. In each and every case we must necessarily find at the end of every explanatory road some ultimates which have simply to be accepted as the fundamental truths about the way things are. And this itself is a contention, not about the lamentable facts of the human condition, but about what follows necessarily from the nature of explanation.' (*God and Philosophy* p 82)

THE ARGUMENT FROM MORALITY

It would be fruitless to examine further efforts to prove the existence of God by logic. But granted that God is not *logically* necessary, may He not be necessary in some other sense? Hume and Kant demolished the classical proofs but Kant was still not satisfied. He felt that although God could not be proved to be necessary for the existence of the world we must nevertheless postulate His existence in order to account for our moral nature. He took a very unusual course. Instead of basing the existence of the moral law on a divine Lawgiver, he argued to God's existence from his conviction that there was a moral law. To quote:

'After we have satisfied ourselves of the vanity of all the ambitious attempts of reason to fly beyond the bounds of experience, enough remains of practical value to content us. It is true that no one may boast that he *knows* that God and a future life exist; for if he possesses that knowledge, he is just the man for whom I have long been seeking. All knowledge (touching an object of mere reason) can be communicated, and therefore I might hope to see my own knowledge increased to this prodigious extent by his instruction. No, our conviction in these matters is not *logical*, but *moral* certainty; and inasmuch as it rest upon subjective grounds (of moral disposition), I must not even say that *it is* morally certain that there is a God, but *I am* morally certain, and so on. That is to say, the belief in a God and in another world is so interwoven with my moral nature that the former can no more vanish than the latter can ever be torn from me.'

The language of this affirmation is both cautious and emotive. When we look at it closely we can see why there has been some disagreement about how it should be interpreted. The chain of speculative *a priori* reasoning is still rejected, yet the certitude which this promised is reached by another route. What Kant appears to be saying is that belief in God is not a purely intellectual matter; nor is it the result of a mystical encounter, so intense that nothing can shake it. To employ the current fashionable jargon, it is 'existential'. We become aware in living our lives that certain courses of action would be *wrong*. There are some things we all feel we just must not do. We may fail to do what seems our plain duty, but we are ashamed afterwards of our weakness. Even the criminal has a code of right and wrong; to betray his associates would be to break it.

There are some things which everybody in his heart feels ought either to be done or avoided. We have to make a choice, and as long as it is not purely prudential—fear of punishment or hope of reward—this is a moral choice. To act morally, then, is to do our duty, come what may, painful or not.

Yet it would be a mistake to suppose that Kant based morality on mere feelings. He believed that man is a rational being and that it is possible by rational reflection to discover a single absolute principle underlying all morality.

THE CATEGORICAL IMPERATIVE

Kant's approach is so different from the traditional view of morality that it repays attention even though many, perhaps the majority of philosophers today, reject it. Certainly it gives cold comfort to theologians, for Kant would be obliged to go some of the way with Humanists who contend that we can have morality without religion. Theologians on the other hand, hold that the idea of God comes first. The Moral Law is seen as a revelation of God's will, and that is why it must be obeyed.

'If God did not exist, everything would be permissible,' said Dostoevsky. This, of course, is what Humanists deny. They say that morality is about what we *ought* to do, not about what *is*. The gods of all religions have issued commands, some of them very cruel commands. The Christian *chooses* the god that seems suited to his own moral sense—he prefers nowadays the loving father of the New Testament (shorn of the hell fire bits) to the warlike Yaweh of the Old Testament, or the amorous Zeus of Greece. Of course, he does not admit that he is selecting a god according to his scruples of conscience; he imagines that his conscience comes from the god he picks.

Kant deals with the problem differently. He utterly rejects the idea that morality is based on a command which our duty is to obey. The arbitrary fiat of an omnipotent Being might be obeyed out of fear or in the hope of reward, but such submission is not a moral act. We have no grounds for calling God good unless we already know the meaning of 'good'. We can conceive what is meant by 'all-powerful' because we have experience of limited power. But how do we derive our notion of 'good'? This is one question which Kant pursued in the *Critique of Practical Reason*. Kant concluded that although morality may lead to religion, it cannot be derived from religion; it is a discovery of reason.

Kant's starting-point is the nature of man, not the nature of God. Unlike all other living creatures, man is endowed with reason. He is also at the mercy of instincts and impulses; and inasmuch as these are not wholly under the control of reason man is an imperfectly rational agent. Because he is imperfect, what he nevertheless regards as his duty—ie what he ought to do—often seems disagreeable. He tends to regard it as a command, or a law outside himself. But a perfectly rational man would not even talk about 'duty' or what he *ought* to do. He would just do it naturally and without effort or resistance. To be rational, then, is to have the power to act disinterestedly and consistently in accordance with principles.

There is only one way of finding out what these principles are unless we take a short cut by appealing to revelation or intuition; we must use our capacity to reason. If, indeed, all men have this capacity—however little they use it—the fundamental principle must be of universal application. It must admit of no exceptions; an impersonal principle free from self-interest, passion or compassion. It gives us an objective meaning of 'good'. This is the famous categorical imperative which is at the core of Kant's system, and it can be expressed as follows: 'Act only on that maxim which you can at the same time will that it should become universal law.'

THE RATIONAL GOOD

Everything tends to the realization of some end result, but only rational beings can be ends in themselves, said Kant. Consequently the moral law is discovered by man, not imposed on him by God. The perfection at which it aims is the creation of a virtuous state of mind; or as Kant puts it, the right sort of *will*. The only thing that is good without any qualification is a good will. This is man's true end, not happiness, not the relief of suffering.

We can see more clearly what this means if we contrast it with opposing views of ethics. Christian morality in its traditional form is based on the supposed divine will. 'In Thy will is our peace,' as Dante expressed it. Kant repudiates the idea that we should submit to a law we did not make for the sake of peace or salvation. Equally he opposes the hedonistic ethics which aim quite simply at happiness; also the utilitarian formula of 'the greatest happiness of the greatest number'. These judge the morality of an act by its consequences. For Kant, however, consequences have nothing to do with morality.

That is not to say that if all men acted from the highest motives there would be no good consequences. If everyone behaved rationally and made laws in accordance with the categorical imperative he would treat his neighbour as an individual with the same rights as himself—never simply as a means to an end but always as an end in himself. And so we should have a world commonwealth in which all members made its universal laws while being themselves subject to those laws. They would live together in peace and happiness.

THE PURPOSE OF LIFE

It is a noble though austere ideal, but is such a utopia likely to be realized? Kant acknowledges that in the conditions of the world in which we live it will not come about. So the human predicament is that we are impelled to strive for ends that cannot be fully realized unless—and this is the point—unless materialism is not the whole truth about man.

To Kant it seemed unthinkable that having staked everything on the life of reason, reality should turn out to be so fundamentally irrational that our highest desires were doomed to frustration. This is presumably why he was impelled to proclaim his faith in God and immortality. He was expressing in technical language what many ordinary people feel when they say that struggling to do their duty does not make sense if annihilation is at the end of the road. Why not eat, drink and be merry if tomorrow we die? If life is no more than a brief journey from Nothing to Nothing it is without meaning, a 'sleeveless errand' without purpose.

Kant recoiled from this conclusion, as well he might, but he took a dubious way out. He smuggled back the concept of purpose which he had demolished in his attack on the classical teleological proof. The latter argues from the fact of order in Nature to an Orderer. Kant explicitly states in the *Critique of Pure Reason* that although we cannot strictly prove that this order is due to the blind working of mechanical laws, it is not inconceivable that this should be so. Yet he reintroduces the concept of purpose in the *Critique of Practical Reason*. He assumes that as in organic life each organ has a purpose or function, so, too, in mental life, reason is the organ which controls action; and we must therefore assume that it also is well-adapted to its function, which is to produce a state of will which is good in itself.

'Such a purposive (or teleological) view of Nature is not readily accepted today,' comments H. J. Paton in *The Moral Law*, 'We need only note that Kant does hold this belief (though by no means in a simple form) and that it is very much more fundamental to his ethics than is commonly supposed.' (p 18)

Aside from any inconsistency in Kant, is there any reason to suppose that unless we can guarantee success in striving for an ideal we are wasting our time? There is certainly no ground for believing that unless God exists and we live for ever there is no point in trying to improve our condition here and now. The late Susan Stebbing in *Ideals and Illusions* gave a Humanist answer:

'Life is not a game for which rules can be prescribed for all; not a rehearsal for a Great Drama the first performance of which is not yet; nor a porch leading us into heavenly courts. It is an illusion to find the value of our lives here and now in a life to come; it is an illusion to suppose that nothing is worth while for me unless I live for ever; it is an illusion to suppose that there is no uncompensated loss, no sacrifice that is without requital, no grief that is unassuaged. But it is also no illusion but uncontested fact that hatred, cruelty, intolerance and indifference to human misery are evil; that love, kindliness, tolerance, forgiveness and truth are good, so unquestionably good that we do not need God or heaven to assure us of their worth.' (p 199)

It is worth noting that Sartre was strongly influenced by Kant's Categorical Imperative though he drew an atheistic conclusion. He agreed with the axiom that we must test our actions by asking whether we are willing for every human being to act as we are about to do. When a man chooses for himself, says Sartre, he chooses for all men. 'Nothing can be better for us unless it is better for all. ... Our responsibility is thus much greater than we had supposed, for it concerns mankind as a whole.' However, Sartre discards the rational framework which Kant erected to guide the moral choice. To the existentialist, virtue consists in the total sincerity of the moral choice rather than in a static conception of goodness. One man may choose to follow Hitler, like Sartre's former master, Heidegger; another, like Sartre, may join the Resistance. Torquemada willed that all men should be Catholics; those who chose differently, provided they were within reach of the Inquisition, were burned alive. In both cases full marks can be given for sincerity and consistency.

Humanists agree with Sartre when he says that values are made by man. If there is no God, there is no one else to make them. But *what* we value surely matters as much as making a sincere (authentic) choice. Sincerity by itself is not enough.

The test of universality looks well on paper, but it is not as helpful as it might appear when we try to act upon it. It poses difficult conundrums in real-life situations. If ethics are autonomous, and consequences are not to count, it is always right to follow one's conscience wherever it leads. But any dangerous monomaniac can be justified by the plea of conscience.

The strength of the personal conviction of being right cannot guarantee that a martyr was, in fact, right in his belief. Martyrs have died for opposed conceptions of truth. Many have died for grotesque superstitions. When people die for principles that we ourselves do not believe in we are apt to call them fanatics rather than martyrs. But the question remains: whatever the truth about a particular issue, why do men feel that it is right to make a stand for the truth as they see it?

As with truth, so with beauty which, together with good, is also a candidate for absolute values.

> *Beauty is truth, truth beauty—that is all*
> *Ye know on earth, and all ye need to know.*

This, too, does not take us very far, though it has the air of profundity which hints at some deeper reality beyond the veil of appearance that is rendered more movingly in Plato's *Symposium*:

'He who has been instructed thus far in the science of Love, and has been led to see beautiful things in their due order and rank, when he moves towards the end of his discipline will suddenly catch sight of a wondrous thing, beautiful with the absolute Beauty: and this, Socrates, is the aim and end of all those earlier labours.'

Socrates gains a glimpse of unity in an eternal realm beyond the shadows on the wall of the cave which are all most mortals can see. As poetry it is magnificent; but it is open to grave objections. That the contemplation of truth can suffuse the mind with a sense of beauty is indisputable; unfortunately, so also can the contemplation of error. The emotion that accompanies our feeling is no witness to its correctness.

There is certainly a connection between some of the most abstract reasoning and beauty. No doubt there are rare souls to whom *Principia Mathematica* is as aesthetically moving as a musical score. Both Bertrand Russell and Henri Poincaré testify to the beauty of mathematics, 'where everything is exact and delightful'. In *Science and Method* (Eng trs p 22) Poincaré writes:

'The scientist does not study Nature because it is useful to do so. He studies it because he takes pleasure in it, and he takes pleasure in it because it is beautiful. If Nature were not beautiful it would not be worth knowing, and life would not be worth living. I am not speaking, of course, of that beauty which strikes the senses, of the beauties of qualities and appearances. What I mean is that more intimate beauty which comes from the harmonious order of its parts, and which a pure intelligence can grasp.... Intellectual beauty is self-sufficing, and it is for it, more perhaps than for the future good of humanity, that the scientist condemns himself to long and painful labours.'

It is easy enough to see how men have been impelled by the sheer strength of such an emotion to postulate the real existence of beauty as an attribute of God. The argument from motion to the Prime Mover, or from cause to the First Cause, seems cold and uninspiring in comparison with that from beauty to the Source and Divine Origin of the Beautiful. As Aldous Huxley wrote in *The Perennial Philosophy*:

'Among the trinities in which the ineffable One makes itself manifest is the trinity of the Good, the True and the Beautiful. We perceive beauty in the harmonious intervals between the parts of the whole.'

But let us face the problem squarely. There is beauty in the explosion of an atomic bomb. One of its inventors, P. Morrison, wrote in *Science News* No 2:

'The column itself is mainly a cloud, just like any thunderhead, except for the dust and vapour it holds, radioactive and generating heat.... As the column rises like the smoke from a chimney it may come to what is called an inversion by the meteorologists. This is a layer of air warmer, instead of cooler, than the air below it. When such a layer is reached the gas of the column will spread out and rise no longer. This is the formation of the mushroom. But some of the gas of the column is still being warmed by radioactivity. This gas is warm enough to break the inversion layer, and the column sends another stem from the first mushroom cap. This too mushrooms, now very high in the air, perhaps six to eight miles. All of these grand and ironically beautiful phenomena can be seen in the moving pictures of the attacks on Hiroshima and Nagasaki.'

The first atom bomb was a squib compared with the H-bomb; even so, we can understand why Morrison should feel the irony of speaking of the 'beauty' of an iridiscent cloud which destroyed some 60,000 people in Hiroshima, injuring 100,000. In this instance the Good and the Beautiful do not seem to harmonize as they certainly should if these values have an objective existence, either in Plato's sense as Eternal Ideas, or as ideas in the mind of God.

ARE THERE MORAL ABSOLUTES?

The issue is between objective values and subjective values, between absolute standards and relative ones. Theists usually rest their faith in an absolute moral law on the existence of a Supreme Lawgiver. Without this assumption they believe that the moral order of the world would collapse. The case is clearly put by Hastings Rashdall in *The Theory of Good and Evil* (1907):

'An absolute moral law, or moral ideal, cannot exist in material things. And it does not exist in the mind of this or that individual. Only if we believe in the existence of a Mind for which the true moral ideal is already in some sense real, a Mind which is the source of whatever is true in our own judgements, can we rationally think of the moral idea as no less real than the world itself. Only so can we believe in an absolute standard of right and wrong, which is as independent of this or that man's actual ideas and actual desires as the facts of material nature. The belief in God, though not (like the belief in a real and an active self) a postulate of there being any such thing as morality at all, is a logical presupposition of an "objective" or absolute morality. A moral ideal can exist nowhere and nohow but in a mind; an absolute moral ideal can exist only in a mind from which all reality is derived. Our moral ideal can only claim objective validity in so far as it can rationally be regarded as the revelation of a moral ideal eternally existing in the mind of God.'

A. E. Taylor also argues that if we believe in absolute values we must believe in God:

'If the implications of the moral law are what Kant, and though less explicitly Butler, take them to be, consideration of it leads us not merely to our acknowledgement of "one God" but of "one God almighty, creator of heaven and earth, and of all things visible and invisible".' (*Does God Exist?*)

But are we justified in believing in moral absolutes? It is not enough to say that we all *feel* that there are some acts that cannot be justified in any conceivable circumstances. This feeling may even be universal; but some acts which arouse revulsion are by no means the same for all men everywhere. It is one thing to claim with Professor Taylor that 'it is as much in the nature of man to be conscious of a difference between right and wrong as it is to be alive to a difference between male and female'. It is quite another thing to assert that all men agree completely about what is right and wrong. They do not and we have to inquire how different views—equally strongly held—originate. This is partly a matter of history and partly a problem of psychology.

It may be that the differences in moral codes are sometimes exaggerated, but when we strip them of rules plainly designed to meet the needs of a particular type of society, the basic agreement with which we are left turns out to be little more than the bare essentials for any sort of tolerable social life.

'Thou shalt not kill' is a safeguard against the anarchy that would result from freedom to murder. Not all killing is classed as murder—as it should be if the prohibition were inborn or the expression of an absolute imperative. 'Thou shalt not steal' is only meaningful in a society which approves of private property, and Jesuit moralists reasonably argued that a starving man could steal—a commonsense proposal which shocked Pascal and which tacitly acknowledges that circumstances alter cases.

The belief in a moral law—and therefore in a divine Lawgiver—is a survival from those ancient civilizations which made no distinction between laws of Nature and morality. A breach of the moral law was believed to disturb the very course of Nature, bringing pestilence, famine and drought as a punishment. This line of thought is no less anachronistic when it is expressed in more refined language.

NATURALISTIC EXPLANATIONS

The secularization of thought has progressed so radically that a purely naturalistic explanation can be given of the differences we find in moral codes, and of the conviction we feel that our own values are absolutely binding. Kant would have been scandalized by the suggestion that conscience is no more than a conditioned reflex. Yet the elimination of the supernatural from morals has made conscience, as well as the origin of species, an object of scientific study.

Whether conscience is actually the product of a social conditioning or of an infantile attitude to a parent—the Freudian super-ego—it is in either case an entirely natural development. There is no longer any need to look for a transcendental cause.

We must postpone a full discussion of what a secular morality implies. What we have been concerned with here is a different question: whether there is an absolute moral law, which must be obeyed whatever the consequences. If, for example, it is our absolute duty to be unselfish, it would be wrong to commit a selfish act even if it promoted widespread happiness. Or if, as Pope Paul decreed, contraception is contrary to the will of God, it must be rejected even though millions of people are thereby doomed to misery and starvation.

There is no need to mourn the passing of such a moral

strait-jacket. It has done immeasurable harm in the course of its brutal history. The fact is that morals have always been devised by man, only he has mistakenly attributed their authorship to God. There is not the slightest reason to fear that once this is recognized we shall fare worse than when religion was thought to provide the one possible basis for responsible social conduct. The history of religion is a sufficient refutation.

FIVE

GOOD AND EVIL

IF you believe in God you must also believe that he permits evil to exist. Indeed, the traditional Christian doctrine is that evil will survive the end of the world and endure for ever. The damned proclaim the glory of God as loudly as the heavens. Consequently, if the existence of good is proof that there is a God, so is the existence of evil. The paradox can be stated in several ways. If God is all-powerful and permits evil, how can He be infinitely good; and if He is infinitely good and permits evil, how can He be all-power-ful?

The problem does not arise at all for the Humanist because he does not attach the same meaning to 'evil'. In religious usage evil is a consequence of sin. When the creation of the world was completed 'God saw everything that he had made, and behold it was very good'. Evil only entered the world because of sin. In the religious sense evil and sin go together.

There is no place in the Humanist's vocabulary for 'sin' if it means disobedience to God; unless you believe in God the word is redundant. It follows that if Humanists still speak of 'evil' they employ the word in a different sense from the Christian. For Humanists evil is a form of suffering, and the problem is not to explain why suffering exists, but how it can be removed. A secular morality is based on a resolve to use our human resources to the maximum in the effort to free mankind from the misery brought about by hunger, disease and frustration. The struggle is not against some abstraction called 'Evil' but against specific, clearly defined evils in the above sense. There will be no final, all-out victory with universal happiness as the prize. The way to happiness lies in the struggle.

MAKING NECESSITY A VIRTUE

The metaphysical problem of why evil exists is on a level with the child's question, Why is grass green? It is a problem only if you believe that the world was made by a loving and all-powerful God. Then, of course, your ingenuity is taxed to the utmost to reconcile the irreconcilable.

As William James asked: 'Does a fountain send forth at the same time sweet and bitter water?' If you assume the existence of that odd sort of fountain—because you believe that it makes the world more intelligible—you have to think of an answer.

Our whole philosophy of life may depend on the way we regard this question of evil. In one sense all practical philosophy, and certainly the great religions, owe much of their survival-power to the success with which they seem to solve the problem of discord in the universe, war in heaven, suffering upon earth. Is evil the fault of man or God? Or is there some malevolent Power which thwarts, at least for a time, the will of God? Or are there two equally matched principles of Light and Darkness? Is it possible that God is indeed all-loving, but not all-powerful?

Theologians sometimes distinguish between instrumental evil and intrinsic evil. The former is like the frustration from which a child suffers; we do not allow a child to play with a loaded gun, lest it come to harm. Physical pain may be an instrument of good; thus toothache warns us that our teeth are decayed, and there might be grave danger to health if we had no such warning. But why should Omnipotence give us teeth that decay? The usual answer seems to be that we are lucky to have teeth at all, that it is as unreasonable to expect to have teeth which cannot ache as to ask for a square circle.

The scandal grows when pain in general is exalted because of its alleged 'purifying' power. On this view sickness is to be welcomed as an opportunity for practising the virtue of patience, poverty for displaying the virtue of holy submission and enabling the rich to practise philanthropy. Thus, according to the Papal Encyclical *Rerum Novarum*:

'The pains and hardships of life will have no end or cessation on earth.... To suffer and to endure, therefore, is the lot of humanity.... No strength and no artifice will ever succeed in banishing from human life the ills and troubles which beset it.'

Again, the Encyclical *Caritate Christi Compulsi* states:

'There are two means with which to cope with the increasing misery of the times, prayer and fasting. Let the rich carry out the fasting by almsgiving. And let the poor, and all those who at this time are facing the hard trial of want of work and security of food—let them in a like spirit of penance suffer with greater resignation the privations imposed upon them by these hard times and the state of the society which Divine Providence, in an inscrutable but ever-loving plan, has assigned to them.'

Such a plan is inscrutable indeed. It may be urged that the pains of this mortal life are not to be compared with the joys to come; but they seem unevenly distributed if the poor man's virtue is meekly to starve while virtue for the rich man consists in flicking a few crumbs from his overladen table. As Joseph Needham remarks:

'Proletarian misery in this world has been constantly lightened by promises of comfort and blessedness in the world to come—an exhortation which comes well enough from the ecclesiastical ascetic who does not spare himself, but very ill from the employer of labour or the representative of the propertied classes.' (*Christianity and the Social Revolution*—A symposium)

INTRINSIC EVIL

What is intrinsic evil? Evidently it cannot be the misunderstood action of a guiding hand. Buddhism teaches that life itself is an intrinsic evil, but as Buddhism is not (in its original form) a theistic doctrine, it is not faced by the same thorny problem as Christianity. The Christian has to explain how evil can exist without God's being responsible for it.

The traditional solution is to divide the responsibility for most evils between Satan and man, both of whom were endowed with free will; but even when this is done, some evil remains to be accounted for, some things seem ugly and painful and irrational (hence the term 'surd evil'), and the blame is hard to fix either on man or the Devil.

One way out of this difficulty is to deny that evil has any positive existence. Something of this sort was suggested by Aquinas. Evil is not the presence of something, for which God is accountable, but the absence of something; just as darkness is not a reality in itself, but merely the absence of light.

'What lamp has Destiny to guide her little children stumbling in the dark?' as Omar Khayyam asked. They always stumble, and they certainly hurt themselves. If a man falls down a hole in a street at night, we hold the Corporation responsible for not lighting the usual warning lantern. They would be ill-advised to plead that they are not responsible for darkness, because darkness is not 'real'.

A more plausible view is that we simply cannot explain the fact of intrinsic evil. It is part of an inscrutable plan. Mere finite intelligence cannot expect to understand it. 'God moves in a mysterious way, his wonders to perform.' We go over a children's hospital and see the innocent victims of meningitis, and wonder—as needs we must—what part of the Divine Design these interesting bacteria play. We shake our heads and conclude that it is all a profound mystery. We would not have created such microbes ourselves, if we had had the power—in fact we are doing our best to exterminate them—but it is blasphemous to doubt the Divine Wisdom. And so our optimism is not impaired.

EXONERATING GOD

Leibniz, a contemporary of Newton, offered a solution which has been much derided, though some modern theologians are more indebted to him than they care to acknowledge. Leibniz was caricatured by Voltaire as Dr Pangloss—one of those incurable optimists who drive people who have to live with them into deepest pessimism.

Roughly, his solution was as follows: An infinite number of things are possible, but some things are not possible in combination or simultaneously. For things that are possible together, Leibniz coined the useful term 'compossible'. He concluded, therefore, that this was 'the best of all possible worlds'.

It is shallow, on this view, to blame God for pain. God could have created an inanimate world, without pain, but not an animate world. If you are capable of feeling pleasure you must be also capable of feeling pain; to wish things to be otherwise is to wish that there were Euclidean triangles whose angles do not add up to two right angles.

God cannot do the impossible, C. S. Lewis tells us:

'His omnipotence means power to do all that is intrinsically possible, not to do the intrinsically impossible. You may attribute miracles to Him, but not nonsense. There is no limit to His power. If you choose to say "God can give a creature free-will and at the same time withhold free-will from it" you have not succeeded in saying anything about God: meaningless combinations of words do not suddenly acquire meaning simply because we prefix to them the two other words "God can". It remains true that all things are possible with God: the intrinsic impossibilities are not things but nonentities. It is no more possible for God than for the weakest of His creatures to carry out both of two mutually exclusive alternatives; not because His power meets an obstacle, but because nonsense remains nonsense even when we talk it about God.' (*The Problem of Pain*, 1940)

On this view there can be no inconsistency between the

toleration of evil in the world and any of God's attributes. If we object that although the evil may be consistent with divine Reason, it seems difficult to reconcile it with divine Love, Lewis is ready for us. Our idea of Love is all wrong. We are altogether too soft-hearted:

'We want, in fact, not so much a Father in Heaven as a grandfather in heaven—a senile benevolence who, as they say, "liked to see young people enjoying themselves," and whose plan for the universe was simply that it might be truly said at the end of each day, "a good time was had by all." Not many people, I admit, would formulate a theology in precisely those terms; but a conception not very different lurks at the back of many minds. I do not claim to be an exception; I should very much like to live in a universe which was governed on such lines. But since it is abundantly clear that I don't, and since I have reason to believe, nevertheless, that God is Love, I conclude that my conception of love needs correction.' (*Ibid*)

C. S. Lewis's confession is interesting. He would like to live in a universe run on indulgent lines, rather than one in which Spartan discipline prevails. He would like nature to be good-nature; but he has been informed that 'God is Love', and so, since he cannot alter his ideas of the universe, he has to alter his ideas of love. One cannot help feeling that, to Lewis, God is rather like a schoolmaster of the stern, old-fashioned type who informs him as he raises the birch rod—what he tries most dutifully to believe—that 'this hurts me more than it hurts you.'

The schoolmaster walks the wards of the children's hospital, sternly reproving any sentimental whimpering, and perhaps not altogether happy about the use of anaesthetics. He seems to have come straight from the world of St Augustine, who preached the damnation of unbaptized infants. Or from the world of Geneva, in which, under Calvin's rule of saints, a child was beheaded for striking his parents.

Should we not rather call such a 'reign of terror' a 'reign

of love'? For, as Lewis reminds us, in sober metaphysical language, 'Love and Kindness are not coterminous.' More poetically, in Dante's phrase, Love is 'a Lord of terrible aspect'.

A DUALISTIC SOLUTION

All the alleged moral pointers to the existence of God point just as surely to the existence of the Devil. If God is not responsible for evil, and if someone has to be, surely an Anti-God must be postulated. This is a solution of ancient and respectable ancestry which entered Europe from Persia and is implicit in some deviations from traditional Christianity. Dualism is at least as reasonable an explanation of the world we live in as Monism.

Zoroaster, who lived about 1000 BC, taught that there were two cosmic Powers, Ahura Mazda (Ormazd), associated with Light, and Agra Amainya (Ahriman), associated with darkness. The universe was their battle-ground. Ormazd is not omnipotent, but he created all the good things; Ahriman created all the evil things. The angels of Ormazd fight the demons of Ahriman. Nevertheless Ormazd will win in the end.

Zoroastrianism inspired a famous heresy called Manichaeanism, which flourished in the third century AD, and taught that material things were all evil. Manichaeanism assumed dangerous proportions, attracted St Augustine and penetrated into India and even China. It also had affinities with the Gnostic heresy, a blend of Christianity and theosophy reaching back to earlier mystery-cults, as exemplified in the works of Marcion and Bardesanes. For these heretics, the entire world of matter was satanic; it sprang from a primeval kingdom of darkness and disorder which attacked a primeval kingdom of light and goodness. Thus there resulted an inextricable mingling of good and bad, beauty and ugliness, order and disorder, in creation.

Religious Dualism may not explain, but it does seem to reflect. the situation we actually find more adequately than religious Monism. It gave rise to curious trends within orthodox Christian theology, notably to a belief that somehow a mighty being, inferior to God, but immensely powerful, twisted and warped the divine creation. Dualism does not try to explain away the existence of evil; it fastens the blame on Satan.

Dr W. R. Matthews writes:

'When we contemplate the details of this evolution, we have the inescapable impression of a confusion and a tendency to degeneration which are somehow inherent in the world of life. We must not here embark upon the question of the meaning of the Fall, but we may note that the myths which have expressed the idea of "something gone wrong" may have been very fantastic, but they have at least given dramatic form to a character of the world which does not disappear as we come to be better acquainted with the facts.' (*Essays in Construction*)

The exciting prospects offered by sheer Diabolism may partly explain the vogue enjoyed by C. S. Lewis. He writes:

'It seems to me, therefore, a reasonable supposition, that some mighty created power had already been at work for ill on the material universe or the solar system, or, at least, the planet Earth, before ever man came on the scene: and that when man fell, someone had, indeed, tempted him.... If there is such a power, as I myself believe, it may well have corrupted the animal creation before man appeared. The intrinsic evil of the animal world lies in the fact that animals, or some animals, live by destroying each other. That plants do the same I will not admit to be an evil. The Satanic corruption of the beasts would therefore be analogous, in one respect, with the Satanic corruption of man.... If it offends less, you may say that the "life-force" is corrupted, where I say that living creatures were corrupted by an evil angelic being. We mean the same thing: but I find it easier to believe in a myth of gods and demons than in one of hypostatised abstract nouns. And after all, our mythology may be much nearer to the literal truth than we suppose. Let us not forget that Our Lord, on one occasion, attributes human disease not to God's wrath, not to nature, but quite explicitly to Satan.'

It is only fair to acknowledge that since the death of C. S. Lewis and the spread of what used to be called Modernism (now supplanted by demythologizing), belief in Satan has faded with the general decline of religion.

'The disappearance of the demons creates a problem for the Christian Theologian,' John Macquarrie frankly confesses. 'He goes to the ancient Christian documents to interpret the religious truths which they contain, and he finds that these truths are tied up with demonic myths to which he can no longer give credence. What is he to do?'

What, indeed! Happily there is a way out:

'We have to reject the demonic mythology, assuredly. But have we not a duty to ask what these ideas meant to the men who made use of them, and to see whether we cannot restate what they said in a form which will be free from outmoded mythical elements, and yet preserve the essential meaning of the death of Christ as seen by the patristic writers, and which they were trying to bring to expression in the ideas at their disposal?' (*Studies in Christian Existentialism* p 212)

ETERNAL PUNISHMENT

If Satan is on the way out, his dark empire must go with him. Even the language of evangelical revivalists has been muted. Billy Graham does not make vast audiences tremble at the thought of hell. There was a time when hell-fire was the Big Deterrent—a kind of religious atomic bomb. The Gospels—the 'good tidings'—not only announced that God loved men but also that if they did not believe it they would be thrown into a lake of fire and brimstone. Believe or be damned was a terrifying message, yet it is the very mainspring of a salvation religion. What, after all, are men to be *saved* from if not from hell?

James Joyce gave a vivid account of a sermon on hell in

Portrait of the Artist as a Young man. It is present as a threatening background in much of Newman's writings. Poor Dr Johnson was oppressed all his life by the morbid fear that he would be damned. It underlies Pascal's famous wager: If you choose to believe that God exists, and you are mistaken, you have nothing to lose; if you choose to deny God, and he does exist, you will go to eternal perdition. Since, if you choose aright, you will gain everlasting happiness, why not play safe?

The savage doctrine of the Fathers and St Augustine was only slightly modified by the logic of the medieval Scholastics. Aquinas consigned unbaptized infants to Limbo, together with virtuous Pagans. But he carried his logic to the extreme of saying that 'in order that the happiness of the saints may be more delightful to them, and that they may render more copious thanks to God for it, they are allowed to see perfectly the sufferings of the damned.... The blessed in glory will have no pity for the damned.' (*Summa Theologica*, III Supp (XCIV) 1–3)

No wonder that John Stuart Mill defiantly declared that if such a God demanded that he should sacrifice his integrity or go to hell, then to hell he would go. Even a modern Catholic finds the official doctrine repellant. Thus Andrew Boyle, a well-known biographer, writes: '... I can say truthfully, echoing the fine indignation of the American writer, Mary McCarthy, as she looked back on her Catholic girlhood, that I would rather spend eternity in Hell than in the company of a divine sadist capable of consigning any creature of his to perdition.' (*The God I Want* ed James Mitchell p 135)

CONTEMPORARY ATTITUDES

Various attempts have been made by the more sensitive Catholic apologists to soften the harshness of the dogma firmly laid down by the Council of Florence in 1439. Mivart's articles published in 1892–3 under the curious title *Happiness in Hell* were placed on the Index.

A book on similar lines by Getins, a Spanish theologian, met a similar fate. In 1932 F. Glorieux advanced an ingenious theory to the effect that at the moment of death, as the soul is separated from the body, it may have an opportunity to repent and so save itself. This met a cool reception.

Pius IX issued an encyclical which conceded, however, that some unbelievers might be saved because 'they suffer from invincible ignorance concerning our most holy religion and lead honest and virtuous lives, diligently observing the natural law and precepts engraved by God in the hearts of all'. (*Denzinger* 1677) But this does not apply to apostates.

It is often said that, of course, nobody *really* believes in hell nowadays. This is simply not true. The mass of practising Catholics, Greek Orthodox and evangelical Protestants are not even aware of the uneasy compromises with which the more liberal Christian intellectual tries to save God from being hardly distinguishable from the Devil. They would regard Professor William Empson's outburst as dreadful blasphemy: 'The Christian God,' he writes, 'the God of Tertullian, Augustine and Aquinas, is the wickedest thing yet invented by the black heart of man.' (*Milton's God* p 250)

The charge is in no way diminished by the plea that the torments of hell are to be understood in a metaphorical sense, that there is no literal fire, only a state of mind. But what is suffering except 'a state of mind?' If as we are told, to be in hell is to be withdrawn from the presence of God, an eternity of despair, a never-ending claustrophobic isolation, this is just as cruel a doom as physical pain.

An eminent Anglican theologian, E. L. Mascall, in *Christian Theology and Natural Science*, complains that the doctrine that 'heaven and hell are states, not places, has done much to eviscerate modern religion'. And Pope Paul, in a weekly general audience, protested: 'Who today speaks of hell? No, the idea is not liked and therefore not discussed. But the teaching of the Church, including hell, must be defended at any cost.' (*The Guardian*, December 4, 1968)

HAPPINESS AS AN AIM

Hell depends on sin, though sin does not entail hell. Sin is rebellion against the laws of God, and if there were no such laws, and no God, 'sin' would be a meaningless term. Nature knows nothing of sin. Man invented the idea of sin when he invented the idea of gods. He did not invent suffering or death. There is no sense in saying that these *ought* not to exist; they are just facts of the conditions of all sentient life. It is how we decide to act in face of such facts that raises the question of what *ought* to be done. The decisions we make constitute our morality.

For example, when a Humanist says that people *ought* to be happy he is affirming what he intends to strive for. He does not promise or expect complete success. He is showing where he himself stands. He has chosen the values by which he intends to give priority to certain actions—ie those likely to promote happiness and reduce misery.

Happiness, then, is what he considers a good consequence, misery what he will treat as a bad one. It is good for people to have enough to eat, bad for them to starve. It is right to prevent famine, wrong to do nothing about it. Suffering that could be prevented is an evil; suffering that cannot be prevented is not strictly 'evil', though it may be tragic, because no responsibility can be fixed. We cannot be blamed for what we did not bring about.

RIGHT AND WRONG

At this point the Humanist may be asked a question which is intended to disconcert him and covertly imply that God is still necessary, or else one thing would be as good as another. Is the decision to label some actions 'right', others 'wrong', only a matter of taste? Unless moral values are objective, why should we condemn Himmler for organizing the slaughter of millions of Jews? Why should we not admit that robbery, murder and treachery are equally valid choices even though in a particular type of society they are punished? For what reason, except our own personal preference, do we call happiness good and misery bad? One way of dealing with this ploy is suggested by Richard Robinson, an Oxford philosopher and classicist, in *An Atheist's Values*:

'*Misery is an evil and happiness is a good*. If anyone denies this, there is nothing to say to him. If he contemplates happy children without any satisfaction, if he calls to mind the vast array of miseries in the world, such as wounded stags, eaten alive by ants, oiled birds battered on rocks, men and women with arthritis or insane depression, and feels no pity or disturbance, there is nothing to say to him. We choose to lessen misery and he does not. We choose to promote happiness and he does not.' (p 48)

In a non-pejorative sense we may even admit that our moral values, like our aesthetic ones, are matters of taste, though it would be safer to speak of sensibility. The insensitive man can watch another being torn to pieces by dogs, or a prisoner being tortured to make him confess, with callous indifference. That vastly more people today have this sensitiveness to suffering than a century or more ago is undeniable. The great Irish famine affected public opinion in England immeasurably less than a famine in far away Asia or Africa does now. In the last hundred years there has been a remarkable extension of the area of sympathy, a kind of expansion of consciousness.

Possibly there is an aesthetic element, too, in our vision of the good life and the good society. We speak metaphorically of some actions being ugly, of performing something 'beautifully'. It is not altogether clear what we are trying to convey, yet the superlative seems fitting. The Greeks had no hesitation in identifying the Good with the Beautiful. It was the highest commendation they could make. Aristotle once said that a man who loves himself will be ready to sacrifice himself 'to take possession of the beautiful'.

OBJECTIVE AND SUBJECTIVE THEORIES

Ethical theories are sometimes divided into two broad classes: those which regard moral values as objective and those which treat them as subjective. Kant is the most famous upholder of the objectivity of values who did not appeal to divine revelation for support. As we have seen, he believed that purely rational considerations could lead us to a standard of conduct that is universally just because we ourselves are rational beings.

A moral law of this kind would be absolute and unalterable. It imposes an obligation that is inescapable no matter what the practical outcome may be. Kant did not start from the premise of a Supreme Lawgiver, but he was driven to postulate a God because a universe of purely physical properties seemed to leave no room for an absolute Moral Law. The Law showed itself only in the actual experience of rational human beings with freedom to choose. If Kant seems inconsistent in appealing to faith where reason finally failed he undoubtedly expressed in a more sophisticated way the feeling so many people have that it does not make sense to believe in absolute values if values are merely manmade.

One alternative to this expedient is to claim that values are objective and known to us directly by intuition. This was the view of G. E. Moore, a Cambridge philosopher who greatly influenced the so-called Bloomsbury Group and paved the way to the absorption with linguistic analysis which came to dominate subsequent developments. Moore was anxious to show that 'good' cannot be a synonym for pleasure, as Bentham thought, or for living 'according to Nature', or furthering the course of evolution to a higher level. Some things, he argued, have intrinsic value—they possess a simple, unanalysable property called goodness, which is a non-natural (but not supernatural) property, as distinct from a natural, but equally unanalysable property like the colour yellow.

He contended that to say that pleasure is good, is surely saying something more than that pleasure is what we desire. The 'something more' is what constitutes an ethical judgment. Consequently Herbert Spencer's view that 'good' merely means 'more evolved' ignores this important difference between a fact of Nature and an evaluation.

Values cannot be derived from facts. What *is* the case is a fact; what we think *ought* to be the case is a value. Moore called the confusion of facts and values 'The Naturalistic Fallacy'.

How, then, can we tell which actual things have the extra property of goodness? On this practical question Moore has no doubts. We recognize it intuitively. 'Once the meaning of the question is clearly understood the answer to it, in its main outlines appears to be so obvious, that it runs the risk of seeming to be a mere platitude. By far the most valuable things, which we know or can imagine, are certainly states of consciousness which may be roughly described as the pleasures of human intercourse, and the enjoyment of beautiful objects. No one, probably, who has asked himself the question, has ever doubted that personal affection and appreciation of what is beautiful in Art or Nature, are good in themselves; nor if we consider strictly what things are worth having *purely for their own sakes*, does it appear probable that anyone will think anything else has *nearly* so great a value as the things which are included under these two heads.' (*Principia Ethica* p 188)

Moore made a subtle and ingenious attempt to establish the objectivity of moral values, but if 'good' is a property, even though it can be known only by intuition, it is a 'fact' of Nature, and by deriving a moral 'ought' from an 'is' he was committing the very fallacy he condemned.

He prided himself on being a philosopher of common sense. After all, he was protesting, almost impatiently, that we *know* that love and friendship are valuable in themselves, that happiness is good and suffering and ugliness are bad, that only a philosopher's view of the world from his study would doubt it. These judgments, he contended, need no elaborate defence. To question them is to indulge in a barren intellectual exercise like trying to prove the reality of the external world. 'If I am asked "what is good?" my answer is that good is good, and that is the end of the matter. Or if I am asked 'how is good to be defined'? my answer is that it cannot be defined, and that is all I have to say about it.' (*Utilitarian Ethics*)

Moore, together with most members of that brilliant Cambridge circle, can be classed as a Humanist in the contemporary sense. But so can Bentham and Mill and the Utilitarians with whom Moore disagreed. It is obvious that once morality is deprived of its religious foundations there is plenty of scope for disagreement about what supports it.

UTILITARIAN ETHICS

Bentham brought the whole subject down to earth by starting with the assumption 'Morality must in the end be to our advantage'. He even claimed on occasions that he wanted to take the word 'ought' out of the language. The plain fact seemed to him that happiness consists in satisfying our wants. What we should aim at, therefore, is the kind of society in which the majority of people have as many as possible of their wants satisfied—'the greatest happiness of the greatest number'.

This principle has been criticized on logical grounds, and derided for less disinterested reasons, but it certainly has a robust good sense. It is the underlying motive of democratic socialism and the inspiration of the modern Welfare State.

Mill's objection that it ignored qualitative differences in various kinds of satisfaction does not undermine the general principle, though it then becomes more difficult to apply. For example, in a somewhat restricted field we have to apply it in deciding what sort of programmes to devise for popular entertainment. Bentham would probably give the mass audience what it wants; Mill would have sided with those who think we should educate the public taste.

Controversy about the nature of an ethical principle still continues unabated. This is to be expected once we abandon the belief that it must be obeyed because it is the will of God. Humanism today is the heir of the Utilitarian tradition in its insistence that man is a social animal, and that a society is good if it is organized for the maximum possible welfare of the majority of people.

An alternative view—which Humanism rejects—is that society should be organized for the production of a cultivated élite. That is why Nietzsche, although he was an atheist, cannot be counted as a Humanist in the contemporary sense.

Welfare, fulfilment, happiness are blanket terms and can be interpreted in many different ways. They cannot be regarded as clearly defined goals; they are more like signposts pointing in the general direction we should take. The centuries-old search for a single all-embracing formula, the Chief Good or *summum bonum* from which all rules of conduct could be derived has been largely given up.

There are a number of things, good in themselves, which make up the richness of a life that is lived to its capacity. We therefore need to create an order of priority. Thus an obligation to our family may conflict with an obligation to society. The scientist who gives military secrets to Russia because he is a dedicated Communist has to choose between being a traitor to his country or false to his conception of right. Dilemmas of this sort are innumerable, and ethical formulae are too general to be of much help.

Despite their rejection of moral absolutes the nineteenth-century agnostics and Utilitarians followed much the same conventions in daily life as Christians. The most drastic attacks on religious dogmas were usually accompanied by the assurance that the rejection of the supernatural

elements in the New Testament does not affect the ethical
precepts.

Marx and Nietzsche alone among the outstanding unbelievers saw the inconsistency of this attitude. They recognized that since Christian morals claimed the authority of a
divine revelation, if there was no such revelation the ethics
of the New Testament had no more privileged position
than the ethics of Aristotle or Spinoza, or any other human
being. The unbeliever must start afresh and build from the
ground up.

THE IMMORALITY OF FAITH

There is certainly one outstanding Humanist value that
conflicts with orthodox Christianity: the emphasis on
Truth. Christians, of course, condemn lying; but although
they do not tell lies to each other, the demand for faith
often involves telling a kind of lie to oneself.

Faith is one of the greatest of Christian virtues. It consists
in believing what you do not know. Moreover, it has been
held—at least by Christ—that not to do this is wicked.
'Blessed are they that have not seen and yet have believed.'
As for those who are not so blessed: 'He will reprove the
world of sin ... because they believe not on me.' (John xx
and xiv) No Humanist could possibly say with Thomas,
'Lord I believe, help thou my unbelief.'

The psychological process of acquiring faith is lucidly
and very candidly explained in a well-known Thomist
manual edited by the late Cardinal Mercier. Since faith in
what is not known cannot be attained by reason it must be
an act of will. 'If it is asked how is it that the will acts upon
the intellect so as to constrain it to assent to what, if left to
itself, it would not assent to, we should say that the part
played by the will is both that of withdrawing the reason
from a too close scrutiny of difficulties which naturally arise
from the obscurity of the material object, and also that of
concentrating attention on the consideration of motives
which make the proposition certain: that a revealed truth

can be believed by a prudent man and ought to be believed.' (*A Manual of Modern Scholastic Philosophy* p 401)

If unbelief is a sin, unless we can be quite sure that we suffer from 'invincible ignorance', the need for prudence is obvious. As Pascal urged, the prudent man tries to be on the winning side. But the very idea of 'withholding the reason from a too close scrutiny of difficulties' is abhorrent to the Humanist. It threatens the very possibility of disinterested inquiry. 'According to me,' writes Richard Robinson, 'this is a terrible mistake, and faith is not a virtue but a positive vice.' (*Op cit* p 119)

T. H. Huxley formulated the principle of Agnosticism in opposition to the religious view that faith is a virtue: 'This principle may be stated in various ways, but they all amount to this: that it is wrong for a man to say that he is certain of the objective truth of any proposition unless he can produce evidence which logically justifies that certainty.' ('Agnosticism and Christianity' *Nineteenth Century* June 1889)

JUDGING BY CONSEQUENCES

A morality which judges the rightness of an action by the consequences is very much concerned with evidence. In framing a social policy it will take into account the findings of the social sciences. It is into this field that the conflict between the absolute ethics of religion and the consequential ethics of agnostic Humanism has already moved. Thus, on the question of crime and punishment, the Humanist will ask whether hanging and long terms of imprisonment really do act as deterrents. The concept of retributive punishment—ie making a man suffer because we think he deserves it—belongs to the religious tradition.

In a manual of Moral Philosophy a Christian defence of the right of the State to punish, and not merely to try to deter or rehabilitate, is stated bluntly. Vengeance, we are told, is natural to mankind, and what is natural cannot be wholly bad. It is wrong for a private individual to take the matter into his own hands, but it is right for the State to do so:

'If punishment is never retributive, the human race in all countries and ages has been the sport of a strange illusion. Everyone knows what vengeance means. It is a desire to punish someone, or to see him punished, not prospectively with an eye to the future, for his improvement, or as a warning to others, but retrospectively and looking to the past, that he may suffer for what he has done. Is then the idea of vengeance nothing but an unclean phantom? Is there no such thing as vengeance to a right-minded man? Then there is an evil element, an element essentially and positively evil, in human nature.... We cannot admit such a flaw in nature.' (*Moral Philosophy* Joseph Rickaby SJ pp 169–70)

This attitude is entirely repudiated by Humanism. Punishment for its own sake seems senseless. Whereas for religion the wrong-doer is a sinner, for the Humanist he is a disordered or immature personality. Somewhere, possibly in early childhood, he may have failed to respond to the process of socialization, and if so, he should be regarded as a misfit.

Sexual aberrations are not 'sins', even at their most repulsive; they are usually symptoms of an arrest in development. Hence the active part played by Humanists in the reform of the laws against homosexuality. As Barbara Wootton pointed out 'the concept of illness expands continually at the expense of the concept of moral failure'. (*The Twentieth Century* May 1956)

THE SACRED AND SECULAR

Another legacy of religious teaching is the phrase 'the sacredness of life'. The secularist does not regard life, or anything else, as 'sacred', though the term might be retained to give greater emphasis to the value placed on life in the scale of priorities. The powerful religious opposition to reform of the abortion laws was mobilized under this emotive slogan. Whether or not a pregnancy should be terminated must be judged in accordance with evidence of the individual and social consequences, in the Humanist view. And so, too, must the still undecided issue of euthanasia.

The problems of sex and marriage, and the allied question of censorship, also give rise to a collision between the two types of morality. Those who believe that marriage is sacred because it is a sacrament regard it as indissoluble. Whether the prohibition of divorce leads to great hardship is dismissed as beside the point. Consequences are irrelevant.

Equally, if birth control is against the law of God it must be rejected despite the misery caused by the population explosion. The ruling of Pope Paul in *Humanae Vitae*, although it merely reaffirmed previous rulings, caused a serious mutiny in the Catholic Church. To most non-Catholics it seemed nonsensical and even wicked.

Public opinion has swung recently against absolute rules. The vast majority of people today take the commonsense view of the Utilitarians that rules are made for man, not man for rules, and if their application results in obvious unhappiness they must be amended. The Victorian agnostics were more preoccupied with what could be believed; the modern world has moved on to a new phase—what should be *done*.

The so-called Permissive Society is the outcome of a growing tolerance which, however, has not yet gone as far in Britain as in Scandinavia and Holland. It is also a symptom of the confusion between a new morality and a very old amorality.

THE MORALITY OF HUMANISM

The morality of modern Humanism starts from the choice of a way of life. There are many possible styles of life competing for our allegiance and they require different and often conflicting programmes of action. The Christian

ideal is holiness—conformity to the will of God as revealed
by the Church or the Scriptures. The Communist ideal, by
contrast, is this-worldly, and it aims at constructing a new
society in conformity with the will of the Party. The
Humanist ideal is also this-worldly, and its aim is the
maximum possible fulfilment of every individual and the
removal of as many obstructions to this end as the unrestricted use of scientific knowledge permits. It is inspired by
a well-grounded faith that our rapidly growing understanding of ourselves and of the laws of Nature is already
advanced enough to reduce a vast amount of the misery
caused by disease, malnutrition and poverty.

We cannot ensure that people will be happy, but we can
at least remove many of the obvious causes of unhappiness.
This is a freely chosen goal, and no further reason can be
given for selecting it among rival goals. If the Christian
objects that we cannot justify it, one reply would be that
neither can he justify obeying God's will. It may be prudent
to obey an omnipotent Being, but that does not entail that
such a Being's will is 'good'.

There is no way of *proving* that we ought to increase happiness and decrease misery to anyone who does not feel that
this is self-evident. The fundamental principle which sets
our sights is not, however, a statement of a fact but of a
decision. We shall need all the facts we can obtain to carry
it out, and the most effective way of using them will, of
course, give rise to disagreement and rational debate. The
rules of conduct we must devise—and our criticism of existing rules—require detailed evaluations in the light of our
estimates of probable consequences. The means we employ
cannot be separated from the end; if we will the latter we
must will the former.

To say that a certain style of life is good is not at all like
saying that grass is green. The former is a value-judgment,
a commitment, not a description. It announces the direction
we intend to follow. We cannot *prove* to anyone who denies
it that the rules necessary to live in this way are 'right', but

we can give cogent reasons for commending them. The basic choice is far from being mere caprice, but it does imply that we are free to make such a decision. This raises the thorny problem of freewill versus determinism which must next be considered.

SIX

FREEWILL AND DETERMINISM

There is no more intractable controversy in the history of thought than that which has raged between the determinists and the advocates of freewill. Unless the issue is very clearly stated we are liable to lose our way in a maze of purely verbal argument.

The religion of the ancient Greeks encouraged a type of fatalism. Greek tragedy is overshadowed by the concept of a mysterious Destiny, to which even the Olympian gods were subject. The religious idea of Fate was 'secularized' by Leucippus and Democritus as abstract Necessity. Everything that happened was attributed to the movement of material atoms, and everything was consequently determined—ie ruled by Necessity. Against this, Epicurus raised his voice in defence of freedom, declaring that he would sooner be a slave to the old gods of the vulgar than to the Necessity of the philosophers.

The Stoics restored personality to this abstract concept, but on a higher level than that of the primitive idea. For them, Gilbert Murray tells us, Necessity 'is like a fine thread running through the whole of existence—the world, we must remember, was to the Stoics a live thing—like that invisible thread of life which, in heredity, passes on from generation of living species and keeps the type alive'.

The Christians also had a notion of a thread in the hereditary guilt transmitted from Adam. The Stoics, however, did not regard man's nature as inherently tainted; on the contrary, as long as man acted in accordance with his true self, he was in harmony with the Reason underlying the world, the mind of Zeus.

Aristotle taught that man had the power to choose

between good and bad actions; indeed, if he had no such power, why should the virtuous be rewarded and the wicked punished? The views of both Aristotle and the Stoics powerfully influenced Christian theologians when they came to grapple with the problem of God's omnipotence and man's freedom.

CHRISTIANITY AND FREEDOM

For centuries the problem of freewill was formulated for the most part in theological language. Obviously if man deserves punishment for doing wrong he must be capable of doing right. Christianity is therefore committed to a belief in freewill. Or, so it would seem, but the situation is not as simple as it looks. Granted that God is omniscient, He must know in advance how a man will choose. He must therefore know who will be saved and who will be damned. But if an individual's actions are completely predictable, what can we mean by calling him a free agent?

As if this were not enough there is the further difficulty that owing to the sin of Adam, all men have a natural propensity to sin. To what extent does this unfortunate inheritance diminish their responsibility? And what of the responsibility of God for a state of affairs that seems unjust by human standards? Why should the innocent suffer because of the guilty?

One answer is that it is all an inscrutable mystery, as Lotze humbly acknowledged. 'Our finite wisdom has come to the end of its tether and we do not understand the solution which yet we believe in.'

However, this refuge in what Spinoza called 'the asylum of ignorance' has nothing to recommend it. The Christian, if he wishes to debate at all, should give a better answer than this. Some light, one would have thought, would be thrown on the subject by the Scriptures, but when we turn to them we find such ambiguities that confusion is worse confounded.

The orthodox doctrine of Original Sin, forgiven at baptism,

simply cannot be found in the Biblical record. Much of it is, no doubt, derived from the interpretations of the Pauline writings. But there is no agreement about the meaning, for example, of the fifth chapter of the Epistle to the Romans. In Romans viii, 29–30, some people claim to find justification for the doctrine of Predestination:

'For whom he foreknew, he also foreordained to be conformed to the image of his Son, that he might be the first-born among many brethren; and whom he foreordained, them he also justified; and whom he justified, them he also glorified.'

The best, but by no means wholly successful, attempt to clear up the muddle in the early Church was made by St Augustine of Hippo, in the first part of the fifth century. Augustine claimed to follow Paul in teaching that God had predestined the elect to be saved. No merit, no amount of natural virtue, could entitle any individual to be saved. Thanks to Adam, sin had been inherited; and it was like a disease that had been handed down. Even new-born babes had inherited this spiritual leprosy; if they died without being baptized they would be damned.

A more humane, and possibly more pagan, view was advanced at the same time by Pelagius, a British monk. He argued that Adam injured himself alone, not the whole of mankind; that new-born children are in the same condition that Adam was before the Fall; that human nature is not so deformed that virtue is impossible without supernatural aid.

One point at issue was: Who takes the initiative when, for example, an adult, like Augustine, is converted? Did Augustine approach God, and because of his approach receive grace? Or did God approach Augustine, having marked him down from eternity for conversion? This, incidentally, lies behind the sort of question that Humanists sometimes ask believers; How do you *begin* to have faith?

St Augustine did not supply a permanently acceptable answer. The whole controversy was reopened centuries later. But Augustine's emphasis was on the first approach by

God, who makes a gift that no man can deserve; the Pelagian emphasis was on the first approach by man, who receives according to his deserts. In the case of new-born children, the question of deserts (resulting from free choice) does not arise; to Augustine that meant that they deserved nothing, and so were damned; but to Pelagius that, since they did not deserve to be damned, they would be saved.

It is useful to bear in mind these two streams of thought, which came into such prominence in the fifth century, because they later broadened into twin rivers. The Roman Church attempted a compromise, but Luther and Calvin returned to the Augustinian doctrine. According to Luther, man has no more power to turn to God than a stone, unless God makes the first move. Man is totally depraved.

MEDIEVAL SOLUTIONS

So long as the problem of determinism was stated in purely theological language, the deeper significance of it remained hidden. Neither Augustine nor Luther was, in the technical sense, a philosopher. It is not easy to give a straight answer to the question of whether they supported freewill or determinism, because the implication of those terms was not sufficiently appreciated. To a non-Christian one thing seems plain enough: Adam, at least, was supposed to have exercised freewill in an unequivocal sense. The depravity of his descendants was due to Adam's free choice of evil before he was 'tainted'; and henceforth, according to one strand of Christian thought, freedom of choice was hindered by an inherited bias.

Aquinas, in the thirteenth century, proposed a way out of the apparent contradiction that if man's nature possessed this bias the will could not fairly be said to be free. Aquinas saw that an important philosophical question was involved —whether the order of things was rational or whether it was the result of a divine caprice. On the cruder versions of Predestination, one would almost imagine the names of the elect and the damned to have been drawn from a hat.

To Aquinas, as to many of the Greeks, the Order of Nature seemed the expression of the divine Reason. Aristotle had compared the ordered movements of the heavenly bodies with the marching forth of Homer's armies before Troy. The starry heavens and human reason were evidence of the existence of a directing mind behind the bewildering flux of change. Thus we get the foundations on which Christian Rationalism was later built.

Aquinas saw that from the Christian point of view it was essential to explain the psychology of God as well as the psychology of man, in order to resolve the contradictions of freewill and determinism. The solution he proposed was that to be free meant obeying the voice of reason rather than the promptings of impulse.

Even God obeyed his reason. God made no purely arbitrary decrees. The divine Will was in harmony with the divine Reason. God is not a despot, demanding blind submission. God's laws and commandments are rational; and if we would be rational we must obey them. In the technical language of philosophy, the divine Reason is 'logically prior' to the divine Will.

Aquinas defined freedom as 'the faculty of choosing what leads to an end' (*Summa Theologica* I q 62, a, 8). In other words, free choice is always between means and not ends. The will seeks happiness; in that sense every choice is determined. But the intellect may present us with rival material means of obtaining happiness; and we may, foolishly, choose something that is inferior.

The problem is partially illustrated by the medieval conundrum of 'Buridan's Ass'—doubtfully attributed to Jean Buridan, a French philosopher, who was born about 1288 and studied under William of Ockham, in the University of Paris. Suppose an ass were placed between two loads of hay, equal in quantity and quality and the same distance from him: would he starve to death because of his inability to choose? Those who hold that the will must choose the greatest good offered to it must hold, it is argued, that the will would be paralysed if presented with two absolutely equivalent good objects.

It might be mentioned, in passing, that modern psychologists give instances of such 'paralysis'. A neurosis is brought about by some emotional conflict. During war the conflict between the sense of duty and the instinct of self-preservation sometimes leads literally to paralysis of an arm or leg or to hysterical blindness. On similar lines, Pavlov induced hysterical symptoms, not indeed in asses, but certainly in dogs.

What was, to start with, an obscure theological conundrum, gave rise to a profounder philosophical problem in the Middle Ages. If we trouble to penetrate the theological formulation we shall see in this, as in other Scholastic debates, the seeds of controversies that are still very much alive today though they are expressed in more sophisticated language. Today we are not specially concerned about the self-imposed difficulties of theologians; but the philosophical aspect of their discussion is worth examining. Before turning to the modern form of the debate let us take a final glance at the family quarrel within the churches.

COLLECTIVE GUILT

For the Christian, as we have seen, freewill is thought to absolve God from responsibility. It is a device whereby the guilt of much of the evil in the world is fastened on man. The mass of moral and social evil can be attributed to man's mis-use of freewill.

What, however, is meant by man? If Adam sinned and was punished, well and good; but is it just that all his descendants should have the dice heavily loaded against them? There is a tendency among contemporary Christian writers to hint obscurely at a sort of collective man.

Dr Alec R. Vidler is not noticeably disturbed by the possibility of the innocent suffering with the guilty:

'The fact is that, when men, corporately or individually, in the exercise of their freedom choose evil, then, sooner or later, in one way or another, punishment, disaster, follows. This is God's way of teaching us in the bitterness of experience that evil is evil and damnable, and that He is a righteous God who cannot and will not tolerate wickedness in His world. And the fact that in the working out of the consequences of sin the comparatively innocent suffer with and for the guilty is evidence of our human solidarity. We are members of a race, bound together in good and evil, not isolated atoms.' (*Good News for Mankind*)

C. S. Lewis tried to express this sort of 'solidarity' in more metaphysical language:

'That we can die "in" Adam and live "in" Christ seems to me to imply that man, as he really is, differs a good deal from man as our categories of thought and our three-dimensional imaginations represent him; that the separateness—modified only by causal relations—which we discern between individuals is balanced, in absolute reality, by some kind of 'inter-animation' of which we have no conception at all. It may be that the acts and sufferings of great archetypal individuals such as Adam and Christ are ours not by legal fiction, metaphor, or causality, but in some much deeper fashion.'

It would be too kind to call this a mystical explanation; it is just plain nonsense. Freewill is invoked to account for the existence of evil, but the argument—for what it is worth—is wrecked by the doctrine of the Fall of Man, entailing a hereditary bias to evil which makes the exercise of freewill extraordinarily difficult, if not impossible. Because we have freewill we are responsible for our actions; and yet, when temptation comes, our hand is forced, and we do not so much fall deliberately as fall because we are too weak to stand.

What sort of an 'explanation' is this? It is no explanation at all. It is as though, through Adam's sin, we all suffered from partial, if not total blindness, and were then called sternly to task for stumbling against an obstacle that we could not properly see.

Whatever the merits of the doctrine of freewill it does not carry out here the programme for which it was intended. It fails to shift responsibility from God to man. It fails also to reconcile divine goodness and omnipotence with the fact that the innocent suffer with the guilty. It creates even more difficult problems for religion than those it seeks to solve.

A return to the determinism first advanced by the Greek Atomists marked the new secular approach which matured with the success of Newtonian science and emerged, full-fledged with Laplace in the eighteenth century. Admittedly Spinoza had already developed a thorough going determinism on metaphysical grounds, but it remained for Laplace to set the seal of scientific authority on the belief in an unbroken (and unbreakable) chain of cause and effect.

Spinoza (1632–1677) wrote:

'The decisions of the mind are nothing save desires, which vary according to various dispositions.

'There is in the mind no absolute or freewill; but the mind is determined in willing this or that by a cause which is determined in its turn by another cause, and this by another, and so on to infinity.

'Men think themselves free because they are conscious of their volitions and desires, but are ignorant of the causes by which they are led to wish and desire.'

SCIENTIFIC MECHANISM

The French materialists of the Enlightenment were out and out determinists. La Mettrie argued for uncompromising mechanism in *L'homme Machine*. He said that every atom in the universe obeys laws. Every atom in the human body must therefore move according to the same laws which govern the motion of the planets. So there cannot be such a thing as freedom of choice. Everything a man feels or thinks follows the same blind, mechanical necessity as the planets. Man is a complicated piece of clockwork.

Diderot (1713–84) made a slightly different point:

'Since I act this way, anyone who can act otherwise is no

longer myself; and to declare that, at the moment I do or say a thing, I could do or say another is to declare that I am myself and someone else.'

But it was Laplace, writing from his position as an eminent astronomer and mathematician, who stated the case with such clarity that until the beginning of the present century the libertarians despaired of refuting him on scientific grounds and were forced to appeal either to intuition or metaphysics. In his *Philosophical Essay on Probabilities* (1773) he wrote:

'We ought to regard the present state of the universe as the effect of its antecedent state and as the cause of the state which is to follow. An intelligent being who at a given instant knew all the forces animating nature and the relative positions of the beings within it would, if his intelligence were sufficiently capacious to analyse these data, include in a single formula the movements of the largest bodies of the universe and those of its lightest atom. Nothing would be uncertain for him: the future as well as the past would be present to his eyes.'

John Stuart Mill (1806–73) was also convinced that man was no exception to the rule for causal law. It was only ignorance of the data that made it impossible to predict exactly how a man would behave. He held: 'That, given the motives which are present to an individual's mind, and given likewise the character and disposition of the individual, the manner in which he will act might be unerringly inferred; that if we knew the person thoroughly, and knew all the inducements which are acting upon him, we could foretell his conduct with as much certainty as we can predict any physical event. This proposition I take to be a mere interpretation of universal experience, a statement in words of what everyone is internally convinced of.'

Thomas Henry Huxley (1825–95) as a biologist, saw no real escape from determinism:

'We are conscious automata endowed with free will in the only intelligible sense of that much-abused term—inasmuch as in many respects we are able to do as we like—but none the less parts of the great series of causes and effects which, in unbroken continuity, composes that which is, and has been, and shall be—the sum of existence.'

Another biologist, Ernst Haeckel, in his popular account of evolution, *The Riddle of the Universe*, was convinced that the controversy was over and the libertarians routed:

'The great struggle between the determinist and the indeterminist, between the opponent and the sustainer of the freedom of the will, has ended today, after more than 2,000 years, completely in favour of the determinist. The human will has no more freedom than that of the higher animals, from which it differs only in degree, not in kind.... We know that each act of the will is as fatally determined by the organization of the individual, and as dependent on the momentary condition of his environment, as every other psychic activity. The character of the inclinations was determined long ago by heredity from parents and ancestors; the determination to each particular act is an instance of adaptation to the circumstances of the moment wherein the strongest motive prevails, according to the laws which govern the statics of emotion. Ontogeny teaches us to understand the evolution of the will in the individual child. Phylogeny reveals to us the historical development of the will within the ranks of our vertebrate ancestors.'

THE LIBERTARIAN CASE

The libertarian case, however, also appeals to scientific evidence. Alternative arguments in its favour are drawn (*a*) from intuition (*b*) from metaphysics.

The bluntest statement of direct insight is the famous retort of Dr Johnson: 'Sir, I know the will is free and there's an end on't.' This certainly corresponds to what most ordinary people feel. They hesitate between alternatives and often after a considerable struggle they make their choice. If the experience of choosing is an illusion, it is asked, why should it have ever arisen?

Sir William Bragg, the physicist, also appealed to direct experience, though he does not—and we need not—call it 'intuition'.

'It is true that Nature's operations move with machine-like precision, and that all her processes, whenever we are able to repeat them, follow the rules of the experimental laboratory. But it is also true that we have another laboratory, wherever we meet our fellow-men, and that there also we learn by experience, and make observations on which we base thoughts and actions. We feel that we have some control over what we do, and may act selfishly or unselfishly. If the lessons of the two laboratories seem to contradict each other, the clash is not even so definite as that in which in the physical world may set the wave theory and the particle theory in apparent contradiction, if we confuse the uses to which the two theories may be put.' (*Scientific Progress*)

A more detailed account of what the experience of freedom involves is given by L. L. Whyte in *The Next Development of Man*:

'To unitary man freedom means the power of the subject to choose, not arbitrarily or in opposition to the course of Nature, but in accordance with his own nature, that is, in continuity with his past. On the other hand the necessity in nature does not imply compulsion or constraint or even the determinism of a mechanical causality, but the continuity of form in natural processes. The experience of freedom and the recognition of necessity can therefore be translated respectively as the sense of being able to think and act in continuity with one's own past and the perception of the continuity of form in natural process. To unitary man there is no distinction between such freedom and such necessity, continuity of development is the form both of objective necessity and of subjective freedom. The continuity of natural processes has the character of the development of form. The recognizable identity of each person lies in the continuity of development of his own characteristic form.

Freewill, the exercise of choice, selection—these lead to the course which develops the person's characteristic form. There is nothing arbitrary in freewill and nothing constraining in natural law; continuity of development is common to both. Freedom and necessity are the subjective and objective, the spiritual and material aspects of this continuity seen by dissociated man.' (p 234)

EXISTENTIALISM AND FREEDOM

Freedom to choose is, of course, basic to all forms of Existentialism. Whereas philosophy since Descartes gave great prominence to theories of how we come to know objects independent of our immediate experience, the Existentialists broke new ground by focusing attention, not on what we perceive, but on how we decide what to *do*. They pointed out the dangerous inadequacy of theories of knowledge which picture man as the passive recipient of sensations from which he infers the existence of a world outside the circle of his immediate consciousness.

Man, insists Sartre, is not just a spectator of life, he is an actor in the drama—and ultimately the tragedy—of human existence. Hitherto, philosophers have concentrated on the problem of the intellect and neglected the most distinguishing characteristic of a human being, which is the *will*. If the will is not free there is no sense in talking about the power to make a moral choice. There is no such thing, in that case, as choice.

Sartre has constructed the most radical philosophy of freedom that, has yet been conceived. It starts with a sharp distinction between the world of blind, inanimate nature and self-consciousness, between the world of *things* and of *persons*. It denies that man is at the mercy of heredity and environment. He is not something already finished, completed, unalterable; he is something in the making. And he—by what he freely chooses to do with his life—is continuously *making himself*. The only thing he cannot choose is not to be free. 'Man is condemned to be free.'

This may seem a sombre conclusion to what at first sight appears as an exhilarating philosophy. It is sombre because the freedom to choose our own style of life, our own values, is doomed to futility by our final extinction. Our choice is not whether to obey the moral law; there is no absolute moral law. We may think we must choose to submit to the will of God, or reject, but this is illusory because there is no God. The only absolute is freedom itself, and this does not mean that sometimes our actions are entirely original and creative, and at other times determined: 'Man cannot be at times free and at other times a slave; either he is always or entirely free or he is not free at all.'

Again, 'Man is responsible for what he is. Thus, the first effect of Existentialism is that it puts every man in possession of himself as he is, and places the entire responsibility for his existence squarely upon his own shoulders.'

The emphasis on responsibility may seem to contradict the sense of frustration which led Sartre to exclaim 'Man is a useless passion'. It leads him somewhat inconsistently along the road taken by Kant—the assertion that a moral decision must be universally applicable.

'Nothing could be better for us unless it is better for all. If, moreover, existence precedes essence, and we will to exist at the same time as we fashion our image, the image is valid for all and for the entire epoch in which we find ourselves. Our responsibility is thus made greater than we had supposed, for it concerns mankind as a whole.... In fashioning myself I fashion man.' (*L'Existentialisme est un humanisme*)

TRUTH AND FALSEHOOD

A different line of attack on determinism is taken by the late Morris Ginsberg. 'If it be maintained that a man's judgments are themselves completely determined, that he cannot help making the judgments he makes, the answer is that this makes nonsense of all knowledge.... If all judgments were causally necessitated they would all be on the same level and it would be impossible to distinguish some as true and others as false. Sense and nonsense would all be equally necessitated. The whole notion of going by the evidence would lose all its meaning if in forming a judgment we were completely unable to resist the violence of present desire, the effects of past habits, the persistence of ancient prejudices or the forces of the unconscious.'

For example, if Freud is correct in thinking that our beliefs and actions are the outcome of unconscious motivation, how could Freud know that he was not in the same predicament? How could his theory then be said to be true? To the indeterminist, not only are the scientific search for truth and repudiation of wishful thinking undermined by such a theory, but so are other moral judgments. If all our actions result from instinctive drives and conditioned reflexes, how does man differ from other animals?

Animals ought also to be considered as morally responsible as man if the determinists are right, contends Professor C. A. Campbell, replying to Moritz Schlick, the Logical Positivist. 'It is quite possible, by punishing the dog who absconds with the succulent chops designed for his master's luncheon, favourably to influence its motives in respect of its future behaviour in like circumstances. If moral responsibility is to be linked with punishment, as Schlick links it, and punishment conceived as a form of education, we should surely hold the dog morally responsible. The plain fact, of course, is that we don't. We don't, because we suppose that the dog "couldn't help it": that its action (unlike what we usually believe to be true of human beings) was simply a link in a continuous chain of causes and effects.' (*In Defence of Free Will, with Other Philosophical Essays* p 23)

We need not linger over the objection that men are not like machines as this is no longer seriously advanced in its original crude form. Obviously no one could hold that men behave like cars because it would be nonsense to hold a car responsible for breaking down. But highly sophisticated machines have been invented and they provide useful models of the operation of the brain and nervous system. The school of psychology which employs the concept of 'stimulus and response' to interpret learned behaviour might seem to leave no room for freedom, but this is not necessarily the case according to D. E. Broadbent. He points out that heredity and environment do not always act in a simple straightforward way. They can produce a complex system which will control its own detailed actions.

'There is no contradiction in attaching words such as "responsibility" to a self-regulating system, since once it is launched it is its own master: and yet we may well seek out the principles by which its regulation is achieved. In theological terms, to say that a creature has free will does not make it any the less a creature, deriving its being from sources outside itself. It would be idle to pretend that we now know the detailed way in which the machinery of moral choice revolves: but we do at least know that important animal or human actions do not follow single, isolated outside causes, as a billiard ball moves in response to a blow of a cue.' (*Behaviour* p 45)

RATIONAL CHOICE

Some libertarians take a short-cut through the difficulties raised by their opponents. They admit that every effect must have a cause, but they say that the cause of moral choice is to be found in the person himself. He is not the sport of external forces; not merely the product of heredity and environment. We are—as Sartre claimed—to some extent the masters of our destiny.

If we make a rational decision after weighing the pros and cons the cause is our application of human reason. Again, if someone could predict that we would act in a certain way and we heard the prediction, we could change course. So even in principle, the precise predictability that is required by Laplacean determinism is not really possible. A choice can be a creative act, bringing about something genuinely new, and not just the outcome of past influences.

Henri Bergson made this approach from an intuitionist angle. He held that we do not discover truth by the intellect; on the contrary, the intellect falsifies our experiences. The intellect constructs an abstract scheme, according to which one state of consciousness succeeds another, instant by instant; and this sort of scheme must land us in complete determinism. Actually, he argues, the flow of consciousness cannot be thus divided up into instants of time; true knowledge of it can be obtained only by direct insight, or intuition. Hence the paradox that we are convinced that we are really free, though intellectual arguments all show that we are determined. Our freedom consists in our ability to create the future, and that would be impossible if we were slaves of the past.

But do *all* intellectual arguments show that we are completely determined? A novel twist was given to the old debate by an advance in physics which seemed to suggest that the Law of Universal Causation, which no one hitherto had seriously doubted, does not always hold. Heisenberg's Uncertainty Principle states that it is impossible to predict the behaviour of a particle from its momentum and position, because when one of these factors is known, the other eludes detection. The act of observation interferes with the result.

The more accurately we measure the momentum the less determinate becomes the position. Yet if the particles which make up larger objects—tables, stars, the human body—cannot in any exact sense be precisely assigned both momentum and position, they behave very differently from the grosser matter which science studies. The laws of macroscopic world do not apply to microscopic entities.

SCIENCE AND CAUSATION

This entirely alters the previous way of looking at Nature. Macroscopic objects do, indeed, *seem* to behave just as though universal causation were true. The planets keep to their orbits, nautical tables can be relied on, every-day life can be carried on. But this uniformity—which seemed to be the grand design of an intelligent First Cause —is really the result of statistical probability. Considered in aggregate, the random movement of individual particles gives the appearance of order and precision. It is the kind of order which enables insurance companies to estimate the average duration of life, though they cannot say which individual will die before, say, the age of seventy.

'I do not think,' said Eddington, 'that there is any serious division of opinion as to the decease of determinism. If there is a division among the scientists it is between the mourners and the jubilants.'

Heisenberg himself said: 'The question whether from a complete knowledge of the past we can predict the future, does not arise because a complete knowledge of the past involves a contradiction.'

It might be thought that the inability to bring atomic particles into the web of cause and effect is due to the inadequacy of our instruments, and that one day we shall be able to do the trick. This was Einstein's view:

'I firmly believe, in company with most physicists, that the quantum hypothesis will eventually find its exact expression in certain equations which will be a more exact formulation of the law of causality.'

But the majority opinion entertains no such hope. The passing of physical determinism is greeted as another land-mark on the road to greater understanding of the processes of Nature. Schrödinger writes:

'Whence arises the widespread belief that the behaviour of molecules is determined by absolute causality, whence the conviction that the contrary is unthinkable? Simply from the custom, inherited through thousands of years, of thinking causally, which makes the idea of undetermined events seem complete nonsense, a logical absurdity.'

As might be expected, religious apologists welcomed the alleged breakdown of causality. It seemed to offer a way out of the conflict between religion and science on the freewill issue. They must have been disappointed that the scientists did not follow them.

Schrödinger is emphatic: 'The net result is that quantum physics has nothing to do with the free will problem. If there is such a problem, it is not furthered a whit by the latest development in physics. To quote Ernst Cassirer: "Thus it is clear ... that a possible change in the physical concept of causality can have no immediate bearing on ethics."' (*Science and Humanism* p 67)

And Eddington, though he believed in freewill, did not hold that the random movement of atoms in the brain could guarantee it. 'Could we pick out one atom in Einstein's brain and say that if it had made the wrong quantum jump there would have been a corresponding flaw in the theory of relativity?' he asked. 'It seems that we must attribute to the mind power not only to decide the behaviour of atoms individually but to affect systematically large groups—in fact to tamper with the odds on atomic behaviour.' And this implies that there is a fundamental difference between living and dead matter and an idealistic conception of mind. (*The Nature of the Physical World* pp 313-14)

Whatever hopes there may have been that modern physics would provide a loophole for the libertarians, the fact is that cold comfort can be derived from physicists themselves. To many people, reviewing the arguments for and against, it must seem that, like other great philosophical controversies, the honours are even. But when a controversy threatens to end in stalemate we are bound to ask whether the terms in which it has been stated are satisfactory? Are we saying what we really mean? What do we mean for example by 'free' and 'will'? Perhaps this is not the best language to use.

MAN AND MACHINES

No one today would assert that we possess a 'will' in the

plain sense that we have a nose. So it is misleading at the outset to ask 'Is the will free?' Again, suppose there are some events in the universe which are uncaused: does that help? Do we *want* to prove that our actions are purely random? Is that the sort of freedom we need? How can random actions possibly give a sense of moral responsibility —which is what the argument is basically about?

Another notion which arouses strong emotional resistance is that man is a 'machine', but this may be because we think of the rather simple artefacts that belong to the pre-electronic, pre-computer age. Machines can now be made which appear to learn from experience and correct their mistakes. Claims are advanced for them which would have seemed fantastic a decade or so ago. 'There is no obvious reason why we should not build machines like human beings or even some day build human beings themselves if anyone were so minded,' according to F. H. George. For example: 'It is surely easy to imagine—such machines have been in simple cases actually constructed—a machine that has the capacity to record its environment and react in accordance with its recorded environment and that part of its past environment that has been stored. The machine could be capable of making generalizations if only on the basis of probabilities of a frequency kind based on what the machine itself records. This means that the machine will vary its behaviour according to the nature of its environment, and we shall not necessarily know what its behaviour will be in advance for any particular environment.' ('Finite Automata'; *Philosophy*, Vol XXXII No 24)

It may be objected that such a machine will not be able to feel or show the aesthetic appreciation that is characteristic of a natural man. F. H. George denies that it would be so restricted:

'Many people have assumed that automata cannot—and could not—paint, or draw, or write poetry. The reason for this assumption is that while we may agree that robots may be made to go through the motions, they will not have the appropriate accompanying feelings. But why not?

Who is to say that we cannot in principle build a machine that has the same emotions that humans have? ... It is doubtless true that the sort of emotions that humans go through are closely related to the materials used in their construction, and we do not know enough yet to construct a robot from colloidal protoplasm, but would anyone care to assert that a construction in such terms was impossible?' ('Thinking Machines'; *Philosophy*, Vol XXXII No 121)

It is likely enough that many people will accept the challenge and make such an assertion. However, if a robot is identical in all essential respects with a natural human being, the question of whether it can act 'freely' still arises. The upshot of this discussion is that neither physics nor cybernetics provides a conclusive answer. In the quest, however, the meaning of the terms has become clarified and to some extent the original formulation has changed.

Freedom is not finally seen as random, motiveless action —that is no way of establishing human dignity and moral responsibility. Freedom is the absence of constraint. The free man does not act under the blind compulsion of instinct but with rational foresight.

The conscious effort that accompanies a voluntary action is absent from an involuntary action. We need not use such words as 'will' or 'volition' to describe the difference, but it is convenient in ordinary language to say that when a deliberate choice has been made between alternatives, the reasons offered for the choice are the cause of the action. Provided the alternatives are within our power to carry out we lay ourselves open to praise or blame. With such modifications both the determinist and the indeterminist can retain the concept of moral responsibility, which is all that matters in the practical living of our lives.

SEVEN

THE ORIGIN OF RELIGION

THE rise of Rationalism in the nineteenth century was dominated at first by Darwinism. It was natural that the concept of evolution should be applied to the development of human society and its ideologies. Obviously vast changes of outlook had taken place from ancient times onwards. Attempts were made to correlate these changes with the social structure and with advances in science and technology. Marx regarded religion as a reflection and rationalization of a class society. Comte thought that progress had occurred in stages: magic and religion were transmuted in a more sophisticated society into metaphysics, and he believed that in the end metaphysics was destined to give place to science. Freud, on the other hand, sought the genesis of magic and religion in psychology.

All these theories agreed that religion is a natural phenomenon. Its key-words, such as God, Soul, Conscience, could therefore be examined as objectively as any other matter of scientific study. There was nothing essentially mysterious about them. They had entered the language at some historical point and for various reasons they modified their meanings. They could not have arisen unless they satisfied some social or psychological need. One problem is therefore to account for the fact that the belief in a supernatural world managed to survive in a period when the success of science seemed to bring all human experience into a purely natural frame.

The supernatural explanation of the origin of the universe and the destiny of man is not based on evidence but on tradition. It is an account that has been handed down from generation to generation. 'It is not my word but my

Mother's word...' A cry from ancient Greece that finds its echo in those tribal societies where all things are justified or condemned on the authority of Custom. But traditions and customs charge; and no matter how old they are they must have had a beginning. If we believe that man descended from an ape-like ancestor we must suppose that not more (and probably less) than a million years ago speech was used for intelligent conversation for the first time.

For three-quarters of the Palaeolithic Age, *Homo Neanderthalensis* was one of the prototypes of man. *Homo Sapiens* had not yet appeared. The problem which orthodox theologians had to face is that Neanderthal man is a different species from *Homo Sapiens*. Yet Neanderthal man made stone implements, used fire, and buried his dead with a care that suggests rudimentary religious feeling. Did this clumsy, grotesque, and even pathetic experiment in humanity come into existence before or after the Fall?

DEFINITIONS OF RELIGION

Whether we describe the cults in vogue among prehistoric man, and certain aborigines that still survive, as religious or magical, is a matter of definition. Professor Leuba, in *A Psychological Study of Religion,* collected forty-eight definitions of religion. It would not have been difficult to double the number.

We must not be misled, however, by what is sometimes called 'the fallacy of the True Meaning'. There is a welter of observed phenomena in the religious field, and the anthropologist or psychologist selects and classifies for his own convenience. When we examine the various definitions proposed from this point of view we are no longer bewildered. We are not necessarily confronted by a conflict about the facts, but by different methods of classification.

The sense in which Frazer uses the word 'religion' is clearly stated in *The Golden Bough*:

'By religion, then, I understand a propitiation or conciliation of powers superior to man which are believed to direct and control the course of Nature and of human life.'

According to R. H. Thouless, 'Religion is a felt practical relationship with what is believed in as a superhuman being or beings.' This is vaguer and wider, but neither of these definitions would include early Buddhism. They assume that one or more gods is an essential ingredient in all religion. Matthew Arnold's view of morality touched with emotion might be applied to godless Buddhism. According to Hegel: 'Religion is the knowledge possessed by the finite mind of its nature as Absolute Mind.'

The Cambridge philosopher McTaggart, like the early Buddhists, was an atheist, but he would not have disclaimed the epithet 'religious'. In *Some Dogmas of Religion* he proposed the following definition:

'Religion is clearly a state of mind.... It seems to me that it may best be described as an emotion resting on a conviction of harmony between ourselves and the universe at large.'

The French sociologists who collaborated in *l'Année Sociologique* stress another aspect of religious phenomena. Thus Durkheim writes:

'Religion is a unified system of beliefs and practices relative to sacred things—that is to say, things set apart and forbidden: beliefs and practices which unite into one single moral community, called the Church, all those who adhere to them.'

On this view religion is a social phenomenon. It is what we do as members of a group, a kind of collective-thinking and mass-emotion which strengthens the sense of solidarity. But for A. N. Whitehead, on the other hand:

'Religion is what the individual does with his own solitariness.... If you are never solitary, you are never religious.

'Religion is the art and the theory of the internal life of man, so far as it depends on the man himself and on what is permanent in the nature of things.'

Clearly the individual that Whitehead is thinking about

is a member of a civilized community, whereas Durkheim and Frazer have in mind the primitive. Among primitives the true solitary is the magician. As Durkheim points out, there has never been a Church of Magic.

THE AGE OF MAGIC

It has been maintained that there are three great world-systems of thought, corresponding to three stages in the evolution of culture: Magic, Religion, Science. Perhaps the first advocates of this classification were a little too anxious to make a neat schematization. However we choose to classify the confused mass of facts and guesses which challenge us, there will be awkward items that stubbornly refuse to fit into the patterns we devise. It is extraordinarily difficult to be certain what modern primitives really believe; and it seems almost impossible to enter into the state of mind of the prehistoric hunters who have left us only a few heaps of stone, some carvings and the paintings like those in the dark recesses of the caves of the Dordogne and Altamira. Are we entitled to assume that the mental processes of Palaeolithic man were similar to those of aborigines still found in a pre-agricultural stage? Are we even safe in supposing that the mind of the primitive works in much the same way as our own?

Levy Bruhl once tried to show that the latter assumption is mistaken. He argued that primitive mentality scorns the law of contradiction and cannot be judged by the standards appropriate to civilized man, although we ourselves have a primitive layer underneath our intellectual development. This theory was strongly contested by Frazer:

'The myth of the illogical or pre-logical savage may safely be relegated to that museum of learned absurdities which speculative anthropology is constantly enriching with fresh specimens of misapplied ingenuity and wasted industry.'

These are extreme positions, but it is generally recognized nowadays that the early anthropologists were too ready to give an intellectual explanation of the origin of primitive beliefs. The tendency has grown since the early work of Robertson Smith to look for the origin of myths in the rites performed, rather than to seek to account for the rites as the natural consequence of previously held myths.

By dressing-up periodically to represent the Spring, we may come to believe in the existence of an independent being, the god of Spring, just as we might come to believe in the real existence of Father Christmas. In the course of the pantomime or the dance, when mass-suggestibility is at its height, stories may be told, and later on embroidered. Durkheim, Jane Harrison and many others, have contended that in this way myths and legends are generated by ritual.

The Australian aborigine who leaps in imitation of the kangaroo does so because he thinks that he assists in the multiplication of kangaroos. In parts of Germany and Austria the peasant thought he could make the flax grow taller by dancing or leaping high: the higher the leap the taller will be the flax that year. It would be straining the meaning of the word to describe these actions as 'religious'. They belong to the pre-religious stage, the primitive world-system of magic.

THE MEANING OF MANA

Frazer was taken to task for regarding magic as a sort of bad science. Be that as it may, these magical ceremonies seek to bring about the desired result largely by mimicry, and the magicians certainly believe that if the traditional acts are correctly performed they will be efficacious. There is no question of being dependent on the whims of super-natural beings. The ancient Egyptians believed that if a man knew the right spells even the gods would have to obey him. So if we classify these phenomena according to ritual (the thing done) rather than myth (the thing believed) we have a definite standard.

There is a great difference between leaping in the air to make flax grow and praying to God for a good harvest

Gods who are petitioned and offered sacrifices in the hope that they will grant favours belong to the religious, as distinct from the magical, stage of mankind. A useful definition of a god would be 'a supernatural being who is worshipped'.

Primitive man, as far as we can judge, was innocent of worship. He indulged in picturesque mimicry, partly because he thought that it really would ensure success in the chase and so increase the food supply, and partly no doubt because it also gave him a pleasurable and valuable sense of tribal solidarity. He was concerned to tap the mythical source of power indicated by the Polynesian word *mana*. This was conceived as a sort of spiritual electricity which inhered more powerfully in some objects than in others.

Gold, ochre, certain shells, amulets, bull-roarers were 'sacred'. They were full of *mana*. So were blood and semen and the objects that symbolized them. There was *mana* in lightning, in the wind, the earthquake and running water. The same concept is found among North American Indians under the name of Orenda and Wakonda, in Morocco as Baraka, and among the Egyptians as Hike.

Much has been made of the varying opinions held by anthropologists regarding the relation of religion to magic, but this must not be allowed to obscure the crucial question of whether in the lowest cultural stage we find societies who do not worship gods. Such a stage, if it exists, could not be explained in terms of orthodox Christianity. Indeed, Augustine went so far as to deny the possibility that human beings lived at the antipodes, on the ground that it would be impossible for them to be acquainted with the truths of revealed religion.

EVOLUTION OR THE DEVIL?

An argument that frequently occurs in Christian apologetics is that after the Fall the human race lost the vision of God and saw 'in a glass darkly'. The similarity between savage rites of communion and baptism and the Christian sacraments is explained as being due to a distorted view of divine truth.

The Christian Fathers, for example, were perfectly aware of the resemblances between the pagan mysteries and the Christian Eucharist. After describing the institution of the Lord's Supper, Justin Martyr goes on to say:

'Which the wicked devils have imitated in the mysteries of Mithra, commanding the same thing to be done.'

Tertullian also says that 'the devil by the mysteries of his idols imitates even the main part of the divine mysteries. . . . He baptises his worshippers in water and makes them believe that this purifies them from their crimes . . . Mithra set his mark on the forehead of his soldiers; he celebrates the oblation of bread: he offers an image of the resurrection and presents at once the crown and the sword; he limits his chief priest to a single marriage; he even has his virgins and ascetics.'

When the Spanish Conquistadores first encountered the eucharistic ceremonial of the Mexicans they immediately concluded that they were witnessing a Satanic parody of the Mass.

No sensible person would advance such a theory today. A much more subtle argument is sometimes advanced to protect the belief in God from the charge that it is a mere refinement of primitive superstition. This line of defence owed a great deal to the work of F. B. Jevons, and its present form may be summarized as follows.

A god is a spirit with a proper name. An impersonal potency, like *mana*, is not even a spirit, still less a god. The idea of a personal spirit, which develops in the so-called animistic stage, is an advance on the idea of an impersonal spirit; again the idea of a single supreme God is an advance on the idea of many gods. We may rightly conclude that the evolution of religious ideas is characterized by several stages: (1) Pre-animistic or magical, with impersonal spirits; (2) Animistic, with numerous personal spirits; (3) Polytheistic, with the worship of many gods; (4) Monotheistic, with the worship of one God.

But this does not mean, we are told, that one God has evolved in a straight line from many gods, many spirits, and originally from a vague impersonal force:

'If we choose to speak of this unfolding or disclosure as evolution, the process, which the history of religion undertakes to set forth, will be the evolution of the idea of God. But in that case the process which we designate by the name of evolution will be a process of disclosure and revelation. Disclosure implies that there is something to disclose: revelation, that there is something to be revealed to the common consciousness—the presence of the Godhead, of divine personality.' (*The Idea of God* F. B. Jevons)

The Christian who embarked upon a journey of discovery about the ancient world already believed that God existed; and so for him the evolution of the idea of God as studied by anthropology cannot be the whole story. It is sometimes alleged that the evolutionary stages mentioned above have no basis in fact. The Jesuit anthropologist, Father Schmidt, claimed that there is evidence of Monotheism in the most primitive societies. Andrew Lang used to cite the All-Father of the Australian aborigines as an example of primitive Monotheism. To some extent this is a dispute about facts.

WERE THERE ALWAYS GODS?

The last of the Tasmanians died in 1890. They were even more primitive than the inhabitants of the Australian mainland. According to Dr Nixon, the first Bishop of Tasmania, no trace can be found among them of any religious usage or even sentiment, unless indeed we can call by that name the dread of a malignant and destructive spirit which seems to have been their predominant, if not their only, feeling on the subject. (*Aborigines of Tasmania* R. L. Roth)

The Veddahs of Ceylon are described by all who have

come in contact with them as harmless, truthful and mono-gamous. They go about nude, and share all game and honey with the community. They do not appear to have any idea of gods or immortality. The Yahgans, so primitive that they are unclad despite the bleak climate of Tierra del Fuego, do not appear to have any religious beliefs. Accord-ing to the French ethnologists, Deniker and Hyades:

'We have studied the Yahgans very closely from this point of view during the year we spent among them and have never detected the least allusion to any kind of cult or religious idea.' (*Mission Scientifique du Cap Horn*)

The aborigines of Australia comprise a number of tribes at slightly varying levels. Some of them have a conception of a unique, pre-eminent being called variously Bunjil, Daramulun, Baiame, Nurunder. According to one version, he once lived on earth and ascended into heaven. He makes thunder and rain. He made men by fashioning an image out of clay and breathing into its nostrils. Then there is Murtu Murtu, who made a noise like a bull-roarer with his mouth. He taught the ideas passed on in the important initiation ceremonies. He was killed by wild dogs, who tore his body to pieces. Bits of his flesh fell to the earth, and out of them the natives now make bull-roarers.

It was natural enough for missionaries who first heard these stories to conclude that the Australians believed in a single God who had created the world. They seized upon the term All-Father, as used by Howitt in his authoritative study of tribes of South-east Australia. But Howitt em-phasized very clearly that this being was never worshipped. If we define a god as a being with a proper name who is wor-shipped we must conclude that the Australians are godless.

Spencer and Gillen, whose study of Australian tribes is now a classic, give an interesting account of an initiation ceremony. The novice submits to a painful ordeal, and everything possible is done to terrify him. At last he re-ceives the great revelation 'that the spirit creature, whom up to that time, as a boy, he has regarded as all-powerful, is merely a myth, and that such a being does not really exist, and is only an invention of the men to frighten the women and children.

'The central Australian natives—and this is true of the tribes extending from Lake Eyre in the south to the far north and eastwards across the Gulf of Carpentaria—have no idea whatever of the existence of any supreme being who is pleased if they follow a certain line of what we call moral conduct and displeased if they do not do so. They have not the vaguest idea of a personal individual other than an actual living member of the tribe who approves or disapproves of their conduct, so far as anything like what we call morality is concerned. Any such idea as that of a future life of happiness or the reverse, as a reward for meritorious or as a punishment for blameworthy conduct, is quite foreign to them.' (*Northern Tribes of Central Australia* 1904)

The theory that the Australians have a natural monotheism is therefore difficult to maintain. Those who approach the subject with a religious bias are tempted to interpret the confusing facts favourably for their own beliefs. But if we restrict ourselves to evidence, there are two alternatives. Either the Australians acquired their ideas from some external source, or the ideas now held have evolved in the course of thousands of years.

The once popular Diffusionist School, represented by G. Elliot Smith and W. J. Perry, claimed that the Australians received many of their conceptions from ancient Egyptian voyagers. If that is the case, clearly the aborigines give no support to the view that pure monotheism is the natural theology of a primitive man.

There is no way of deciding the issue conclusively, of course, but even if the All-Father idea is taken seriously, it by no means follows that this concept always existed. The evidence analysed by Durkheim can be interpreted quite differently. Durkheim calls attention to the widespread belief in a mythical ancestor of the tribe. He contends that as the

tribes travel about and members of different clans inter-
mingle, so an inter-tribal mythology is established. The All-
Father is thus an ancestral spirit who has won a pre-eminent place. (*Elementary Forms of Religious Life*)

MAN INTO GOD

In this conflict of theories there are two strongly opposed
strands of thought:

(1) Euhemerism originated from a Greek philosopher,
Euhemerus, who lived about 300 BC, and taught that the
gods are merely men who lived long ago and who have
since been glorified in pious memory. The Diffusionists
follow in some respects this principle of Euhemerus when
they hold that the Australians' claim to have been taught
their myths by mysterious ancestors is the truth. The ancestors, on this view, were intrepid Egyptian mariners. So, too,
Osiris was a real man who invented agriculture and became
deified.

(2) A rival theory regards gods and heroes, as 'collective
representations'. According to this, the name of a clan, for
example, is not the name of a particular individual who
gave rise to it. There was no such individual man as
Heracles, and when we read about his exploits we are really
reading a garbled version of the deeds of the clan of which
Heracles is the mythical ancestor.

Again, a group of ritual dancers, taking part in some
actual ceremony, may be personified as a Spirit. But this is a
different type of personification from that of a natural
phenomenon such as Dawn. An actual human being is
dressed up as Spring, Winter, the Old Year; a succession of
such pantomimes begets a belief in a being over and above
the real performers, just as a succession of Lord Mayor
Shows might beget a belief in *the* Lord Mayor. The god,
says Doutté, in *Algerian Magic*, is the collective desire personified.

It is clearly too simple to say that a bull-god or a horse-
god, is the inevitable projection of people in whose econo-

mic life bulls and horses play the leading part, though the symbol chosen will undoubtedly represent what the community values. Poseidon, for example, is sometimes represented grasping a fish in one hand, a trident in the other and seated on a bull. This confusion is due to the fact that to begin with Poseidon was the Cretan Minotaur, half-man, half-bull, worshipped by islanders who were fishermen, agriculturalists and herdsmen. The monstrous symbol, however, tells us more than that: it betrays the existence of a primitive ritual in which the king put on a bull's head and horns, and possibly his hide and hoofs, in order to obtain for himself and his people the fertility and potency, 'the tremendous mana of the bull', as Gilbert Murray calls it. Lord Raglan wrote:

'Myth is never fictitious, since it is always the story of something that real people do or did; on the other hand, it is never historical, because it is always the story of something which was done not once but many times. Myth and ritual are complementary; ritual is a magic drama to which myth is the book of the words, which often survives after the drama has ceased to be performed.' (*Death and Rebirth*)

This is more subtle and fruitful than the crude theory that the gods are merely transmogrified men. As A. M. Hocart writes in *Kingship*:

'The Euhemerists came nearer to the truth in so far as they recognized that the prime interest of man has always been man: so they looked to human actions to explain myths. Where they erred was in limiting themselves to those actions which are least capable of making a deep impression on tradition—that is, transient events enacted once for all. At the time a great battle, a tragedy of the palace, the sad fate of lovers, may fill men's minds, but after the first blaze these sensations go out, while customs continue to smoulder on during the ages.'

THE CHRISTIAN EXPLANATION

It is impossible for us to do more than glance at the dark

labyrinth of ancient superstitions. Magic is not merely an infantile make-believe, and myth is not idle day-dreaming. Both contain important clues to the structure and history of primitive society. To unravel these clues would be no more than an interesting academic pastime if it were not for the fact that these primitive ideas are still enshrined in the dogmas of the leading religions.

The corner-stone of traditional Christianity is the doctrine of the Fall. Whatever compromises are made by theologians with the theory of evolution, there remains the problem of early man's religion. The dim period when Palaeolithic hunters roamed over the world, fashioning flint tools, making amulets, disposing of their dead with care, is consequently of great significance. Those who accept the dogma of the Fall are hard put to it to square their theology with the results of archaeological and anthropological research.

The traditional Christian has at least two alternatives to consider. (*a*) He can argue that man fell so abysmally from the state in which he had direct contact with God that he lost the very belief in the existence of God. The consequence of eating the fruit of the tree of knowledge was that everything he knew was blotted out of his mind. Ever since he has been slowly and painfully groping his way back through the various stages of animism, polytheism and monotheism. It is possible, on this view, to accept an evolutionary theory of the origin of religion. (*b*) On the other hand, it may be held that man did not fall quite so far as this. He remembered something of Eden. If we look far enough back we shall see that it is true of the entire human race.

> *Not in entire forgetfulness*
> *And not in utter nakedness,*
> *But trailing clouds of glory do we come*
> *From God who is our home.*

Whichever view is accepted, the theologian is not

ashamed to appeal to scientific evidence for support. Those who hold (*a*) appeal to Freud. According to W. Robinson 'We do not have to go to Augustine or John Calvin for a doctrine of total depravity. We find it more securely in Freud, but without any accompanying doctrine of Redemption.' (*Whither Theology?*) Freud's own theory that religion is an illusion is conveniently overlooked.

Those who hold (*b*) are willing enough to believe that primitive man was harmless and friendly, and that the horrors of war and human sacrifice belong to a later, degenerate stage of society. This is sometimes regarded as providing confirmation of the Fall from a state of primal innocence.

THE GOLDEN AGE

The myth of a Golden Age of pristine innocence and understanding is held to be supported by the claim that some primitives, notably the Australian aborigines, had a pure monotheism with a high moral tone. In *Primitive Man as Philosopher*, Paul Radin declared that 'orthodox ethnology has been nothing but an enthusiastic and quite uncritical attempt to apply the Darwinian theory of evolution to the facts of social experience'. Ethnologists, he says, have held 'the curious notion that everything possesses a history; until they realize that certain ideas and certain concepts are ultimate for man as a social being, as specific physiological reactions are ultimate for him as a biological being they will make no progress'. Among these ultimate concepts is monotheism.

The theory that the human race entered upon the earthly scene trailing clouds of glory, that the widespread legend of a Golden Age of innocence contains an element of historical truth, does not appeal solely to the Christian. It was hailed, for example, by Aldous Huxley and those for whom much of modern progress merely spells the multiplication of gadgets, and is really a degenerate downward movement into a robot age. Huxley believed that prehistoric man

knew the elements of the perennial philosophy—a term
which he applied to his own theosophical system, though it
was invented by Leibniz and is also used by Catholics to
describe Thomism.

According to Huxley, mankind indulged in profound
speculations before any recorded history. How it is proposed to verify this strange statement is not very clear.
Huxley seemed satisfied to say that there is no reason to
doubt it:

'It is highly significant that, among many contemporary
primitives, two thought-patterns are found—an exoteric
pattern for the unphilosophic many, and an esoteric pattern
(often monotheistic with a belief in a God not merely of
power, but of goodness and wisdom) for the initiated
few.... Strange openings and theophanies are granted to
quite small children, who are often profoundly and permanently affected by these experiences. We have no reason
to suppose that what happens now to persons with small
vocabularies did not happen in remote antiquity.' (*The
Perennial Philosophy* p 27)

But the most imaginative recent attempt to describe the
religious consciousness of man before and after the Fall was
made by C. S. Lewis in *The Problem of Pain* (1940).

PARADISAL MAN

Like Aldous Huxley, Paul Radin, and others, Lewis
held that prehistoric man knew a great deal more than we
commonly suppose. 'We forget that our prehistoric ancestors made all the most useful discoveries, except that of
chloroform, which have ever been made.' This is certainly a
promising start; and, of course, it all depends on what you
care to call 'useful'. He is cautious enough to cast his recon-
struction in the form of a myth; not, he assures us, a myth
in the sense of a symbolical representation of non-historical
truth (as the Protestant theologian Dr Niebuhr regards it),
but in the Socratic sense, 'an account of what may have been
a historical fact'.

C. S. Lewis suggests that the bodily frame of man may well have come into being as the evolutionists say; such a creature may even have been clever enough to make the things which a modern archaeologist would accept as proof of its humanity. So much for the Neanderthal prototypes whose skulls and artefacts have been examined.

'Then in the fullness of time, God caused to descend on this organism both on its psychology and physiology, a new kind of consciousness which could say "I" and "we", which could look upon itself as an object, which knew God, which could make judgments of truth, beauty and goodness, and which was above time in that it could perceive time flowing past.'

This self-conscious creature was not merely *Homo sapiens* but Adamic or Paradisal man. Like a Yogi, he could control the automatic functions of digestion and circulation, he could sleep and keep awake as long as he chose and decide when to die.

'Since the processes of decay and repair in his tissues were similarly conscious and obedient, it may not be fanciful to suppose that the length of his life was largely at his own discretion. Even now we meet rare individuals who have a mysterious power of taming beasts. This power the Paradisal man enjoyed in eminence.'

It is a pity that no date can be assigned to this Edenic period of human history; apart from that, however, we cannot complain of dearth of information:

'I do not doubt if the Paradisal man could now appear among us, we should regard him as an utter savage, a creature to be exploited, or, at best, patronised. Only one or two, and those the holiest among us, would glance a second time at the naked, shaggy, bearded, slow-spoken creature: but they, after a few minutes, would fall at his feet.'

Suddenly (again the date is missing) everything went wrong. Through an act of self-will the Paradisal lion-tamer lost the power to control the beasts, his digestion, and his life-span. 'Our present condition, then, is explained by the fact that we are members of a spoiled species.'

Such are the fantasies advanced by some of our most brilliant writers and acutest intellects. There is, of course, not the slightest reason to suppose that prehistoric man was a philosopher, as Aldous Huxley alleges, or a kind of Mahatma. The evidence, patiently sifted by discipline of scientific method, is all the other way.

PRIMITIVE TOTEMISM

Evidence of what the Palaeolithic hunters believed in is meagre, but it points to magic rather than religion, if the latter is defined as the practice of propitiating gods. Both in Babylonia and Greece there is evidence of a period before the gods were given proper names. The Babylonian epic, which contains a creation myth, speaks of a time 'when of the gods not one had arisen, when no name had been named, no lot had been determined, then were made the gods'. There is a well-known passage in Herodotus about the Pelasgians, or aboriginal inhabitants of Greece:

'Formerly the Pelasgians on all occasions of sacrifice called upon gods (theoi) as I know from what I heard at Dodona; but they gave no title nor yet any name to any of them.'

An important rite in primitive Greece was associated with the *Agathos Daimon* or Good Spirit. This spirit had no proper name. The Olympian gods, like Zeus and Hera, had names and distinct individualities, but they belong to an historically later period. Intermediate between the conceptions of a purely impersonal force, like *mana* and a clear-cut god, are semi-personal beings. They are spirits or *daimones*. Some of them become gods later on; others remain at the stage of mythical hero and ancestor.

There are important similarities between the conceptions of the early Greeks and Cretans and the ideas of societies as low in the human scale as that of the Australian blacks. One common factor is the social behaviour and beliefs associated with totemism. We cannot possibly understand primitive magic without studying this most bizarre of all beliefs. Totemism, according to Frazer, is 'an intimate relation which is supposed to exist between a group of kindred people on the one side and a species of natural or artificial objects on the other side, which objects are called the totems of the human group'.

A totemic society is composed of clans. Each clan bears the name of some animal, bird, vegetable or occasionally an inanimate object. (But it should be remembered that at the totemic level there is no sharp distinction between animate and inanimate; everything in the world is believed to be more or less alive.) Thus the totem of the kangaroo tribe will be a kangaroo, of the emu clan, an emu. Members of these clans regard a kangaroo or an emu, as the case may be, as one of their kinsfolk; it is related to them by blood, and normally they will not kill it. Under the system known as exogamy a clansman must marry out of the clan; a child may take the totem of its mother or father, but the totem of the mother must be different from that of the father.

All religions have legends of gods transforming themselves into birds and beasts. Eve was tempted by a talking serpent in the Garden of Eden. Zeus took the shapes at various times of a snake, an eagle, a swan, a bull, a shower of gold. Apollo is associated with the lizard. Demeter with the pig, Athenae with the owl. Dionysus appears as snake, bull, goat and lion. The animal-headed gods of Egypt instantly spring to mind, and it is generally thought that they evolved from totems of the various tribes that inhabited the Nile valley before the formation of an Egyptian kingdom. Wherever we find arbitrary prohibitions of certain types of food we may suspect that the taboo had its origin in totemism.

Totemism fulfils an important social function. It organizes the supply of *mana* (and indirectly of real food) and it stabilizes social order in the primitive phase before authority is vested in a king. But it is magical rather than religious, because all authorities agree that the totem object is never worshipped. The totem is not yet a god, but it contains the ingredients from which a god can be made. It gives rise to ceremonies in which collective make-believe is used to mobilize the tribal energy so that the necessary measures can be taken to increase the supply of food and ensure good hunting.

THE FIRST GOD

That totemism was universal may be disputed. Elliot Smith and his followers regarded totemism as an invention of the ancient Egyptians, derived from a superstitious explanation of the placenta. On this theory man, in the godless milleniums before civilization began, wandered across the world in search of objects with magical life-giving properties—blood, ochre, anything red, certain shells and teeth, etc. Gold came to be regarded as a magical substance conferring immortality, and the search for gold sent the Egyptians far and wide, and so they spread many of their own beliefs and much of their positive knowledge.

Whether or not this is accepted—and it is a minority view —for our present purposes we may note that it supports the contention that an age of magic preceded an age of religion. Australians, Egyptians, Babylonians, Mexicans, and Greeks—even prehistoric man, if we may judge from the cave-drawings—sought to identify themselves in magical ceremonies with animals by putting on masks and skins. Their endeavour, like that of the Cretan kings who put on the horns and hide of a bull, was to obtain *mana*. Is it not possible that the priest, medicine man or divine king who regularly donned this bloody garment was the prototype of the god?

'If an old suggestion of my own is right he is the original theos, the incarnate medicine or spell or magic power. He at first, I suspect, is the only theos or God that his society knows. We commonly speak of ancient kings being deified; we regard the process as due to an outburst of superstition, or insane flattery. And so no doubt it was, especially in later times—when man and god were felt as two utterly distinct things. But deification is an unintelligent and misleading word. What we call deification is only the survival of the undifferentiated human theos with his *mana* his *Kratos* and *Bia*, his control of the weather, the rain and the thunder, the spring crops and the autumn floods; his knowledge of what was lawful and what was not, and his innate power to curse or make dead.... What is the subsequent history of this medicine-chief or theos? He is differentiated, as it were: the visible part of him becomes merely human; the supposed supernatural part grows into what we should call a God.' (*Five Stages of Greek Religion* Gilbert Murray p 24)

THE FIRST MONOTHEISM

There are many theories to account for the origin of religion, and there could be no surer sign of the difficulty of the problem. Yet religion must have had a beginning, like any other aspect of human culture, like poetry and drama and science. There must have been a time when men first began to worship gods. Before that time they did not worship gods; and such evidence as we possess suggests that they were preoccupied with a highly practical sort of magic. Whether our earliest ancestors were mainly concerned with the preservation of their individual lives or with the collective food-supply cannot be known for certain.

We cannot be certain that prehistoric man thought and acted like the Australian aborigines; but we can surely say that societies at the totemic level cannot have been wholly different from the Stone Age tribes studied in Australia. And it seems plain that when hunting was replaced by agriculture, when the roving clans settled down in communities and acquired despotic chieftains and even kings, a profound change took place in man's imaginative life.

The tribal spirits who had toiled for the welfare of the group were translated to the sky. In Egypt the actual reigning kings were regarded as gods, sometimes the equals and even the superiors of the gods already ruling in the sky.

After death the souls of the kings went up to the sky-world and joined the other gods. Every tribal group had its chief who could be equated with 'god' when civilization advanced to a certain point.

When the tribal organization was replaced by City States —in Egypt, Babylonia and Greece, for example—every City State had its god. And when one state went to war with another, defeated and absorbed it, the god of the conquered state was either assimilated (ie became an attribute of the victor) or was treated as a demon of the underworld. Hell became populated by the ideological reflections of conquered kings. By studying the mythology of a state it is therefore possible to learn something of its real history. This process of imperial expansion, projected on an imaginary heaven, so that one god becomes loaded with the attributes of the vanquished as with trophies, is known as syncretism. It was almost bound to lead in the end to monotheism.

The first authentic monotheism recorded in history is that of Ikhnaton, who ascended the throne of Egypt as Amenhotep IV in 1375 BC. He introduced the universal cult of Aton, symbolized as the sun's disc.

'In the Old Kingdom the sun-god was conceived as a Pharaoh, whose kingdom was Egypt. With the expansion of the Egyptian kingdom into a world empire it was inevitable that the domain of the god should likewise expand. As the kingdom had long since found expression in religion, so now the empire was to make a powerful impression upon religious thought. ... It was universalism expressed in terms of imperial power which first caught the imagination of the thinking men of the empire and disclosed to them the universal sweep of the sun-god's domination as a physical fact. Monotheism was but imperialism in religion.' (*The Dawn of Conscience* J. H. Breasted)

In one sense it may be argued that the belief in one supreme God is the result of a historical accident, that it would never have occurred to anyone that such could be the case if the amalgamation of ancient cities had not occurred. Or we can regard it perhaps as part of a vast evolution, in which the transformation of tribe into empire was accompanied by the parallel development of totem and ancestral-spirit into god. What is important to recognize is that the term 'god' does not contain a 'true meaning'. We shall learn nothing fresh by devising a definition of the word and drawing deductions from the definition. 'God' is the generic name of many classes of supernatural beings in whom men have believed.

IMPERSONAL GODS

Gilbert Murray shows what widely different connotations were given to the word 'god' in ancient Greece:

'We shall find Parmenides telling us that God coincides with the universe, which is a sphere and immovable; Heraclitus, that God is "day, night, summer, winter, war, peace, satiety, hunger". Xenophanes, that God is all-seeing, all-hearing and all-mind; and as for his supposed human shape, why, if bulls and lions were to speak about God they would doubtless tell us that he was a bull or lion.... "The fact of success" is "a god and more than a god": "the thrill of recognizing a friend" after long absence is a "god": wine is a "god" whose body is poured out in libation to gods: and in the unwritten law of the human conscience "a great god liveth and groweth not old" (Aeschylus).... And without going into the point at length, I think we may safely conclude that the soil from which such language as this grew was not any system of clear-cut personal anthropomorphic theology.' (*Op cit* p 12)

The evidence that before clear-cut personal gods were worshipped there was a stage when more or less impersonal forces were regarded as objects or channels through which the weather and food-supply could be controlled seems very strong. And if magic paved the way to religion proper we should expect to find in the intermediate stage a concern with ritual acts rather than the individual devotion and faith which nowadays seem inseparable from religion.

This is what we do find, according to Robertson Smith, among the early Hebrews. His *Religion of the Semites* first appeared in 1894, and some of the theories he advanced are no longer easy to defend, but he was undoubtedly right in claiming that in the beginning belief was not obligatory. What was meritorious was the act done, not the state of mind or belief. Thus, as is now widely accepted, myth is largely derived from ritual, not ritual from myth:

'Ancient religion was mainly a series of acts. You did not choose it but were born into it. You could not be absolutely irreligious. Religion was a social obligation. You were born into a circle of divine beings as well as kinsfolk. Society was made up of gods and men.'

The kinship of gods and men was at first taken literally. The symbol of kinship is blood; and when the tribal system broke up, the god could not be the physical father of men of diverse kin, and so he became their king, the Father of the people. The Fatherhood of God had therefore evolved from savage customs.

To argue, as theologians sometimes do, that to show how an idea evolved has no necessary bearing on its truth, is logically correct, but it is surely a remarkable coincidence if there is indeed a close parallel between the development of social institutions and the concepts of religion.

There are some critics who would deny that the principal clue to the idea of God is to be found in the history of society. Instead of starting their analysis with the history of the community, they begin with the individual consciousness. Psychological and sociological theories of the origin of religion are not, however, mutually exclusive. They have to explain the same phenomena, and although they start from a different point and use a different language, the two methods of approach should be complementary rather than contradictory. Unfortunately this is often overlooked in the heat of the controversy.

PSYCHOLOGICAL THEORIES

Freud's Theory: According to Freud, religion developed out of totemism; and totemism developed out of a cannibalistic feast among the primal horde, when the violent, jealous father who kept all the females for himself was slain by the sons:

'One day the expelled brothers joined forces, slew and ate the father, and thus put an end to the father-horde. Together they dared and accomplished what would have remained impossible for them singly. Perhaps some advance in culture, like the use of a new weapon, had given them the feeling of superiority. Of course, these cannibalistic savages ate their victim. This violent primal father has surely been the envied and feared model for each of the brothers. Now they accomplished their identification with him by devouring him and each acquired a part of his strength. The totem-feast, which is perhaps mankind's first celebration, would be the repetition and commemoration of this memorable, criminal act with which so many things began, social organization, moral restrictions and religion.' (*Totem and Tabu*)

Remorse for killing the father who stood in the way of their sexual demands resulted in a guilt complex. Henceforth the slaying of the totem animal (father-substitute) and union with the mother were taboo.

It is unnecessary to go into further details of this curious theory, which no one accepts outside orthodox psycho-analytical circles, but it is easy to see how plausibly it can be applied to the numerous myths in which a god is slain and dismembered.

The fact that it is more often the son than the father who is slain in the myths is too easily dismissed by the Freudian doctrine of ambivalence, according to which opposites may be identical, hate being found in love and vice versa:

'In the Christian myth, man's original sin is undoubtedly an offence against God the Father, and if Christ redeems mankind from the weight of Original Sin by sacrificing his own life, he forces us to the conclusion that this sin was murder.

'According to the law of retaliation, which is deeply rooted in human feeling, a murder can be atoned for only by the sacrifice of another life; the self-sacrifice points to a blood-guilt. And if this sacrifice of one's own life brings about a reconciliation with god, the father, then the crime which must be expiated can only have been the murder of the father. Thus in the Christian doctrine mankind most unreservedly acknowledges the guilty deed of primordial times because it now has found the most complete expiation for this deed in the sacrificial death of the son....

'In the same deed which offers the greatest possible expiation to the father, the son also attains the goal of his wishes against the father. He becomes a god himself beside, or rather in place of his father. The religion of the son succeeds the religion of the father. As a sign of this substitution the old totem feast is revived again in the form of communion in which the band of brothers now eats the flesh and blood of the son and no longer that of the father, the sons thereby identifying themselves with him and becoming holy themselves. Thus through the ages we see the identity of the totem feast with the animal sacrifice, the theanthropic human sacrifice, and the Christian eucharist....' (Freud *Op cit*)

Jung's Theory: Jung broke away from Freud on a number of points. Whereas Freudian analysts encourage us to think that religion is an illusion, Jung counsels us to believe in God and immortality if we find it helps us. Jung writes with great obscurity, and he looks, not to social history, but to the Unconscious for the clue to the origin of religion. The Unconscious is represented in the conscious mind by symbols; and Jung holds that the similarity of myths and religious symbolism generally in such widely separated parts of the world is due to the fact that human minds are constituted in the same way. We all inherit an innate, archaic symbolism, and this is the language of religion. In

his *Psychology of the Unconscious,* Jung contends that religion arises from a tendency to regress to an attitude of
infantile dependence on the parent.

No one can doubt that such psychological concepts as the
Unconscious, projection, introversion, etc, throw light on
religious manifestations. Thanks to these explorations of
the mind, it is easier to comprehend ancient phallic worship, the sexual language of so much mysticism and the
frequency of adolescent conversions.

Trotter's Theory: In contrast to the schools which stress
the importance of the sex instinct as a factor, there is the
emphasis on the herd-instinct. This point of view was given
in W. Trotter's *Instincts of the Herd in Peace and War*:

'This intimate dependence on the herd is traceable not
merely in matters physical and intellectual, but also betrays
itself in the deepest recesses of personality as a sense of
incompleteness which compels the individual to reach out
towards some larger existence than his own, some encom-
passing being in whom his perplexities may find a solution
and his longings peace. Physical loneliness and intellectual
isolation are effectually solaced by the nearness and agreement of the herd. The deeper personal necessities cannot be
met—at any rate in such society as has been so far evolved
—by so superficial a union. . . . Religious feeling is therefore
a character inherent in the very structure of the human
mind, and is the expression of a need which must be recognized by the biologist as neither superficial nor transitory.'

By contrast, the diffusionist theory that prehistoric man
was engaged in a world-wide search for substances that
could be regarded as Givers-of-Life may be considered as an
attempt to base religion, not on the herd-instinct, but on
the instinct of self-preservation. Whichever of these factors
is considered to be the more important, it seems probable
that each of them to a varying degree enters into the composition of the religious consciousness.

Psychology helps us to understand the mechanism
whereby impulses and conflicts in the mind are externalized

and then regarded as independent realities. We can gain some knowledge of animism by watching a child infuse his own vitality into a doll, so that it becomes a living thing for him. We ourselves, behave like animists when we kick a door in anger because we have jammed our fingers.

The veneration of the national flag or regimental colours is a survival of totemic thinking. The irrational sense of guilt, the thirst for self-punishment, the ferocity of religious persecutions, are perfectly intelligible in terms of masochism and sadism. But most psychological theories have to meet the criticism that they do not tell the whole story because they deal with man as an individual unit and neglect the social medium in which the content of his consciousness is shaped.

Durkheim's Theory: Just as Jung regards 'god' as the symbol of the Unconscious, Freud of the Father, Elliot Smith of the King, so Durkheim regards 'god' as a symbol of the social group. It follows that changes in social organization will compel a revision of the symbol. Thus we may expect a matriarchal society to worship the Great Mother, and an Empire to tend to monotheism. These forms, however, are comparatively superficial. The function of religion is to affirm the unity of the group, whether of a clan, a tribe, a nation or an empire.

There are rites without gods, and rites from which gods are derived; but there is no religion without a Church: 'A religion is a unified system of beliefs and practices relative to sacred things. . . . The point is not whether mythology is false—that is granted—but how anything so false could endure.'

Durkheim contends that religion satisfies a social need. The believer in religion feels stronger. He has a new power and is raised above ordinary miseries and weaknesses. This comes about when members of the community meet together. The feeling of tribal solidarity is projected as a god. What is personified, reduced to a single comprehensible symbol, is the authority of society.

Malinowski's Theory: The social value of religion is also emphasized by Malinowski:

'Religion and magic on the one hand give man freedom from fear, from despondency, from spiritual and social disorganization. On the other hand they cement and integrate the partial and specific values of conduct and of achievement into one system or several systems, each converging on the central value with its focus of efficiency placed on a world sacred, firm and powerful, just because it remains outside the normal ordinary experience of man.' (*Freedom and Civilization*)

Magic is therefore good for morale. Again:

'Any system of mystical belief arises as a cultural response to the disorganizing fear of adversity and disaster. Every such system consists first and foremost in a dogmatic affirmation, mythologically founded.

'The affirmation declares: "there is a God, who is a source of strength to those who obey his words. There is a providence which can be induced to cooperate with man and make his efforts effective and successful. There are ancestor-spirits, who demand sacrifice and prayer, but who free man from the hindrances of ill-luck and the schemings of his enemies. There is another world, where those who have been oppressed, ill-treated and persecuted here will exist in the glory of strength and pleasure, hence of freedom. There is a force which man can capture and use to master and harness luck and chance through magical rite and spell".'

The Marxist Theory: Superficially there is a good deal in common between Marxism and the French school of sociology in regard to religion, but the difference is deep. For Marx, 'god' is not so much the symbol of the community in general as of a particular kind of community, a society riven by class divisions. The modern Marxist, surveying the vast mass of material that has been collected since Marx wrote, can point to many discoveries that seem to confirm the original thesis that religion is a reflection, on the mental plane, of the material structure of society.

If God stands for king, then king stands for ruling class, not for the group as a whole, and in a classless society the concept would be superfluous. The traditional view that the king is a microcosm of society, so that injury or benefit to him mysteriously reacts on the whole social organism, is regarded as an ideological trick. The function of religion in a class-society is to identify the demands of the ruling class (equated with justice) with the will of God. Belief in the supernatural is due to man's feeling of helplessness in face of the blind forces of nature; but scientific control of natural forces will result in such concepts as 'God' and 'soul' becoming as outmoded as Kepler's angels and phlogiston. The following quotations will make this clear:

'Religious misery is, on the one hand, the expression of actual misery, and, on the other, a protest against actual misery. Religion is the sigh of the oppressed creature, the kindliness of a heartless world, the spirit of unspiritual conditions. It is the people's opium. The removal of religion as the illusory happiness of the people is the demand for its real happiness. The demand that it should give up illusions about its real conditions is the demand that it should give up the conditions which make illusion necessary. Criticism of religion is therefore at heart a criticism of the vale of misery for which religion is promised vision.

'Criticism has torn away the imaginary flowers with which his chains were bedecked, not in order that man should wear his chains without the comfort of illusions, but that he may throw off the chains and pluck the living flowers. Criticism of religion disillusions man so that he may think, act and shape his reality as one who is disillusioned and come to full understanding, so that he may move on his own axis and thus be his own sun. Religion is but the false sun which revolves around him while he is not yet fully self-aware.' (*Introduction to a Critique of Hegel's Philosophy of Law* Marx)

'Religion is a reflection, on the ideological plane, of the

structure of society and it will not disappear until the relations between human beings in their practical everyday life have assumed the aspect of perfectly intelligible and reasonable relations as between man and man, and as between man and Nature. The life process of society, this meaning the material process of production, will not lose its veil of mystery until it becomes a process carried on by a free association of producers under their conscious and purposive control.' (*Capital*, Vol I Marx)

According to Lenin:

'Religion is a kind of spiritual intoxicant, in which the slaves of the capital drown their humanity and blunt their desire for a decent human existence.'

It is evident enough that there is no such thing as *the* Humanist theory of the origin of religion. There are many theories and it is unlikely that any of them expresses the whole truth of the matter. The individual Humanist is concerned only to study the evidence and to arrive at a tentative conclusion that seems to him in harmony with such facts as are at present known. What he plainly must not do it to try to fit the facts into some preconceived belief.

EIGHT

THE PAGAN BACKGROUND OF CHRISTIANITY

No matter how far back we search in history we shall find strikingly similar patterns of belief. There are numerous pagan Trinities. The myth of a slain and resurrected saviour-god is almost universal. There are rites closely resembling baptism and the eucharist. A peculiar sacredness is almost everywhere supposed to reside in blood and in running water. The cross is a pre-Christian symbol, so are the sacred tree, the sacred bridegroom, the lamp and the dove. The divine Mother and holy Child were worshipped in Egypt, Greece and even in China before Christianity was thought of.

Some writers explain all this away in the following ingenious manner. They start by asserting that there is a *real* Trinity. Then they profess to feel no surprise that there should be Trinities in pagan pantheons, even female trinities such as three Moirae, three Gorgons, three Charities, etc. The mystic significance of the number three (and so, no doubt, of the numbers five, seven and twelve) is due to an objective fact.

In the same way, the mystical identification of the sacrificer and the victim, the worshipper and the worshipped, when the sacred flesh of the god is eaten, results from a sort of unconscious pre-cognition. The bemused mind of the heathen must have caught a distorted glimpse of the eucharist centuries before it was instituted.

Yet if a belief still held—say in baptism—can be shown to have originated in a superstition, its truth value, as distinct from whatever social value it may conceivably possess, is surely impaired. It is incontrovertible that kings wear crowns because they were once thought to be gods. We may believe in the social value of monarchy, but we do not nowadays believe that kings are divine.

We need feel no compunction about accepting what has been dismissed as 'the fallacious theory of survivals'. Wherein lies the fallacy? It cannot be doubted that many beliefs still held in civilized communities by learned and intelligent men are survivals from primitive savagery. There are, of course, qualitative differences. The British monarchy is qualitatively different from the divine kingship of ancient Egypt. But through the centuries that divide them certain vestiges of ancient superstition lingered on— the belief in the healing power of the royal touch, for example, which brought crowds flocking to Charles II. The regalia and ceremonial of the coronation can be understood better in the light of our knowledge of the divine Pharaohs. When the assembled peers cry out, 'Let the King live for ever' we may smile at the hyperbole, but millenniums ago the exclamation enshrined a real belief.

If there had been no ancient kingship, is it likely that we would have invented it for ourselves? The crown and sceptre, the investiture and anointing, have lost their original meaning, just as the crown still used in an ordinary marriage ceremony in the Eastern Church has become dissociated from the primitive coronation ceremony. It is one of innumerable fossilized remains of once living beliefs.

The material fossils found in the Alps were at first dismissed by theologians as devices of the devil to mislead the faithful. Shall we not commit a similar mistake if we ignore what might perhaps be called 'ideological fossils'? The structure of the still-surviving mumming plays, and even of Punch and Judy, is curiously similar to the structure of Greek drama, which in turn is similar to the structure of very early fertility and initiation rites. Again, when Oscar Wilde declared that the Mass was a survival of Greek tragedy he was uttering a truth that scholarship has confirmed.

THE GREAT MOTHER

The shadow of the Great Mother looms behind all ancient religions. Whether this concept was known in some crude fashion to Palaeolithic man is a question that is unlikely to be conclusively answered. Stone images of a female form have been dug up, and they probably had a magical significance in the dim period when the ancient food-gatherers—like the Arunta of Australia—did not fully understand the physical meaning of paternity.

As Jane Harrison points out in *Themis*, primitive man sees the mother and son relationship predominant. He projects his own emotions on Nature, and so regards the earth as mother, or foodgiver, and the fruits of the earth as her son, so often symbolized by a blossoming tree. Then the influence of the sky in determining the food supply begins to be felt. The rhythmic changes of the moon are given mythological expression before there is a solar calendar. And there is still another factor, for a matriarchal society will worship a Mother and Son, and a patriarchal society will tend to have a cult of the Father.

Among the first agriculturalists the sowing of crops was regarded as a task for women. They knew the magical secrets and could ensure fertility. The earth was conceived of as the Mother-of-all-Living. As the Homeric hymn-writer sang:

'Concerning Earth, the mother of all, shall I sing, firm Earth, eldest of the gods, that nourishes all things in the world; all things that fare on the sacred land, all things in the sea, all flying things, all are fed out of her store. Through thee, revered goddess, are men happy in their children and fortunate in their harvest.'

And Jane Harrison comments:

'Our religion teaches us to revere a male Trinity; the figure of the Mother is absent. The Roman and Orthodox Churches with a more happy and genial humanism include the Mother who is also the Maid.'

It is impossible to trace here the connection between the

earth-mother (Ge or Gaia) and Rhea (the mother of all the gods) and Demeter (the grain mother). Among the same family of ideas is the mountain-mother of ancient Crete, sceptre in hand and guarded by lions. The Cretan Lady-of-Wild-Things is practically the same as the Thracian Semele, who gave birth to Dionysus. And in Egypt, Isis was regarded as the Queen of Heaven and Star of the Sea.

VIRGIN BIRTH

Sometimes this symbol of the female principle and the source of life and the fruits of the earth is associated with a divine son, sometimes with a lover. The most atrocious logical contradictions were tolerated. Sometimes the love theme is between brother and sister. There is always an atmosphere of miracle, and frequently the sacred mother is a virgin. Quetzalcoatl, the saviour-god of Mexico, was born of the virgin Chimalman. Semele miraculously conceived Dionysus. The Hindu Devaki gave birth sexlessly to Krishna. St Jerome knew the legend that Buddha was born of a virgin. Indeed, a similar story was told of Pythagoras.

Belief in the virgin birth of Jesus is no longer binding on Anglicans. It may have arisen among the early Christians by a mistranslation of a prophecy in Isaiah (vii, 14). Matthew gives the passage as: 'Behold the virgin shall be with child, and shall bring forth a son, and they shall call his name Immanuel' (i, 23). The original Hebrew word translated as virgin means young woman.

One thing is clear; few in the ancient world would have felt incredulous on hearing that a virgin had given birth to a child, or that a man was really a god.

Marriage and birth are important features of the Eleusinian mysteries in Greece. At one very solemn point in the dramatic performance the priest announced: 'Holy Brimo has given birth to a Sacred Child, Brimos.' The ordinary man might well believe that the many goddesses, with their divine sons or lovers were separate beings, but the intelligentsia had no such illusions. It seemed obvious to Plutarch that Osiris and Dionysus, like Isis and Demeter, differed mainly in name. Aeschylus perceived the unity of the mother-goddesses: 'Themis she, and Gaia, one in form with many names.'

THE CHRISTIAN MADONNA

The Christian Church has taken over the plot of a very ancient story and treated fiction as historical fact. In the case of the Catholic Church, it is difficult to see how anyone can fail to notice the identity of the Virgin Mary with the great female divinities worshipped from the dawn of civilization. Not only is the similarity ignored by Catholics, but an audacious attempt is sometimes made to give the Christian version of the Great Mother an air of scientific respectability. Nowadays, of course, the cult stands or falls with the dogma of the Virgin Birth, and although this has lost ground among Protestants it is still vital to the Catholic. F. Sherwood Taylor writes:

'There is no evidence that in the normal course of nature, one conception in 10,000 or more is not a virgin conception; for were it to be so we would be very unlikely to discover it. There is at present the small positive evidence that girls of good character are occasionally known to allege this occurrence in their own cases (I know of two instances). They are, of course, disbelieved; but only on grounds of analogy, not of positive proof.' (*The Fourfold Vision: a study of the relations of science and religion*)

Even if this alarming state of affairs exists there is nothing miraculous about it. But the evidence will strike most people as singularly weak—far weaker, surely, than the evidence that the concept of the Great Mother is 'one in form with many names'.

We can trace the idea back to the remote days of the Sumerian goddess, Innini. Indeed, a serpent-headed goddess was worshipped in Babylonia before 4000 BC—ie before the Flood possibly described in Genesis. Innini played a leading part in the oldest of all plots, the myth of the dying and resurrected god. Time and again we find the same story with different names, and the most reasonable conclusion is that the myth was begotten by a ritual act.

In all these myths great stress is laid on the dolours of the mother (or mistress or sister or both) when the god is slain. There is a descent into the underworld. The details vary, but the association of the goddess with the world of shades is clear; and although there is certainly nothing to suggest such an association in the New Testament narrative, a visit to any Catholic church will show how this archaic pattern has persisted in popular devotions. The Virgin in her various guises—Our Lady of Lourdes, of Fatima, of Mount Carmel, of Guadaloupe—has special powers to ease the lot of those who suffer, not indeed in hell, but in purgatory.

Some popular devotions recall Mahomet's curious mistake in thinking that the Christian Trinity consisted of Father, Mother and Son. In others the Trinity appealed to is 'Jesu, Mary, Joseph'. All this may be formally disproved by reference to strict theology, but we are now concerned with the living reality, not the dead letter. C. G. Coulton mentions the case of a medieval testator who bequeathed his soul 'to allmighty God, my Creatour, Saviour and Redeemer, and Mary, Virgin, Quene of Heaven, Lady of the Worlde and Emporesse of Helle.' (*Five Centuries of Religion*)

In the past the Mother and Maiden had a double function which derives perhaps from the primordial figure of Gaia, rising from the ground. Demeter was both Corn-Mother and Queen of the Underworld. Artemis, the moon-goddess, is equated with Hecate, dark Queen of the Shades, a form of the Babylonian Ereshkigal, Queen of the Land-of-No-Return.

THE SPRING FESTIVAL

What was the ritual that gave rise to these remarkably similar personifications? Frazer, as is well known, regarded it as essentially an example of vegetation magic. It was concerned with the Corn Spirit, Maize Spirit, Rice Spirit, as the case might be. It is enough for our purposes to take the example of Osiris in Egypt:

'The primitive conception of him as the corn god comes clearly out in the festival of his death and resurrection, which was celebrated in the month of Cholak, and at a later period in the month of Athyr. That festival appears to have been essentially a festival of sowing, which properly fell at the time when the husbandman actually committed the seed to the earth. On that occasion an effigy of the corn god, moulded of earth and corn, was buried with funeral rites in the ground in order that, dying there, he might come to life again with new crops. The ceremony was in fact a charm to ensure the growth of the corn by sympathetic magic, and we may conjecture that as such it was practised in simple form by every Egyptian farmer on his fields long before it was adopted and transfigured by the priests in the stately ritual of the temple.'

Care must be taken to distinguish fact from conjecture in *The Golden Bough*, but Frazer himself never confuses the two. He undoubtedly established the existence of a widespread primitive ritual in which the personification of vegetable life played a dominant part. But there were other aspects besides vegetation.

Gilbert Murray writes as follows of the great Dromenon or Spring Festival in Greece:

'The tribe and the growing earth were renovated together; the earth arises fresh from her dead seeds, the tribe from its dead ancestors. The whole process projects itself in the idea of the Spirit of the Year, who in the first stage is living, then dies with each year and thirdly rises again from the dead, raising the whole world with him. The Greeks called him in this stage 'The Third One' (*Tritos Soter*) or the 'Saviour'; and the renovation ceremonies were accompanied by a casting off of the old year, the old garments, and everything that is polluted by the infection of death.' (*Op cit*)

On the Harrison–Murray theory the main features in this

ritual were (1) the *agon*, or contest, (2) the *pathos*, or defeat, (3) the reappearance in triumph, rebirth or *epiphany*. Analysis of Greek tragedies suggests that whereas the stories may come from the epics, nevertheless the ritual forms, the peculiar stage conventions, have descended from the Spring Festival, which was a conflict, a dramatic setting forth of natural happenings, death being followed by rebirth, contest by victory. F. M. Cornford has made a similar analysis of Greek comedy, showing its religious origin. The same process can be seen in the evolution of Olympic games.

More recently, details of this theory have been criticized by Professor George Thomson, who calls attention to the similarity of the pattern to initiation rites. In the initiation of young men we find the equivalent of the *pompe*, or send off, the *agon*, or contest, the triumphal procession, or *komos*. Yet another strand in this interweaving of primitive ideas is the duel between a Fair Man and a Dark Man—mythologized perhaps into Light and Darkness, Good and Evil, though it may originally have stood merely for Summer and Winter. The threadbare pattern has degenerated into the duel between St George and Captain Slasher in our own mumming plays.

Professor Thomson also shows how Tragedy had its origin in the worship of Dionysus:

'The Dionysian worshippers were a secret magical society which preserved in modified form the structure and functions of the totemic clan, out of which it had evolved during the later phases of tribal society. It was composed of women led by a male priest. Its principal rite, derived from initiation, contained three elements—an orgiastic exodus into the open country, a sacrament in which the victim was torn to pieces and eaten raw, and a triumphant return. The ritual was projected as a myth of the passion of Dionysus.

'It ceased to be secret and began to disintegrate. The orgiastic processions became a hymn which was developed most rapidly in the Peloponnese; the sacrament became a passion play. . . .' (*Aeschylus and Athens*)

The plot of a passion play, allowing for differences of detail, is found in many mythologies of the ancient Middle East.

The Babylonian Tammuz was the husband or lover of Ishtar, the Great Mother. Every year Tammuz was supposed to die and pass into the gloomy underworld, and every year his divine Mistress–Mother descended to search for him 'in the land of no-returning, the house of darkness, where the dust lies on the door and the bolt'. The world is sterile and abandoned during the absence of Ishtar, and the death of Tammuz was annually mourned by dirges to the sound of flutes. Some of the laments for Tammuz have been preserved, and the comparison with the Christian Passiontide is remarkable. The sorrows of Ishtar are akin to the sorrows of Mary.

The Greeks changed Tammuz into Adonis, a babe hidden by Aphrodite in a chest and discovered by Persephone. This finds an echo in the story of Moses hidden in the bulrushes. The dead body of Osiris was also concealed in a chest.

Persephone, Queen of the Underworld, refused to give up the lovely Adonis, and finally Zeus decreed that Adonis should abide with Persephone in the nether regions for one part of the year and with Aphrodite in the upper world for another part. At last Adonis is killed by a wild boar, and the mourning Aphrodite is surely another prototype of Mater Dolorosa. Frazer writes:

'In ancient Egypt the god whose death and resurrection were annually celebrated with alternate sorrow and joy was Osiris, the most popular of all Egyptian deities; and there are good grounds for classing him in one of his aspects as a personification of the great yearly vicissitudes of Nature, especially of the corn.

'Osiris reigned as a king on earth, and taught the Egyptians the secrets of agriculture. Like Dionysus he is also the god of the vine, whose cultivation he introduced. His brother Set, with seventy-two others, plotted against him and shut him in a coffer, which was thrown into the Nile. Isis, his sister-wife, wandered in search of him, uttering a loud lament. The coffer drifted ashore at Byblus, and an erica tree shot up and enclosed it. The tree was cut down, and later the body in it was stolen and dismembered by the wicked Set. Finally Isis found the broken pieces and through the miraculous intervention of Re, the sun-god, Osiris was restored to life. Henceforth, he reigned over the dead in the underworld.

'In the resurrection of Osiris, the Egyptians saw the pledge of a life everlasting for themselves beyond the grave. They believed that every man would live eternally in the other world if only his surviving friends did for his body what the gods had done for the body of Osiris. Hence the ceremonies observed by the Egyptians over the human dead were an exact copy of those which Anubis, Horus and the rest had performed over the dead god. . . . In this way every dead Egyptian was identified with Osiris and bore his name. From the Middle Kingdom onwards it was the regular practice to address the deceased as Osiris So-And-So, as if he were the god himself. . . . The thousands of inscribed and pictured tombs that have been opened in the valley of the Nile prove that the mystery of the resurrection was performed for the benefit of every dead Egyptian; as Osiris died and rose again from the dead so all men hoped to arise like him from death to life eternal.'

Is it so very fanciful to see in Extreme Unction and Requiem Masses a reflection of this more ancient blend of magic and religion? The cluster of ideas which Christianity inherited—collective guilt, taboo, scapegoat, saviour, death, resurrection, the divine and sorrowing mother—takes us back beyond the great Spring Festival in primitive Greece, though the latter is far enough to establish the existence of a substratum of ideas that remained, as it were, radioactive until, and even after, the appearance of Christianity.

To quote Murray again:

'The life of the Year-Daimon, as it seems to be reflected in Tragedy, is generally a story of Pride and Punishment. Each Year arrives, waxes great, commits the sin of Hubris, and then is slain. The death is deserved, but the slaying is a sin; hence comes the next Year as Avenger, or as the Wronged One re-arisen. "All things pay retribution for their injustice one to another according to the ordinance of time." It is the range of ideas half suppressed during the classical period and evidently still current among the ruder and less Hellenized peoples which supplied St Paul with some of his most famous and deep-reaching metaphors: "Thou fool, that which thou sowest is not quickened except it die." '

THE THEME OF REBIRTH

The rebirth theme may or may not have had a different origin from the Spring vegetation rites. There are those who think that it goes back to totemic (pre-agricultural) society:

'The rite of the second birth is widespread and universal over half the savage world. With the savage to be twice born is the rule. By this first birth he comes into the world; by his second he is born into the tribe. At his first birth he belongs to his mother and the women folk; at his second he becomes a full-fledged man and passes into the society of the warriors of his tribe ...' (*Themis* J. E. Harrison)

There are various types of ritual. The Kikuyu of East Africa re-enact their birth, and at the end of the mimicry the boy cries like a baby and is washed. Sometimes the initiate is washed in blood—either in his own or in that of an animal. Who can help recalling, when one realizes the tremendous magical significance always attached to blood, the familiar Christian symbols? The devotees of Mithra were also drenched in the real blood. The Christian differed from the rival, contemporaneous creed and was physically immersed in water and only metaphorically washed in the saving 'blood of the Lamb'. Jane Harrison writes:

'More often the new birth is simulated or imagined as a

death and resurrection, either of the boys themselves or of someone else in their presence. In South-East Australia an old man is buried in the presence of the initiates and after much singing he rises from the grave. Among other totemic tribes the initiate puts on the skin of an animal, and his subsequent ritual disappearance and reappearance signify his death and resurrection. He puts on a bear skin, for example, as the Christian metaphorically puts on Christ. He gets rid of the old Adam metaphorically; but in earlier ceremonies an old man is sometimes actually buried. As the Anglican Baptism service states: "O merciful God, grant that the old Adam in this child may be so buried that the new man may be raised up in him."'

The position is summed up by E. O. James as follows:

'Since the catechumen was reborn to eternal life (ie, he "died to live") as a result of the baptismal lustration, and was united sacramentally to the risen and triumphant Saviour in a bond which endured beyond the grave, so in the last rites he was again anointed, absolved, exorcised, communicated, washed, clothed, re-animated (incense and holy water). Having fought and struggled with supernatural foes, he was carried in a solemn procession through all the stages of his perilous journey to live and reign for ever in eternal light. . . . Underlying the ritual pattern there is the age-long quest for life ever renewing, interpreted in terms of a death and resurrection cultus—a dying to live— in which the salient features of the coronation ceremony are repeated to secure the rebirth of the soul beyond the grave. If in the Christian rite it is no longer supposed that the soul is deified, its goal is nevertheless a state of bliss visualized as a solar paradise. Souls will become kings and queens in heaven where they will reign for ever and wear "the crown of glory".' (*Christian Myth and Ritual*)

There can be no question that these pagan ideas were active at the beginning of the Christian era. Christian apologists sometimes speak as though Judaism was mysteriously insulated against the beliefs of surrounding peoples. On this point Canon D. C. Simpson writes:

'Official Palestinian Judaism might—and it did with all its strength—resist the imposition of the worship of the gods of Hellenism and draw up minute regulations as to the correct etiquette and behaviour of the devout Jew in regard to the images of pagan gods, and refuse to allow the Roman eagle to be placed upon a porch of the Temple, but it could do no more than check—it could not entirely arrest—the invasion of Egyptian and Oriental, Greek and Roman ideas. Thus facilitated, Greek ideas must have spread at least among some sections of the Jewish people, and have produced a recrudescence of earlier phases of superstitions, mythological speculations and magical rites, and may indeed have added new ones.' (*Christianity in the Light of Modern Knowledge*—Symposium)

THE MYSTERY GOD

There were a number of rival mystery-religions in the Roman Empire when Christianity took shape. They can be traced back to very primitive societies in which an important ceremony concerned communion with the god by eating his flesh and so becoming virtually identified with him. The theory of gift-sacrifice, in which the god is placated by libations and burnt offerings is a later development; but the sacramental eating of the god—which persisted in the mystery cults—arose from the primitive object to obtain *mana*.

Out of the original communion feast, with this object in view, grew such gods as the horned Iacchos, Zagreus and Dionysus Tauromorphos. They were mystery-gods, vague, deeply exciting, potent and in intimate contact with the worshipper, as opposed to the Olympian gods, who were cold and aloof, 'things known rather than things felt'. In the Christian scheme, God the Father has become for the popular worshipper as aloof as the Olympians; but Christ, especially in the eucharist, is a mystery-god.

EATING THE GOD

An alleged early example of eating a sacred animal to obtain *mana* is the sacrifice of a white camel in the Mount Sinai region, which persisted down to the fifth century and is described by St Nilus. The uncooked flesh and blood of the camel had to be entirely consumed before daybreak. The significance of this rite was first discerned by Robertson Smith:

'The plain meaning is that the victim was devoured before its life had left the still warm blood and flesh ... and that thus, in the most literal way, all those who shared in the ceremony absorbed part of the victim's life into themselves. One sees how much more forcibly than any ordinary meal such a rite expresses the establishment or confirmation of a bond of common life between the worshippers, and also since the blood is shed upon the altar itself, between the worshippers and their god. In this sacrifice, then, the significant factors are two; the conveyance of the living blood to the godhead, and the absorption of the living flesh and blood into the flesh and blood of worshippers.' (*Religion of the Semites*)

Despite the objections that have since been raised to Robertson Smith's interpretation, there is only one modification that need be made. Gilbert Murray speaks of his 'almost prophetic insight', but states that 'he spoke too definitely of the sacrifice affording communion with the tribal god. There was no god there, only the raw materials out of which gods are made.'

It would be easy enough to find parallels. The Ainos of North Japan and the Gilyaks of Eastern Siberia capture a bear and feed him richly for the sacrifice. Finally, after leading for a time a life as pampered as that of the divine kings of old, he is slain. The flesh is divided and cupfuls of the blood are drunk by the men.

The same type of ceremony is to be found in Tibet. Jevons, in his *Introduction to the History of Religion*, quoted a Catholic missionary who witnessed a parallel to the Mass in Tartary:

'This I do affirm, that the devil so mimics the Catholic Church there, that although no European or Christian has ever been there, still in all essential things they agree so completely with the Roman Church, as even to celebrate the Host with bread and wine: with my own eyes I have seen it.'

Similar sentiments were felt by the priests who accompanied the Spanish Conquistadores. The Aztecs made a dough image of Huitzipochtli every May and December; it was broken in pieces and eaten by the worshippers. The Incas made a pudding of ground maize and sprinkled it with the blood of the slain victim before distributing it to be consumed by the people. Many Protestants, of course, would not hesitate to affirm that this widespread ceremony is evidence of the magical nature of the Catholic doctrine of Transubstantiation.

We must note, however, that some of these cults had already vanished from the scene when Christianity appeared. The Bacchic Feast of Raw Flesh was a memory of a savage past, and the Athenian festival called the Bouphonia, in which an ox was slain and brought to life again in mimicry, even being stuffed with straw and yoked to a plough, was no longer performed. What is difficult to ascertain is the extent to which the Dionysian cult and its Orphic modifications continued to make themselves felt underground.

Ideas are seldom annihilated, though they undergo many changes. Orphism was a religion that penetrated Greece and South Italy from Persia in the sixth century BC. According to Murray:

'The Orphic congregations of later times, in their most holy gatherings, solemnly partook of the blood of a bull, which was by a mystery the blood of Dionysus-Zagreus himself, the Bull of God, slain in sacrifice for the purification of man.'

According to J. M. Robertson:

'A sacrificial banquet was one of the most universal features of ancient religion, being originally the typical tribal ceremony; and though among the Jews it had been to a remarkable extent superseded by sacrifices without communion, the usage was once as general with them as with the Gentiles.... The presumption is that such a banquet was connected with the Semitic God-name Jesus or Joshua before the Christian era; otherwise we must conclude that a sect of "Jesuists", starting from the bare belief in the sacrificial death, adopted arbitrarily a kind of rite which was identified with the heathen worships of the surrounding Gentiles, and adopted also the Gentile sun-worshippers' practice of assembling by night. Paul's Corinthian converts are described as frequenting the table of Jesus ("the Lord") and the table of daemons—that is, of heathen Gods or demigods. As the less orthodox Jews had long dabbled in similar mysteries, there is every probability that private 'Holy Suppers" had been practised even in Jewry by some groups long before the Christian period, whether or not in connection with the name of Jesus "the Saviour". The gospel phrase 'blood of the covenant", points to a standing usage, the original form of which was probably the mutual drinking of actual human blood by the parties to a solemn pledge.... It is further probable that the idea of a mystical partaking of an atoning or inspiring "body and blood" was of old standing in the same kind of connection. Such a practice was certainly part of the great Asiatic cults of Dionysus and Mithra; and as the ancient idea of a sacrificial banquet in honour of a god usually was that in some sense the worshipped power was either eaten or present as partaker, it is more than likely that any banquets in connection with the Syrian worships of Adonis and (or) Marnas (each name "the Lord") carried with them the same significance. In early Christian usage the ministrant of the eucharist spoke in the person of the founder, using the formulas preserved in the gospels; and as the priest in the cult of Attis also personated the god, there is a strong presumption that the same thing had been done in Jewry in the pre-Christian period, by way of modifying a still older usage in which a deified victim was actually slain and eaten. For such an ancient Jesuine eucharist (revived, perhaps, as old mysteries were apt to be among the Jews, no less than among other ancient peoples, in times of national disaster) a new meaning may have been found in the story of an actually slain man Jesus, whose death took a sacrificial aspect from its occurrence at the time of the atoning feast.' (*A History of Christianity* pp 20–21)

Critics were not slow in pointing out the amount of conjecture in this and similar passages. On such questions as these we must either frame hypotheses on the flimsy evidence available or leave the matter alone. The best Christian authorities now cautiously acknowledge the possibility of a Jewish sacramentalism and of a considerable infiltration, despite all resistance, of pagan ideas in Palestine in the period of the historic Jesus.

The existence of baptism is plain. John the Baptist practised it before the ministry of Jesus, and it continued in some independence of Christianity after John's death. But there were other sacramental cults, as Canon D. C. Simpson shows:

'That Oriental ideas of a very pronounced character had already entered Palestine, and had successfully established themselves in some circles—whether in the train of Hellenism in general, or directly from the Orient—is put beyond dispute by the peculiar beliefs and practices of the Essenes. The members of this rigorist and ascetic sect of Palestinian Judaism, retaining as they did many distinctively Jewish beliefs and doctrines unaltered, modified certain dogmas and added others. They formulated for themselves a code of practical life which was perhaps partly Greek—possibly Pythagorean—but which was also in part certainly of Oriental and especially of Persian origin. In particular, the

Essenes' sacramental treatment of common meals should warn us against a too hasty judgement in favour of the commonly accepted view, that not only in its origins was the Jewish sacrificial system not sacramental, but that also in New Testament times it was necessarily and always regarded merely as "a good deed" to be performed, lacking all sacramental efficacy, and conveying no "grace" whatsoever to those who took part in it. Indeed it is far too hastily assumed that, whatever may have been the extent to which the specific ideas and practices of the "mystery religions" held sway outside Palestine, and influenced the thought and practice of the Judaism of the Diaspora and of European Christianity, they did not enter Palestine at least sufficiently early to be reckoned among the religious ideas in which our Lord was educated, and in regard to which He sought to educate His disciples at the Last Supper.' (*Op cit*)

The view that sacramental ideas were innate in the Jewish sacrificial worship and were presupposed in the words of the Last Supper is also expressed in *The Development of Sacramentalism* by J. W. C. Wand (1928). Those who accept a more or less Catholic doctrine of the eucharist may find support to a limited extent in Judaic sacramentalism, but naturally they recoil from any suggestion that these ideas had a common origin in primitive magic. The truth seems to be that the earliest Christian conceptions were subjected to two streams of influence, pagan and Jewish. The pagan influence was more Oriental than Greek, and the most conspicuous parallels at that time to Christianity are to be found in Mithraism.

THE RELIGION OF MITHRA

Mithra or Mithras originated in the primitive Aryan religion. The story goes that the first creation of Ahura Mazda was a wild bull; and this reminds us that in Persia, as in Greece, the bull was the recognized channel by which the mysterious power of *mana*, subsequently sublimated into 'grace', reached the worshipper. Mithra, like Osiris and Dionysus, was a Saviour-god; and like Prometheus he was the friend and benefactor of man. He was born from rock, and according to the ancient myth he wrestled with the sacred bull and carried it to the obscure cave which had been the scene of his nativity, the date of which was December 25.

The slaying of the bull by Mithra was frequently depicted by ancient artists in the grottoes where his worship took place. The blood flowing from the dying, holy beast gave rise to all other animals and corn.

There were other incidents in Mithra's career which suggest familiar stories. He saved mankind from a great drought by firing an arrow at a rock and starting a spring of water. He also saved mankind from perishing in a great flood. Before ascending into heaven, when his work on earth had been completed, he held a farewell banquet. His followers commemorated this by a solemn sacramental meal, though water was used instead of wine.

Mithraism developed many astrological ideas. It taught that the soul had descended through seven planetary spheres, becoming more loaded with impurity at each stage. After death it ascended through the seven spheres; and this was symbolized by the seven grades of initiation through which the initiate passed. S. Reinach writes:

'Mithra granted the petitions of them that pray to him. Those who are initiated into his mysteries, in caverns like that where he first saw the day, receive after death his powerful protection against those enemies beyond the tomb who threaten the tranquillity of the dead. Furthermore, he will one day give to them a better life and has promised a resurrection.... It is obvious that the creed of Mithra had many elements in common with Christianity.' (*Cults, Myths and Religions*)

The most famous Mithraic rite was the sacrifice of a bull though sometimes a ram was substituted. The animal was slain above a pit covered with boards. The votaries standing

in the pit were splashed with holy blood, which was believed to confer a new divine life. The candidates were 'born
again into eternity' (*renatus in aeternum*). Thus the central
point of the religion was to secure immortality; and murals
in the Mithraic chapels that have been found depict Mithra
welcoming into Paradise his faithful followers, where they
will enjoy a heavenly banquet. Mithra is usually shown
with a halo, for he is identified with the 'unconquered sun'
(*Sol invictus*).

Not much fault has been found with the moral tone of
Mithraism. Its service was conceived as a warfare against
the powers of evil. It was a kind of ritualistic Salvation
Army, and its followers regarded themselves as soldiers in
the Army of God (*militia dei*). It made a strong appeal to
the Roman soldiery, and might have become a serious rival
to Christianity.

In Reinach's view the movements of the Roman Army
and the great slave populations account for the spread of
Mithraism. It began to move from East to West in 400 BC,
but it was not established until the reign of Trajan, about a
century after Christ:

'Ninety years later the Emperor Commodus was himself
initiated into the mysteries of Mithra, and by the end of
the second century of the empire there was not a part of the
Roman world where Mithraism had not its votaries. In the
third and fourth centuries it continued to spread, despite
the competition of adolescent Christianity. For a moment,
the conversion of Constantine stemmed its course; then
came the pagan reaction under Julian, and another outburst of energy. In the fifth century it disappeared along
with paganism in general, but not without leaving profound traces in the minds of the Eastern populations.' (*Op
cit*)

E. R. Bevan, however, considers that the extent of
Mithraism has been exaggerated:

'The fact that monuments connected with the worship of
the Phrygian Great Mother or of Isis or of Mithras are

found in places far apart in Europe has probably given a
false idea of the popularity of these cults in the west.... To
speak of Mithraism as a rival which ran Christianity hard
and almost captured the Roman Empire—language which
has often been used by scholars in the past—seems exces-
sive.'

Dr Bevan gives eight reasons why he thinks that Christianity owed only a superficial debt to Mithraism—and indeed, to pagan mystery cults in general:

'(1) The Divine Being whom the Christians worshipped as
Lord was someone who had only a short while before been
known as a real Man upon earth, not a nebulous figure in
an imaginary past. As for believing that the Christian belief
was derived from the pagan myths of Zagreus or Osiris or
Attis, that can be supposed only by cranks for whom historical evidence is nothing. The death, at any rate, of Jesus
was an unquestionable fact admitted by everybody, and the
belief that Jesus was risen again certainly began in the
primitive community of his disciples almost immediately
after his death—among a group, that is to say, of Aramaic-
speaking Jews in Palestine, the people least likely to be influenced by Hellenistic mystery religions.

'(2) Osiris and Attis were not divine beings who had become men, but beings subject to death, slain against their
will, who had become gods.

'(3) The worshippers of Isis and Attis belonged to local
congregations rather than to a widespread church.

'(4) The service of Attis and Isis lacked the high morality
of the Hebrew tradition. Mithraism was an exception in
this respect and does seem to have contained an element of
moral strength. This was because it had its roots in the
religion of Zoroaster, which was more like the religion of
the Old Testament than anything else outside it.

'(5) Baptism had its antecedents in the synagogue rather
than in the pagan mystery association. As for the eucharist,
before the initiate (of Mithra) there was set a piece of bread
and a cup of water over which the priest uttered a ritual

formula. Here, where the resemblance existed, the Christian Fathers took note of it. They said it was due to a deliberate imitation of the Christian eucharist by devils.

'(6) Unlike the pagan mystery cults, the services of the Church were not secret.

'(7) Still resembling Judaism, Christianity was marked by an intolerance quite unlike the temper of the pagan mystery religions.

'(8) The important thing to grasp when we look at that bewildering medley of religions in the first century AD is that they belong to two main types—the type for which the time process was a vanity, to which Greek Stoicism and Hellenistic mystery religions belonged, and the type with a strong eschatological outlook represented by Zoroastrianism, Judaism and Christianity.' (*Christianity in the Light of Modern Knowledge*—Symposium)

It is evident that Dr Bevan raises some issues that scholarship alone cannot decide. Once more we are confronted with the question: Are these parallels coincidences, or can we correlate them? If deliberate plagiarism be the charge, it is impossible on the evidence available to decide which of two religions running side by side borrowed most from the other, though Mithraism was on the scene in some form much earlier. We can, however, leave aside the possibility of conscious borrowing, as Reinach advises. He points out that this was a charge that was not even brought against the Christians by Julian the Apostate (who followed Mithra):

'We should do well, I think, to imitate this discretion, leave the word plagiarism alone, and attribute the startling likeness between the two religions to one influence operating identically on both—the influence of those old conceptions which, dating from a period undoubtedly earlier than the literary legends of paganism, yet retained their hold on the masses throughout the ancient world, and constituted a mystic environment which conditioned the form of Christianity and Mithraism alike.'

Dr Bevan does not squarely face this issue. In his anxiety to show how little the Judaic–Christian tradition was affected by Hellenistic mysteries he does not seem to have noticed the significance of his admission that it had something in common with the eschatological outlook of Zoroastrianism. It is a matter of detail which non-Christian influence penetrated; the interesting question is whether the ideas of Christianity are unique so that it was impossible for them to have evolved in the same way as it must be admitted that other religions evolved—changing and spreading as the result of the familiar processes of diffusion and syncretism.

NINE

THE DOCUMENTS IN THE CASE

THE source book of Christianity is the Bible. Until comparatively modern times it was accepted by all the principal Christian churches as an inspired revelation of God's will. The inerrancy of the Scriptures was firmly believed in by both the Roman Catholic Church and the Reformers. They did not differ about the inspiration of the text but about its right interpretation. As a contemporary Anglican theologian puts it:

'From the days when the canon of the New Testament was finally determined in the ancient Church until the rise of Biblical criticism in the nineteenth century the traditional Christian view of the nature of divine revelation was that it consisted of truth supernaturally communicated to men in propositional form. This divine truth, which was beyond the possibility of discovery by the unaided human reason, was contained in the Scriptures of the Old and New Testaments. The Bible was thus the only source book for our knowledge of revealed truth. Its supernatural origin was attested by miracle and prophecy—that is, by the miraculous occurrences which acompanied the events which its writers described, and by the fact that these writers were able to predict events which came to pass centuries after their own day. The task of the theologian was therefore to discover the meanings of the scriptural words— their literal, allegorical, moral and anagogical meanings— and then to arrange these meanings and present them in the form of a complete system of dogma.' (*Christian Apologetics* Alan Richardson 1947)

The Council of Trent affirmed that it 'receives with piety

and reverence all the books of the Old and New Testament, since one God is the author of each'. This opinion was underlined in 1903 in the Encyclical *Providentissimus Deus*, and Modernism was condemned by Pius X in 1907.

An authoritative commentator tells us:

'Of no human composition, however excellent, can it be said that God is its author. And the divine origin of the Scriptures implies its perfect truth. We know for certain St. Irenaeus argues that the Scriptures are perfect, since they are spoken by the Word of God and by the Spirit. Some few Catholic theologians have, indeed, maintained that the Scriptures may err *in minimis*—ie, in small matters of historical detail which in no way affect faith or morals, though such an opinion has never obtained any currency in the Church.' (*Catholic Dictionary* Addis and Arnold)

In 1909 the Pontifical Commission issued a decree binding on all Catholics. In spite of the blunder made by the incursion into astronomy when Galileo was condemned for holding that the earth moved round the sun, the Church plunged again into scientific controversy by insisting on the biblical doctrine that: (1) all things were created by God at the beginning of time; (2) man was a special creation; (3) the first woman was formed from the first man; (4) the unity of the human race. A further result of the Commission was to warn against the application of historical criticism to the Bible.

However, this is not quite the same as Fundamentalism:

'Just as Catholics are bound to defend the authority of the Bible against the new school of Protestants who have come to treat it as an ordinary book, so they are compelled to withstand the Protestant exaggeration, on the other side, according to which the words of God is contained in Scripture alone. . . . Indeed, if the study of the Bible has been an indispensable requisite, a greater part of the human race would have been left without the means of grace till the invention of printing. More than this, parts of the Bible are evidently unsuited to the very young or to the ignorant, and hence Clement XI condemned the proposition that "the reading of Scripture is for all".' (*Ibid*)

We may wonder what effect the resistance to biblical criticism has on a scholarly Catholic. H. De Smedt, the Jesuit author of *Principes de la Critique Historique*, explains as follows:

'To be called upon to make a sacrifice in these matters presupposes the possibility of a genuine opposition between historical truth and revealed truth. But since such an opposition is quite beyond all question, the critic has no ground for anxiety. It may happen, we agree, that some fact asserted by historical documents of unquestionable authority seems at first sight to be in contradiction with the teachings of faith. But more attentive examination of the fact in question, and the doctrine opposed to it, soon reveals that there is no difficulty in reconciling them, and that the supposed contradiction is in reality only the result of inaccurate knowledge of either or both. And further, even if it should happen that all attempts at reconciliation prove at first to be fruitless, and the most searching examination furnishes no means of agreement—an event which has never yet come within our experience—this need never disquiet the Catholic savant. He will wait again for light without being troubled by the shouts of triumph of the enemies of religion who are always so alert to claim a victory despite the many hard lessons such a hasty folly has brought against them. This patience will be in every respect, and particularly for the sincerity of his faith and the peace of his soul, far preferable to the violent effort he would have to make to twist the evidence of a fact which for the moment stands opposed to convictions reached from a source higher than science.'

THE PROTESTANT BIBLE

The Anglican Church has been far less reluctant to accept the best attested results of biblical scholarship. Thus, in the semi-official *Doctrine in the Church of England*:

'The use made of the Bible as an authoritative source of teaching should be controlled by the following considerations:

(1) The authority ascribed to the Bible must not be interpreted as prejudging the conclusions of historical, critical and scientific investigation in any field, not excluding that of the Biblical documents themselves.

(2) Christian thinkers are not necessarily bound to the thought-forms employed by Biblical writers.

(3) the Biblical writings display a wide variety of literary type.... The supreme spiritual value of some parts of the Bible is not shared by all.

(4) In estimating the relative spiritual value of different portions of the Bible the standard is the Mind of Christ as unfolded in the experience of the Church and appropriated by the individual Christian through His Spirit. That is to say, the stages of the Biblical revelation are to be judged in relation to its historical climax.

'The actual teaching of Christ, as recorded in the New Testament, was conditioned by the thought-forms and circumstances of the time. The record cannot be accepted as always reproducing the *ipsissima verba* of our Lord.'

Dr F. A. Cockin, late Bishop of Bristol, in *Does Christianity Make Sense?* is even more forthright:

'The consequences of the introduction of the critical method have been, of course, nothing less than revolutionary. That its use has in a number of cases been carried too far, resulting in extravagantly destructive views, cannot be denied. Such exaggeration was almost inevitable and sound scholarship has already begun to correct it. But in the main its results have been of incalculable value. It has enabled us to verify past any doubt the substantial accuracy of the record of Hebrew history, of the life of Jesus, and of the origins of the Christian community. It has removed the intolerable difficulties in which the literalist method of interpretation involved the Christian mind, by enabling us frankly to recognize the fact of development in man's apprehension of God, and the economy of God's revelation of Himself to meet that development. And it has put into our hands a tested and established instrument for the discernment of the original meaning of the writers whose words are preserved for us in the Bible.'

These are bold claims, and at first glance the casual reader may not notice the extreme care of the phrasing. What is meant by 'substantial' accuracy? Is it really the case that modern scholarship has given us a clearer view of the historical Jesus? In what way does 'the Doctrine of Development', so artlessly introduced, differ from the famous theory of development suggested by Newman and rather grudgingly adapted to the needs of Catholic theology? No doubt we are in a far better position today to judge the original meaning of the authors of the Scriptures; but we also know that they frequently contradict one another and that their names are not always those accepted by tradition. Let us look briefly at some of the conclusions of biblical critics.

THE OLD TESTAMENT

The effect of nearly a century of scholarship may be judged by the kind of results accepted by an interdenominational conference appointed to recommend what religious teaching should be given in London County Council schools in accordance with the Education Act, 1944. One outcome was *The London Syllabus of Religious Education*, intended as a guide to teachers faced with the problem of giving compulsory religious instruction for the first time in the history of education in this country. The line taken is that the Bible is not inerrant; that it contains a progressive revelation of God, which is why the older portions seem so barbaric; and that it contains a certain amount of myth.

That the books are, in the main, a patchwork of writings set down at widely separated periods is admitted:

'The books of the Old Testament are mostly compilations and many are anonymous. With few exceptions—namely,

parts of Ezra and Nehemiah, some prophetic writings, and
a little of the history—most of the material was first handed
down by oral tradition. Later, collections of this material
were made and written down, and finally, after a number of
additions (introduced often over a period of centuries) and
compilations of similar or differing collections worked over
from time to time by a series of editors and concluding with
a fresh breaking-up of some sections into books, the Old
Testament reached its present form.'

This is what Rationalists had long been saying. We have
only to recall the bitterness with which they were assailed
not so long ago for doubting the truth of Holy Writ to
realize what a victory has been achieved. As S. H. Hooke
writes, 'those who hold that the Bible cannot contain errors
must regard it as the sole authority on every department of
human knowledge'. He goes on to say (with some exaggeration, surely):

'The vulnerability of this position was very early perceived, and it is hard for the Rationalist Press to point out
any errors in the Bible which Celsus has not already pointed
out in Origen's day (*c* AD 185–254).' (*What is the Bible?*)

The significant thing is that until comparatively recently
the errors were not pointed out by Christians; the first impact of biblical criticism produced shock and anger. Subter-
fuges are not lacking in *The London Syllabus* to explain
away what seems scarcely possible for any educated person
to deny. These may do incalculable harm to the mind of
the child; but at least it is a gain that many results of
criticism are incorporated. For example, the *Syllabus*
states:

'For many generations history and legends, songs and
poems, myths and laws (some of the last already in writing)
had been handed down until, in the middle of the ninth
century BC, a man or group of men, living in Judah,
gathered together those they knew and wrote them down.
The resulting document is known as J, since it originated in
Judah, and Yahweh is the name which it most frequently

uses for God. The same was done in Israel in the following century by people who did not know J. This second document is called E, Israel being known also as Ephraim, and Elohim being the name used for God. At a later date J and E were combined, and since many of the same stories occurred in both—with certain variations—these were interwoven, naturally causing discrepancies in the narrative. During the seventh century a group known as the Deuteronomic writers—whose document is known as D—revised the written law and produced a new section (probably Deuteronomy xxii–xxvi) and also supplied a framework for the existing JE, and finally, about a century later, priestly writers added more material, known as P—poetical, legal and statistical—to JED, thus completing that part of the Old Testament, apart from some further editorial comments and amendations. This complicated process accounts not only for contradictions and repetitions in the books but also for the varying conceptions of God. In J He appears as a superman walking in the garden of Eden in the cool of the evening and enjoying the savour of Noah's sacrifice, but in later E He does not appear to man face to face, He speaks from behind a cloud or through the words of an angel. D emphasizes His moral nature and in P He is shown as transcendent, the Creator, above and beyond all that man can understand, the God portrayed by Deutero-Isaiah (eg Isaiah xi).'

What can this mean except that for more than two thousand years a mistaken idea has been propagated by the custodians of revelation? Neither the apostles, the authors of the New Testament nor the members of the various ecumenical councils knew anything about J, E and P.

The Church did not gain this information as a result of the promised guidance by the Holy Spirit. On the contrary it is thanks to the labours of scholars who preferred truth to tradition that Dr Cockin can claim that 'it is no exaggeration to say that we are in a position to understand and appreciate the true nature and meaning of the Bible in a way which has not been possible for any previous generation'.

THE NEW TESTAMENT

It would be a mistake to suppose that critical interpretations are in perfect agreement. There are some facts which are beyond dispute, such as the patchwork compilation of the Old Testament given above. As regards the New Testament, it is generally agreed that Matthew and Luke made use of the Gospel of Mark, which was therefore earlier, and of a collection of sayings of Jesus, now lost, called Q (from the German *Quelle*—spring or source).

Matthew himself also made use of a lost narrative that probably came from the Church in Jerusalem, and this is referred to as M. Again, it is acknowledged that the Fourth Gospel is in a special category and was the latest to appear.

In Q, which may have been a translation of an Aramaic document, there is no mention of the death or resurrection of Jesus; there are no miracles and only two cures—that of the blind demoniac and that of the paralytic girl. Jesus does not claim to be the Messiah, but to possess the final revelation of God's nature.

In Mark there is no account of the birth or childhood of Jesus, and the verses after xvi, 8 are late additions. Matthew is Jewish in tone and contains the formula of Baptism. It is the only Synoptic Gospel to mention the Kingdom of Heaven and the Church. The expression 'Father, Son and Holy Ghost' which occurs in xxviii, 9, is thought to be an interpolation. Luke is written in good Greek (in contrast to the unpolished style of Mark) by the author of the Acts of the Apostles.

The Fourth Gospel is thought to have appeared too late to have been written by John, the son of Zebedee, and the Gnostic tone of it contrasts with the homely simplicity of Mark. Jesus is represented as the divine Logos, the Word made flesh. He is symbolized as the Vine, the Bread, the Light, the Door, the Good Shepherd, the Resurrection and the Way. Those who accept these Gospels as revelation must explain why the various strands contradict each other in the narratives.

The early traditions suggest that, for some, Jesus was a Jewish Messiah prophesying the imminent end of the world; for others he was the mystical Logos; and for yet others he was a human figure. Hence the controversy as to whether he really existed. There were many gospels and many other Christian writings competing for inclusion in the Bible. In 376 AD Athanasius defined the canon of twenty-seven books now in use, and subsequent Church councils gave the official seal of approbation.

If we take the Bible as a whole we can see how gradual the growth of the canon was. The first books that came to be regarded as canonical by the Jews were the *Torah* (Law), better known to us as the Pentateuch (Gr *penta,* five; *teuchos,* book). In the fourth century BC the Torah was regarded as the fullest expression of the words of God. The Prophetic books were added between 250 and 175 BC; and these, together with the Psalms, and of course the Torah, seem to have constituted the scriptures for Luke.

At the time of Jesus there was no Bible in our sense of the word, as the Jewish canon was not closed until the Synod of Jamnia, about AD 90. Sir F. G. Kenyon writes:

'Fundamentally, therefore, the Bible as Christ knew it consisted of the Hebrew Scriptures classified in these three divisions and embodied in leather rolls preserved in the synagogues. No such thing as the Bible in a single volume existed then, or for several centuries after. There was a roll of the Law; a roll (or more probably two or more rolls) of the Prophets; and detached rolls of the Hagiographa. And these rolls were not, at any rate normally, held in private possession. They belonged to the synagogue. Only the trained scholars who understood Hebrew could read them, and although the Rabbis must have had means of private study the educated Jew in general would not be likely to possess a private copy of the Scriptures in Hebrew. Such acquaintance as he had with them apart from hearing them read aloud and paraphrased in the synagogue, was due to the great translation known as the Septuagint, or the Version of the Seventy.' (*Christianity in the Light of Modern Knowledge*)

The Septuagint was a translation into Greek begun about 200 BC and finished by the middle of the second century BC. It contained those books known as the Apocrypha which were excluded from the definitive canon. There were some important differences in the text of the Greek and Hebrew versions. Jerome translated the Hebrew version into Latin (including the Apocrypha), and together with his revised version of the New Testament this forms the Vulgate, which is the official Bible of the Roman Church.

It is an interesting fact that Paul used the Septuagint, whereas Jerome employed the Hebrew version. The Authorized Version of 1611 was a translation into English from Hebrew and Greek. In the middle of the nineteenth century, however, new and important manuscripts were discovered and much has been learned about ancient Syriac and Coptic versions. The Codex Alexandrinus, fifth century, and the Codex Sinaiticus, fourth century, are both in the British Museum; the Codex Vaticanus, fourth century, had reposed in the Vatican Library since 1481, but has only been made accessible recently.

One obvious conclusion to be drawn from these facts is that we can scarcely speak of the truth of *the* Bible. There are many Bibles; and they are translations, or copies, or both. The hand of the copyist is not so dependable as that of the printer. In the course of dictation, or subsequent translation, or copying—inevitable before the age of printing—errors crept in and texts were sometimes added.

The object of criticism is to sort out this veritable jig-saw puzzle of corrupt texts and translations of translations, to reconstruct missing material as the anatomist reconstructs an extinct mammoth from a bone, to go back to the period before the written word supplanted the oral tradition.

The purely philological examination is usually called textual or Lower Criticism; the wider inquiry, which takes into consideration the evidence of ancient history and archaeology, is called Higher Criticism. The detailed findings are too complex to consider here; what is of more concern to us is how all these discoveries have modified the claim that the Bible is a divine revelation. In what sense is the Bible true?

There are various answers, but they can be brought under two headings: (1) Harnack and his successors in the Liberal Protestant tradition reject the fabulous and Pauline-Gnostic elements and regard the Bible as mainly a source of moral truth exemplified by the life of Jesus. (2) Karl Barth and the so-called Confessional Church maintain that the Bible reveals God's dealings with man in history. Associated with some members of this school is a method of interpreting Old Testament history called *typological*, and a mode of thinking called *existential*. These terms are now fashionable and they will presently be explained. To understand their meaning we must examine certain trends in theology during the past hundred years.

THE RISE AND FALL OF MODERNISM

What is called Liberal Christianity, and its offshoot, Modernism, declined steeply in the early part of the twentieth century. It was as 'rational' in intention as its successors—rightly alarmed by the implications—were irrational. The origins of Liberal Protestantism go back at least as far as Kant, but they are particularly associated in Germany with Schleiermacher (1768–1834) and Ritschl (1822–89). Schleiermacher introduced a subjective note by emphasizing the importance of feeling. What was of more consequence than creed was man's consciousness of God. To be redeemed meant to receive this God-consciousness through Christ.

Insofar as Schleiermacher broke with rigid orthodoxy the movement he initiated was among the liberalizing tendencies of the nineteenth century; it helped to frame one possible solution of the dilemmas to come. A more rationalistic liberalism was presented by W. E. Channing, of Baltimore. In a sermon preached in 1819 he said:

'Our leading principle in interpreting Scripture is this— that the Bible is a book written for men, in the language of men, and that its meaning is to be sought in the same manner as that of other books. . . . We grant that the use of reason is accompanied with danger. But we ask any honest man to look back on the history of the Church and say whether the renunciation of it be not still more dangerous.'

The road leading away from tradition very quickly branched in these two directions. On the one hand, revelation seemed to consist in private experience, here and now, consequently a Church was not necessary, and even sacred writings were of secondary value. On the other hand, revelation seemed to consist in understanding correctly certain external happenings, chiefly the life and teachings of Jesus. These tendencies were profoundly affected by the new method of analysing the Scriptures.

The first serious attempt at analytical criticism was made by a group of theologians under the leadership of F. C Baur (1826–60), known as the Tübingen school. Baur applied the philosophy of Hegel to Christianity at about the same time as Marx applied it to Communism. Philosophy apart, the Tübingen school laid emphasis on the clash in the early Church between those who regarded Jesus as the Messiah of the Jews and those who held with Paul that Jesus was the Messiah of the whole world.

Only four Pauline letters (Roms, 1 and 2 Corinthians and Galatians) were accepted as genuine writings of Paul. Matthew represented the early, Jewish type of Christianity, Luke the Pauline opposition. Among the members of this school were Schwegler, Zeller, Volkmar, Lipsius, Hausrath, Weizacker, Pfeiderer and Schmiedel.

The Tübingen theory that Matthew was the earliest Gospel was disproved by the researches of later scholars, notably Harnack and Holtzmann, and the two-document hypothesis (that Mark and Q were the basic documents) was widely accepted. By the beginning of the present century liberal Protestantism had adapted itself to the findings of historical research and was very largely influenced by Ritschl.

As Canon Alan Richardson described it:

'The true gospel is regarded as consisting in the simple facts about and teachings of the historical Jesus, who can thus be objectively portrayed by modern historical research, while the interpretations of St Paul and the other apostles may be discarded as representing values for them which are no longer values for us. Hence the Ritschlians present the history of Christian dogma as pronouncing its own condemnation in the eyes of all unprejudiced Christian people. Harnack worked out this view with massive thoroughness in the learned volumes of his *History of Dogma*. The Creed of Nicea, the formulary of Chalcedon, the dogmatic writings of the Fathers, even the Epistles of St Paul, represent "the work of the spirit of a decadent antiquity on the soil of the Gospel". The chief emphasis is placed upon the contrast between the original Gospel of Jesus and the theological interpretations of the Church, between the Sermon on the Mount and the Nicene Creed. ... So we come to the familiar antithesis, beloved still today of the Rationalist Press, between Jesus and Paul: Jesus taught a simple ethical monotheism; Paul invented Christology and is the real founder of Christianity.' (*Christian Apologetics* p 148)

Ritschl endeavoured to avoid the danger of basing belief on subjective evidence. Nor did there seem to be any need to do so as long as this type of Protestantism could feel that history was on its side. H. R. Mackintosh writes:

'The argument as actually unfolded often appears to rest on the assumption that the Person and life-work of Jesus confront us as a homogeneous piece of "profane" history, the divine import of which is accessible to direct historical inspection, or can be made plain by sober rational deduction from obvious facts. The facts simply *qua* history are revelations.' (*Types of Dogma*)

THE LIBERAL COMPROMISE

The Liberal compromise reached its peak with the publication of *The Rise of Christianity* by E. W. Barnes (1947):

'Some, who have been brought up in the belief that there is a deadly opposition between science and scholarship on the one hand and Christianity on the other, may be surprised that the result of the search is not a spiritual desert: there emerges, I submit, a lovely and satisfying faith which contains the essentials of the great Christian tradition. The time has come when mistaken assumptions of the pre-scientific, pre-critical era must be repudiated.'

If such a programme could be carried out a sort of Christian Humanism might seem to be possible. It would be hardly distinguishable from Unitarianism. But Humanists, whether or not they accept the historicity of Jesus, are mostly in agreement that the clear picture of an ethical teacher such as liberal Protestants require cannot be supported.

A new turn had been given to the inquiry in the early part of the twentieth century by the researches of Albert Schweitzer. He claimed that modern man could not comprehend the historical Jesus with his intense preoccupation with the end of the world. 'The historical Jesus will be to our time a stranger and an enigma.'

An equally negative result comes from the work of the latest type of criticism, the Form-history method; or *Formgeschichte*. Wellhausen (1844–1918), who did so much to establish the order of the documents of the Hexateuch and date the Priestly Code in the Old Testament writings, also showed the importance of endeavouring to classify such clues as we possess to the oral tradition that preceded the New Testament. This led to an important new approach by Martin Dibelius, who published the results of his investigation in 1919:

'It assumes that in the oral period the tradition circulated in separate units which can be classified according to their form.... The separate units are classified into groups, the most obvious of which are sayings and narratives. But the exponents of this method are not content with analysis. They pass historical judgements upon the groups and the units, and then Form-history becomes Form-criticism, which is the name most commonly used in English. There is no agreed terminology about the groups. Paradigms (Dibelius), Apophthlegms (Bultmann), Pronouncement-stories (Vincent Taylor) refer to similar though not the same groups. The names of others, such as Miracles, Myths, Legends, not only classify but pass historical judgements upon the forms.' (*An Introduction to the New Testament* F. B. Clogg)

These are big concessions. For the Protestant Churches, though not for the Roman Church, a new attitude towards revelation had been taken up as a result of nearly a century of scientific and historical scrutiny of the Bible. Rome, as we have seen, was suspicious of the findings of critical scholarship. Anglicans and Free Churchmen accept some of them and compromise according to individual tastes.

Traditionalists such as Sir Frederic Kenyon, contend that there was not time for such elaborate processes as are required for Dibelius's *Formgeschichte* to develop.

'What we are entitled to claim is that the books which we know as canonical were produced within some fifty years of the first century and that the evidence for their text is in all essentials early and good.'

On the other hand, the existence and importance of varying traditions out of which the New Testament as we know it was composed are acknowledged by the best orthodox scholarship. Thus in a series of lectures on 'The Life of Jesus' Professor T. W. Manson sums up as follows:

'One of the principal early by-products of the new movement was a series of streams of tradition about the Founder-Person and his public career. These streams of tradition have their original sources in Galilee and Jerusalem ... the scenes of the Ministry; and in the course of their flow, as it were, form small lakes of standing tradition at various centres of Church life. The first of these of which we have any clear trace was formed probably at Antioch about AD 50. This we call Q. It may be associated with the apostle Matthew. At Antioch also we can locate a body of 'Johannine' tradition and (perhaps between 60 and 70) another which supplied the material peculiar to Matthew (M). This M tradition, along with Q, was used to produce the revised and enlarged edition of Mark which we know as the Gospel of Matthew and may be regarded as the Antiochene Gospel. The earliest form of Antiochene tradition reappears at Ephesus in Paul's letters; it may be that he brought it there in the first instance. Later on we find the Johannine tradition of Antioch taking literary form at Ephesus in the Fourth Gospel and the Johannine Epistles, and at Antioch in the letters of Ignatius. Another reservoir of tradition was formed at Caesarea; and this, in combination with Q, may well have formed the first (and catechetical) draft of Luke's gospel, which later (70-75), by the addition of extracts from Mark, was to become the first part of a public apologia for the new religion. In Rome another body of tradition issued from the teachings of Peter and took literary form in the Gospel of Mark about AD 58.'

According to the continental Form-critics, however, the authors of the Gospels were really editors. It follows that, in the Gospels, Jesus is seen in the perspective of the present position, in terms that can give no comfort to those who rejoiced at the apparent collapse of Liberal Protestantism:

'The result is that New Testament scholarship now generally realizes that it is impossible to write a life of Jesus. No chronological framework for it exists, and the individual traditions inevitably bear the mark of the interests of the apostolic Church.' (*An Encyclopedia of Religion* ed V. Ferm)

HOW TRUE IS HISTORY?

What is an apologist to do in circumstances such as these? There would seem to be two alternatives: he can either reject the critical method altogether, or he can accept its destructive consequences. Actually the need for either of these hard choices is not usually admitted.

One compromise is to accept that the development of criticism has made matters so difficult for liberals of the Ritschl or Harnack school, while evading the negative conclusions about the historical Jesus. To achieve this ingenious solution it is necessary (1) to argue that history is not *really* history, but something else; (2) to contend that truth is not *really* truth, in the plain straightforward sense. E. W. Barnes believed that the historian should be impartial. 'I have sought with firm impartiality to reach the truth, so far as it can be ascertained.' The very possibility of impartial history is, however, often denied. H. W. V. Temperley, in *Research and Modern History* (1930), stressed that the collecting of facts is only a part of history-writing, and C. Oman, in *Memories of Victorian Oxford* (1941), states that even in his own memory the idea that history is a science had perished. 'Not only do we repudiate the ideal of Ranke that history should be colourless, new and impartial. We do not even suggest that it is desirable.'

Reinhold Niebuhr, in *The Nature and Destiny of Man* (1941), wrote:

'It is impossible to interpret history at all without a principle of interpretation which history as such does not yield.'

'What is the word of God in Holy Scripture?' asks W. Robinson:

'Obviously it does not mean that every word spoken in the Bible is a word spoken by God. There are many words in the Bible spoken by men, and there are even some spoken by the Devil; and further, much of the Bible is narrative. The Bible is mainly a book of history. If we examine the Bible as a whole we shall see that it is mainly concerned with "the mighty acts of God"—God in His saving attitude towards His people.... Much confusion has arisen through treating the Bible as if it were a compendium of information about this or that thing, a textbook on geography, or science, or astronomy, or ethics, instead of the book which reveals to us the creative and redemptive activity of God, which is the sure and saving Word of God.' (*Whither Theology?*)

Thus liberal theology, which was moving towards a religion without revelation, was succeeded by another type of theology altogether.

Scientists and Higher Critics alike are put firmly in their places. Intense emotional experience and a changed way of life must be accompanied by dogmatism of a new sort. 'Propositional thinking,' as we are told over and over again, must be replaced by 'existential thinking'.

All this is, no doubt, a symptom of a revolt against reason. The actual creed propounded by the New Theology (as it was sometimes inadvisedly called) struggled for expression in the confused depths of Barth's *Church Dogmatics,* which first appeared in English in 1936.

Barth regarded Faith as a contradiction of Reason. He quotes Luther to the Higher Critics:

'We must take care not to defend the gospel, so that it collapseth. Let us not be anxious; the Gospel needeth not our help; it is sufficiently strong of itself.'

Yet it would be a mistake to suppose that defence of the Gospels, for the Existentialist, means going back to the literalism of the Fundamentalist. The existentialist approach derives from Soren Kierkegaard who originated the Theology of Crisis which enjoyed such a popular vogue in the post-war years. The hope that by stripping orthodox Christianity of supernatural accretions a reasonable and purely ethical religion would survive and be acceptable to modern man is totally rejected. Equally, the attempt to prove the accuracy of the Gospel story by applying standards of historical evidence to the crucifixion and resurrection is dismissed as illusory. The quest for the historical

Jesus is said to be in vain and largely irrelevant.

'Can one learn anything from history about Christ?' asks Kierkegaard. 'No. Why not? Because one can "know" nothing at all about "Christ"; He is the paradox, the object of faith, existing only for faith.... History makes out Christ to be another than he actually is, and so one learns a lot about Christ? No, not about Christ, for about him nothing can be known, he can only be believed.' (*Training in Christianity* p 28)

We can learn nothing about the human personality of the 'God-Man' from the Gospels: 'If the contemporary generation had left nothing behind them but these words: "We have believed that in such and such a year God appeared among us in the humble figure of a servant, that he lived and taught in our community and finally died," it would be more than enough.' (*Philosophical Fragments* p 87)

According to Barth: 'In so far as our world has been touched in Jesus by the unknown world it ceases to be capable of direct observation as history, time or thing.... Jesus as the Christ is the End of History and can be comprehended only as Paradox (Kierkegaard).' (*Commentary on the Epistle to the Romans* p 10)

Thus what seemed to liberal Christians and rationalists serious obstacles to belief are by-passed by describing the apparent contradictions as 'Paradox', and appealing to 'the leap of Faith'. What is important, on this view, is not the story of a Resurrection two thousand years ago, but the 'resurrection' of the individual here and now who experiences the encounter with God and becomes a new man. To be 'contemporaneous' with Christ is possible to all generations because, as Kierkegaard says, there is only one tense to describe the eternal, viz the present.

In what sense, then, are the alleged facts of faith true? Can any plain answer be given to the question: How true is the Bible? We come now to the curious suggestion that from the Fall until the Resurrection there are a number of 'mighty acts of God' which are more than mere history, although they appear in historical guise. God's dealings with Israel as described in the Bible are analogies, enabling us to understand future happenings. History itself is prophetic, because it shows the 'type' of things to come, the 'type' of interaction to be expected between God and man. The Jews are the chosen people; the peculiarity of their history is that it foreshadows the divine drama of the death and resurrection of Christ.

This, presumably, is what Dr Cockin had in mind when he spoke of the 'post-Critical' phase in which we are living. He quoted with approval from Professor Hodgson's *The Doctrine of the Trinity*:

'The revelation of God (in the Bible) is not given in words but in deeds.... It is only of recent years that we have been able to see it standing out clear.'

How clear it is may be judged from the following: 'It means that once we begin really to get the hang of the Bible we find in our hands certain great clues, which, rightly followed, enable us to see the whole development in its true perspective and to distinguish essentials from non-essentials. Among those clues are such themes as the Calling of People of God, Obedience and Apostasy, the Preservation of the True Faith by a Faithful Remnant, the Hope and the Coming of Messiah, the Great Rejection, the Calling of the New People of God, the Christian Church. And among them all there runs the master clue of history as God-centred. The whole drama is the drama of God's activity in Creation and Redemption.' (*Op cit*)

The New Theology seems to face both ways. The Fall is not history in the ordinary sense, and yet it is not myth. 'It is, of course, a true mythos, that is, truth couched in symbolic form.'

'What it means is that there is no historical experience in the race memory of man, let alone any actual experience, except of man in this fallen condition. As a myth bearing the truth of what has happened and of what does happen to man it is profoundly true and can only be denied by those who deliberately close their eyes to facts. It means that not only does man commit sins but that original sin is part of his nature.' (W. Robinson *Op cit*)

By whom was the first sin committed? The old orthodoxy at least gave a straight answer; it was committed by Adam. But the New Theology speaks of 'man' in the abstract:

'We note that man broke a rule and discovered a principle. From a state of innocency he passed to one of moral responsibility: he knew good and evil.... The Bible is about God's double activity: His creative activity and His redemptive activity: and, in both, He is making a bid for fellowship with men.' (*Ibid*)

The difficulties of the agnostic—and the objections of the Catholic, too, for that matter—are evaded by the use of such nebulous language. The story of the Fall is no less a myth when the word is written in Greek; myth is a translation of mythos, and both words mean stories that are false. Sometimes the New Theologians write in such a way that they seem to mean, by myth, what some scientists have meant by the expression 'useful fiction'. A mathematical point is a useful fiction; there is no such thing in Nature but it is of practical convenience to pretend that there might be. Clearly this would be a slippery path for the New Theologian to enter, but he can avoid it only by using imprecise language.

Professor Cornelius van Til has written a scathing account of Barthianism, and he accuses it of denying fundamentals of Christian teaching. He writes as a Calvinist, but even a Rationalist will feel some sympathy with his argument that the issues of an historic Fall and historic Redemption are obscured.

Professor van Til charges Barth with holding that 'the Resurrection of Jesus Christ stands for the idea of the general progress of the human race towards ideal perfection. Miracle is eliminated; and naturally there can be no place for the Second Coming in any literal sense.' (*The New Modernism*)

Whether or not these views are really held by Barth, it is easy to see to what lengths typology may be carried. As a further example of how the new vagueness is expressed with a vehemence that creates the illusion of something being said, we may take Professor Robinson's statement:

'Knowledge of God is one thing, and it may be derived from many sources (in this sense we may speak of General Revelation and of Natural Theology); but the Holy Action of God is quite another thing, and it is this redemptive action of God, which must necessarily be confined to one place and time and have the character of once-for-all-ness which we mean when we speak of "revelation".'

Fashions in theology come and go. Typological interpretation and, 'The Theology of Crisis' are no new things; to return to them is to go back to the period before the rise of critical method. The Humanist is not deeply concerned about a family quarrel among Christians, but he will not be deceived into imagining that existential thinking is a novelty.

It goes back to Pascal, whose recipe for unbelief was to attend Mass and use holy water. Indeed the roots of it can be found in St Anselm: 'The right order of proceeding is that we should believe the deep things of the Christian faith before we presume to discuss them by means of our reason.' (*Cur Deus Homo*, Book I, Chapter 2.) The germ of it is in Augustine's famous saying: 'Understanding is the reward of faith. Therefore seek not to understand that thou mayest believe, but believe that thou mayest understand.'

DID JESUS EXIST?

It is refreshing to turn from the ambiguities of contemporary theologians to the plain question of whether—apart from faith—there are grounds for believing, not merely in some details of the Gospel narrative, but in the actual existence of Jesus himself. Until very recently the various theories to the effect that the 'Jesus of History' was a composite figure made up of myths from various mystery-religions ceased to be taken seriously. However, the discovery of the Dead Sea Scrolls has led to a reassessment by John Allegro, a Paleographer who has been working on the decipherment of these important documents. The controversy is sometimes described as that of mythicists versus historicists. The best known defenders of the mythicist theory are:

J. M. Robertson, author of *Christianity and Mythology* (1900); *Pagan Christs*; *The Historical Jesus*; *The Jesus Problem*; *Jesus and Judas*.

Thomas Whittaker, author of *The Origins of Christianity* (1904).

W. B. Smith, author of *Ecce Deus* (1906). (American.)

Arthur Drews, author of *Witnesses to the Historicity of Jesus*. (German.)

P. L. Couchoud, author of *The Enigma of Jesus*; *The Book of Revelation*; *A Key to Christian Origins*; *The Creation of Christ* (1924–39).

L. Gordon Rylands, author of *The Evolution of Christianity*; *The Beginnings of Gnostic Christianity* (1927–40).

Edouard Dujardin, author of *The Ancient History of the God Jesus* (1938).

The myth theory goes back to the eighteenth century, when Volney published an essay suggesting that Jesus was a solar myth derived from Krishna. A similar view was put forward by Dupuis. In 1840 Bruno Bauer, then professor of Theology at Bonn, claimed that Jesus was an invention of Mark, who wrote the earliest Gospel at the beginning of the second century.

In 1900, J. M. Robertson's *Christianity and Mythology* drew attention to the possible implications of *The Golden Bough*. A novel feature of Robertson's contribution was the theory that the traditional story of the passion and resurrection of Jesus arose out of a ritual drama in connection with the cult of Joshua. In primitive times that cult had involved human sacrifice. Vestiges of the ancient cult persisted in Samaria and Galilee, but the old barbarities were toned down to a sacramental meal followed by a mimic crucifixion and resurrection.

Jesus, Robertson points out, is the Greek form of the Hebrew name, Joshua. He considers that Mark ix, 38 shows that exorcism was performed in the name of Jesus or Joshua in pre-Christian times. In itself this does not take us far, but Robertson claims that the story of Barabbas supplies an important additional clue. In the canonical Gospels this clue does not appear, but a version well-known to Origen (in the third century) reads: 'And they had then a notable prisoner, called Jesus Barabbas ... "whom will ye that I release unto you? Jesus Barabbas or Jesus which is called Christ?"' Now Barabbas means Son of the Father; and as Jesus is a form of Joshua, Jesus Barabbas can be translated Joshua, Son of the Father. So far so good; the next step involves a leap.

It was quite common in primitive sacrifice for the son to be a substitute for the father. An echo of this may be detected in the story of Isaac; and again, as Frazer comments on an early form of the Passover, 'the one thing that looms clear through the haze of this weird tradition is the memory of a great massacre of the first-born', though some scholars disagree.

Another clue noted by Robertson is thought by many critics to be even less substantial. Philo, a Jewish Gnostic and a contemporary of Paul, tells of an anti-Semitic riot in Alexandria, where he lived. The enraged mob seized a lunatic named Karabas, dressed him in a mock robe, crown and sceptre, and acclaimed him in Aramaic as the Lord. At once the ancient pattern of mock-coronation springs to mind; and there are no grounds for thinking that it had passed into oblivion. There is still a trace of it in the buffoonery of All-Fools' Day. Robertson contends that Karabas is a mistaken rendering of Barabbas.

It is necessary for Robertson to postulate the continuance

of a ritual drama, associated with Joshua, until after the Fall of Jerusalem in AD 70. Passion plays were admittedly not uncommon in the ancient world. The myth of Osiris was enacted in earliest times in Egypt. It is well established that Greek Tragedy was derived from the Dionysian Mysteries. What is required in the case of the supposed Joshua cult, however, is a different kind of secularization; instead of ritual begetting myth, which becomes frank fiction, myth begets what purports to be fact. At a certain point the make-believe is taken for reality; the saviour-god who was slain and rose again in mimicry every spring is given a local habitation. Play-acting becomes mixed up with violent, historical events.

These events were the disasters that overtook the Jews in AD 70. Some of them had dreamed of a warrior Messiah who would overthrow the power of Rome. Things turned out differently, and if the Jews as a whole had accepted a revolutionary role they would not have been tolerated in the Empire. They would not have been licensed to practise a religion that seemed so strange to the Roman—a licence that was subsequently withdrawn from the Christians once it became clear that they were not merely a Jewish sect and were, indeed, repudiated by official Jewry.

CHRISTOS AND CHRESTOS

This rejection by the Jews of what seemed a subversive heresy led the votaries of Joshua to proselytizing activities among the Gentiles, according to Robertson. Messiah, which means 'Anointed One', was translated into Greek as 'Christos'; but it became confused with the word 'Chrestos', which means Good. Chrestos was a special title of the underworld gods of the Samothracian mysteries, also of Hermes, of Osiris and of Isis. In short, Chrestos is the appellation of a mystery-god.

Robertson writes:

'The two words were pronounced alike; and the coincidence is often such as would be made by ancient thinkers, wont to lay great stress on words. In the gospel phrase so loosely rendered "my yoke is easy", the Greek adjective is *chrestos*; in the epistles *chrestotes* is the word used in the phrase "the goodness of God"; and in the familiar Pauline quotation from Menander "good manners" is in the Greek *chresta ethe*. Among the Pagans again, this epithet constantly figures on the kind of tomb called *heroon,* erected to distinguished persons ... who in consequence of this very epigraphic formula came in later times to be regarded as Christian martyrs.... There was thus on the Christist side an appeal to Gentiles on the lines of a name or badge already much associated with Gentile religion, and attractive to them in a way in which the name Christ, as signifying the "one anointed", would not be.' (*A History of Christianity*)

The confusion is illustrated by a letter which the Emperor Hadrian wrote from Alexandria:'Here the worshippers of Serapis are Christians, and those who call themselves Bishops of Christ are devotees of Serapis.' And Suetonius speaks of Claudius expelling the Jews from Rome in AD 49 for rioting under the instigation of Chrestos.

According to Robertson, the cult of Joshua the Messiah, translated into Greek as Iesous Christos, spread among the Gentiles. Membership was given to those who accepted the rite of baptism. The initiates were called Mystae, like those of all rival religions. When Paul speaks of being 'crucified with Christ' it is no mere metaphor.

Robertson concludes:

'The Gospels as we know them are a baseless fabric of myths of action and myths of doctrine leaving on scientific analysis "not a wrack behind" save the speechless crucified Messiah of Paul's propaganda, only in speculation identifiable with the remote and shadowy Jesus ben Pandira of the Talmud, who may have died for some forgotten heresy a hundred years before Christ.'

The Talmud is a collection of rabbinical writings divided into two parts: (*a*) the Mishnah, or oral teaching, written between AD 90 and 220, which does not mention either Jesus or Christianity; (*b*) the Gemara, or 'completion' written between AD 220 and 500, which tells of Jesus ben Pandira, who was put to death (according to one version) in the reign of Alexander Jannaeus 103–78 BC. We read:

'On the eve of the Passover, Jesus the Nazarene was hung. During forty days a herald went before him crying aloud: "He ought to be stoned because he practised magic, has led Israel astray and caused them to rise in rebellion. Let him who has something to say in his defence come forward and declare it." But no one came forward, and he was hung on the eve of the Passover.'

VARIETIES OF MYTHICISM

Whittaker, Drews, Rylands and Dujardin accept a great deal of Robertson's theory and make fresh contributions. The details of their agreements and disagreements must be sought in their works. What is common to them all is the idea that a mythical being came to be regarded as having really lived on earth. What they all deny is the euhemeristic view of a real man who became deified.

Whittaker claims that a statement by Origen shows that the postulated passion play must have been continued until the second half of the second century. He also draws attention to a passage in the Roman prophetic books known as the Sibylline Oracles, dating from AD 80, which identifies Joshua with the Christian Jesus:

'Then shall one come again from heaven, an excellent hero; He who spread his hands on a tree of beautiful fruitage; best of the Hebrews all, who stayed the sun in his course once, bidding him stay with words that were fair and lips that were holy.'

Lenin became acquainted with the writings of Arthur Drews, and the mythicist theory is widely accepted by Russian Communists. Drews, however, like W. B. Smith, was a theist. He considered himself to be merely purging Christianity of legendary dross.

Dujardin, seizing on the identification of Jesus with Joshua, seeks to trace the cult of totemism. Joshua was 'the son
of Nun', which means 'fish'; and Dujardin contends that
the cult of an eel-god persisted into the second century. He
points to the symbolization of Jesus as a fish in the catacombs; but Howell Smith comments that although there
are paintings of fishes, none of them has the appearance of
an eel.

When, according to the mythicists, did the change from
legend to history occur? Dujardin suggests that there was
an hallucination after a secret sacramental meal shared by
Galilean fishermen and peasants who had migrated to
Jericho when Herod Antipas founded the city of Tiberias
in honour of the emperor. The scene of this ritual meal was
Gilgal (one of the many ancient cromlechs, like the setting
where 'Samuel hewed Agag in pieces before Yahweh'); and
the date was AD 27. Peter and some others believed they had
seen the risen god.

The story spread among the Greek-speaking Jews of the
Dispersion. At first the main import of the message was
essentially Jewish—the end of the world was at hand. The
note was changed after the fall of Jerusalem, and the politi-
cally subversive character of the movement became effaced.

Rylands, who made a close study of Gnosticism, stresses
the Gnostic element in the Pauline Epistles and holds that
the earliest Gospel—which, it is widely agreed, we do not
now possess—is best represented by the apocryphal *Gospel
of Peter*, dated in its present form about AD 140. He considers that the Odes of Solomon, discovered in 1908, are pre-
Christian. If that is accepted, a sect must have existed before the date assigned to the historical Jesus, who revered
Christ as the Logos, which is the divine Reason or Word in
a mystical context, and is equivalent to the 'Wisdom' of
the theosophical Jews.

The concept of Logos has affinities with the Egyptian
Thoth, who was the Heart, the Tongue, the Mind of Re,
the sun-god. Whatever Thoth named sprang into existence.

He was identified with Hermes by the Greeks and a vast Hermetic literature came into being between 50 BC and AD 150, though some authorities date it later.

Esoteric doctrines undoubtedly flourished in Alexandria in the time of Philo, who appears to have known nothing about the historical Jesus, though he calls the Logos 'Christ'. He speaks of it also as 'First begotten Son of God', and 'Heavenly Man'.

Couchoud does not think that the idea of an historical Christ occurred to anyone before the second century. Christianity resulted from a fusion between the Christos of Jewish Messianism and the Chrestos of Gnosticism; hence its contradictions. He holds that the most primitive version of the Gospel is that of Marcion, a Christian by birth and a sea-captain. According to Marcion's Gospel, Jesus was not born of Mary but descended from Heaven in the likeness of man. Most scholars, however, regard Marcion's work as a distortion of Luke's Gospel.

W. B. Smith takes a somewhat different line. He identifies Jesus with the saviour-aspect of Yahweh. The pre-Christian sect who worshipped Jesus were Nazarenes, a name derived from nazar ('to keep' or 'to guard'). Smith mentions a papyrus, dated by some authorities as second century BC, but by others as third century AD, which contains the formula, 'I adjure thee by the God of the Hebrews, Jesus.' It is therefore suggested that Christianity is a continuation of Jewish monotheism, and that the Gospels were originally devised as allegories to veil an esoteric teaching.

THE HISTORICIST CASE

One general criticism often brought against the various forms of the myth theory is that the evidence is meagre and the constructions strained. The complaint is also made that there is too much readiness to dismiss texts that do not fit in as forgeries or interpolations. Also, there are obvious dangers about postulating a secret cult or a secret meaning. But all who consider this perplexing problem without having first made up their minds on *a priori* grounds must admit that the mythicists have shed some light at least on dark places. They call attention to one outstanding fact that can hardly be denied by the secular historian, namely that there are certain categories, certain forms of thought and imagery, which no new religious movement seems able wholly to avoid. Whether these categories are due to socio-logical of psychological causes is a matter of controversy. But while admitting that a very great deal of the traditional Christian picture is mythical, the historicists do not admit that a human Jesus can be eliminated altogether.

A fair and lucid presentation of the historicist case is made by A. D. Howell Smith in *Jesus Not a Myth* (1942). He regards the evidence in favour of Robertson's Joshua cult as thin. The Sibylline text quoted by Whittaker is 'very interesting but throws no light whatever on the alleged pre-Christian Joshua (Jesus) cult'. As for the Passion play:

'Even if some dramatic mystery has helped to shape the Gospel accounts of the last days of Jesus, the statement of Robertson that whoever added the Passion story to the First and Second Gospels was transcribing from a dramatic text seems to go far beyond the data.

'If the Christian movement was, as W. B. Smith alleges, a protest against idolatry, "a crusade for monotheism" in which Jesus is simply Yahweh in another guise, why does the New Testament repeatedly distinguish between Jesus and God, making one the Son and the other the Father? Why was he credited with a virgin birth, an expiatory death, and a physical resurrection? ... If the object of the Gospels was to preach monotheism, why, as F. C. Conybeare per-tinently says, is there no text that "betrays on the part of Jesus, their central figure, any such crusading spirit? Jesus everywhere assumes his hearers to be monotheists like himself—he speaks as a Jew to Jews—and perpetually re-minds them of their Father in heaven."'

Again, why should Jesus be made to say that his own generation would not pass away before the Messianic Kingdom is established by authors who, if they wrote as late as the Mythicists contend, must have known that no one of that generation could be alive?

'But to place a long-worshipped mythical figure in Judea under the Roman Emperor Tiberius, and to make him suffer at the hands of Pontius Pilate, was a daring thing to do, and the motive for so doing has never been explained by the mythicist,' Howell Smith continues. He refers to Papias, Bishop of Hieropolis, who wrote before AD 150:

'There is no doubt, however, that those with whom Papias conversed were convinced that they were removed by only a few decades from the immediate followers of Jesus. Such historic links do not exist in the case of any of the Saviour gods of the mystery cults.'

One of the strongest points Howell Smith makes is that the mythicists favour a very late dating of the Gospels. Couchoud puts their composition approximately between 135 and 142. E. W. Barnes, in *The Rise of Christianity*, also relegates the Gospels to the second century. Those who uphold the traditional dates have taken heart from two comparatively recent discoveries: (1) The Chester Beatty papyri, a group of Scriptural manuscripts ranging in date from the second to the fourth century, and therefore older than either the Codex Vaticanus or the Codex Sinaiticus, which were hitherto believed to be the oldest extant authorities for the text of the Greek Bible; (2) the John Rylands Papyrus, found in 1935. According to Sir Frederic Kenyon:

'It is a tiny fragment, measuring only about 3½ by 2¼ inches, bearing on both sides of it portions of a few verses of the Fourth Gospel, ch xviii, 31–3, 37, 38; but its importance lies in the fact that papyrological experts agree in assigning the date of its writing to the first half of the second century. Small therefore as it is, it suffices to prove that a manuscript of this Gospel was circulating, presumably in provincial Egypt where it was found, about the period AD 130–150. Allowing even a minimum time for the circulation of the work from its place of origin, this would throw back the date of composition so near the traditional date in the last decade of the first century that there is no longer any reason to question the validity of the tradition.'

Yet how are we to measure the 'minimum time' for the Gospel to reach Egypt? The new discoveries show that the very late dating favoured by some critics cannot be easily defended, but they by no means establish the traditional view. Howell Smith, after considering this papyrological evidence, concludes as follows:

'In the light of all the evidence so far available we seem justified in regarding Mark, or an earlier version of it, as having been composed about AD 70, just before, or just after, the destruction of Jerusalem; Luke as a work of about AD 80, unless, as seems probable, its author knew the writings of Josephus, in which case this Gospel must have been composed after AD 96; and Matthew as dating about AD 100, with additions made perhaps twenty years later.'

The references found in the work of the historian Josephus (AD 37-100) raise the question of forgery. This is discussed from a Jewish point of view by Robert Eisler; and the Talmudic evidence has been dealt with from the standpoint of a modern Jew by Joseph Klausner in *Jesus of Nazareth* (1922). F. C. Conybeare writes as an historicist and Rationalist in *The Historical Christ* (1914), which is described by a Christian scholar, Professor F. C. Burkitt, as 'the best refutation of the various theories that the Gospel story is not historical at all, but wholly mythical'.

Other contributions of unquestioned importance are Albert Schweitzer's *The Quest of the Historical Jesus* (Eng trans 1910); Maurice Gogol's *Jesus the Nazarene; Myth or History?* (1925) and *The Life of Jesus* (1932); and Charles Guignebert's *Jesus* (1935).

THE QUMRAN SCROLLS

In 1947 some Hebrew documents were found in jars hidden in a cave above the Dead Sea. It was one of the most exciting archaeological discoveries of the twentieth century. They are still being deciphered and an erudite controversy continues about the dating of the scripts and its significance. A scroll of Isaiah together with apocryphal writings, including a commentary on Habbakuk yield some highly interesting results.

The commentary interprets the biblical text in the light of contemporary events. There are references to a 'Teacher of Righteousness', also called 'the Master of Justice and the elect of God' who was tortured and executed by a wicked high priest. As a judgment for this crime, Jerusalem was captured on the Day of Atonement. The captors were said to worship their regimental standards. In the future, it was predicted, the martyred Master would return to judge Israel and all nations, and those who believe in him will be saved.

According to Professor Dupont-Somer, one of the team of Jewish, Christian and Humanist scholars, the evidence points to the existence of an austere religious sect calling itself the 'New Covenant'. They were bound together by an oath similar to that of a mysterious sect referred to by the Jewish historian Josephus as Essenes. There is no mention in Josephus that they believed in a Messiah, but the belief was rooted in Judaic tradition. Whether or not the Qumran community were identical with the Essenes, they had much in common both with that sect and the first Christians. They rated celibacy above marriage, held property in common and despised riches. They believed in a heaven-sent leader who was cruelly put to death and who, they confidently predicted would return in glory on the Day of Judgment.

The Habbakuk commentary, according to Professor Dupont-Somer, and the majority of scholars, can be precisely dated. The first High Priest is Aristobulus II, who was taken prisoner by Pompey in 63 BC. He was succeeded by Hyrcanus II, who reigned until 40 BC. The capture of Jerusalem in 63 BC by the Romans bears out the references in the Commentary, except that it did not fall on the Day of Atonement, and there was no High Priest still surviving the massacre of the priests by the Zealots.

There are discrepancies and extraordinary parallels with the beliefs of the primitive Christians in a Messiah who had been put to death and whose imminent return would herald the end of the world. The Christians also preached the 'New Covenant'. In Luke and Corinthians we read that Jesus said at the Last Supper: 'This cup is the New Covenant in my blood.'

John Allegro expects that even more revolutionary implications will be found when all the scrolls are deciphered. It may well be that the Mythicist case will be given more solid support than it seems as yet to have found. If so, the Gospel story may turn out to have been post-dated by a century. Alternatively the story of an unidentified Essene Messiah may have become attached to a real leader, with other legendary material, who was actually crucified under Pontius Pilate. The more moderate interpretation is favoured by Archibald Robertson:

'The Dead Sea evidence, then, does not prove that no Messiah suffered death under Pilate. But it destroys the uniqueness of the event. It puts the "myth or history" issue in a new setting. Hitherto it has been usually assumed that we have to choose between two alternatives: either there was a single Jesus whose life and death provided the peg on which the Christian religion hangs or there was no Jesus at all except a mystery-god. The Dead Sea discovery forces us to consider a third possibility—already conceded as such by J. M. Robertson. It is that more than one historical figure went to make the legend; that mythical material, floating around, was attached first to one such figure and then, when he was forgotten, to another; that the Gospel Jesus is a conglomerate of two or perhaps of many such.' (*The Rationalist Annual* 1952)

TEN

HAS RELIGION DECLINED?

THAT the twentieth century has witnessed an unprecedented decline of religious practice is an understatement. In Communist countries, with the exception of Poland, religion has been driven underground either by direct or indirect persecution. Following Marx's dictum that 'religion is the opium of the people' the Establishment in Russia and her satellites, and also in China, is militantly atheistic. This accounts for a vast segment of the population of the world, in many parts of which religion, where it survives at all, is virtually an underground or despised movement.

The Roman Catholic Church has been faced everywhere, not only with a leakage of the laity, but a serious drop in vocations for the priesthood and monastic orders. Judged by church attendances Protestantism has also suffered from widespread public withdrawal except in the United States where outward conformity is still to some extent a mark of social respectability.

Yet an American Existentialist philosopher can write: 'The central fact of modern history in the West—by which we mean the long period from the end of the Middle Ages to the present—is unquestionably the decline of religion. No doubt the Churches are still very powerful organizations; there are millions of churchgoers all over the world; and even the purely intellectual possibilities of religious belief look better to churchmen now than in the bleak days of self-confident nineteenth century materialism. A few years ago there was even considerable talk about a "religious revival", and some popular patriotic periodicals such as *Life* magazine gave a great deal of space to it; but the talk has by now pretty much died down, the movement, if any, subsided,

and the American public buys more automobiles and television sets than ever before.' (*Irrational Man* William
Barrett p 20)

In England, surveys reveal that less than 10 per cent of
the population are regular churchgoers. It would be a
mistake to think, however, that the decline in religious
practice is the consequence of scepticism following what is
sometimes called 'the Victorian landslide of Unbelief'.
From the beginning of the Industrial Revolution the new,
urbanized working class showed an indifference to the
Church in contrast to the attitude of village communities.

The census of 1851 gave the total population as 18 millions, and church attendance was 40 per cent, though the
majority of non-attenders were working class. The drift to
the towns broke all connection with the simple rural structure of 'parson and squire'. Gradually, the middle classes
became infected with a similar apathy. The statistics of
York, the seat of an Archbishop, are typical of this social
change. One might expect that a city with such strong religious traditions would be one of the last bastions to fall,
but it was not so. In York in 1901, one citizen in seven
attended Church of England services, but in 1948 the figure
had fallen to one in twenty-one.

The natural reaction of the Protestant Churches was to
draw closer together and seek a united front against the
common enemy—not so much against conscious unbelief as
indifference. The Russian orthodox Church, shorn of its
wealth and power under the Czarist regime, felt the same
impulse to restore the lost unity of Christendom. Even the
Roman Catholic Church, decades before *aggiornamento*
and Vatican Council II, permitted cautious feelers to test
the possibility of finding common ground in a rapidly
changing world. None of the Churches could afford the
complacent self-assurance of an earlier age. Somehow they
had to find a new way of carrying their message to a public
with whom the old lines of communication had gone dead.

The more radical apologists, such as Rudolph Bultmann

not only realized that to the bulk of non-churchgoers, there was a credibility gap to be bridged; they felt they could only do so by jettisoning what the average, secularized man could no longer accept. Bultmann's solution was to 'demythologise' the Gospel. So, too, with a somewhat different emphasis, Dietrich Bonhoeffer contended that 'religion' as well as 'myth' must be discarded. The paradox of 'non-religious Christianity' startled the orthodox while appealing to those Christians to whom the Modernism of a previous generation had become outmoded. In his *Letters and Papers from Prison*, posthumously published after his execution in a Nazi concentration camp, Bonhoeffer wrote:

'Man has learned to cope with all questions of importance without recourse to God as a working hypothesis. In questions concerning science, art, and even ethics, this has become an understood thing which one scarcely dares to tilt at any more. But for the last hundred years or so it has been increasingly true of religious questions also: it is becoming evident that everything gets along without "God", and just as well as before. As in the scientific field, so in human affairs generally, what we call "God" is being more and more edged out of life, losing more and more ground.' (p 145)

This is described as 'man's coming of age', but it would be wrong to suppose that either Bonhoeffer, Bultmann or the radical Christians who employ such language have reverted to the language of the nineteenth-century agnostics. They are merely trying to make what they believe to be the essentials of Christianity more acceptable to 'modern secular man'. It entails a drastic criticism of 'institutional Christianity', by which is meant the official Churches.

From another angle the Churches themselves indulged in frank self-criticism. The mistakes of the past—the record of bigotry, persecution and blindness to social justice—are now humbly admitted. Above all, the fragmentation into sects is seen as a major stumbling block and a scandal. Hence the emergence of the Ecumenical Movement.

THE ORIGIN OF ECUMENISM

Tentative moves towards reunion were made early this century. The first World Missionary Conference, held at Edinburgh in 1910 and the formation of an International Missionary Council in 1921, may be said to have brought the Ecumenical Movement into effective existence. In 1948 the World Council of Churches was formed, and in spite of misgivings and some resistance on the part of sections of the non-Roman Catholic Churches it was sufficiently advanced by 1961 that at the Third Assembly, held at New Delhi, more than two hundred Church bodies from all parts of the world were represented, and the Vatican sent observers.

Hopes ran high that at long last the Churches would move out of what the ecumenists called 'the Christian ghetto'. The optimists saw the founding in 1947 of the Church of South India, which was a union of episcopal and non-episcopal bodies, as a model of reunion of Protestant Churches. The Church of England and the Methodists agreed to vote on a Service of Reconciliation which would end the episcopal barrier if 75 per cent were in favour. In July 1969 the houses of Convocation could muster only 69 per cent although the Methodists voted 77 per cent for unity.

The election of Pope John XXIII in 1959, however, soon revealed that the winds of change were also blowing through the hitherto hermetically sealed windows of the Vatican. His bold decision to re-open the Vatican Council of 1870—which had been hastily prorogued on the arrival of victorious Italian troops in Rome—showed that there were liberal elements within the Catholic Church which had caught the new ecumenical spirit. The Archbishop of Canterbury was quick to seize what seemed to be an opportunity to end the Cold War that had existed since the Council of Trent closed all avenues of compromise. He had long been a passionate advocate of reunion both between the Protestant Churches themselves and Rome.

Unity was in the air everywhere. Meanwhile Humanists also gathered their scattered forces and in 1952, at Amsterdam, founded the International Humanist and Ethical Union, with Sir Julian Huxley as President.

Humanism was seen as a major enemy by those ecumenists who looked to reunion as a means of bringing about a religious revival. In the report of a commission on evangelism presented to the Church Assembly in 1945 Humanism is described as 'the age-long lie'. By 'laying the stress on scientific training, which results in a mentality unwilling to take anything on trust, it is made difficult to believe on faith.... The cumulative result of modern education is, thus, to reinforce the humanistic view of life, if only by making it harder for man to understand and to accept the Christian faith.' (*Towards the Conversion of England*)

Since then, however, there has been a change of front and Humanists are almost embarrassed by the compliments paid to them by Church leaders. Reviewing *The Humanist Outlook* (edited by A. J. Ayer) in *The Spectator* the Archbishop of Canterbury wrote: 'Humanism has come to mean a reverence for man and a concern for his dignity, morality and happiness, linked with a belief that these ends are best served by the advance of the scientific outlook.'

A significant symptom of this more tolerant attitude of modern Churchmen to their traditional opponents is the substitution of 'Dialogue' for 'Debate'. Vatican Council II led to a series of high level 'dialogues' with Catholics, Humanists, Marxists, Mahommedans, Hindus and Buddhists under the direction of Secretariats for Non-Christians and Non-believers. In a speech at the Pontifical Urban University dealing with the call for dialogue with atheists Cardinal Marella is quoted as saying: 'The enemy of dialogue is he who denies the existence of true and authentic values in non-Christian religions ... considering the ethical-religious patrimony of non-Christian humanity as a realm of shadows and errors.' (*Catholic Herald* November 29 1968)

CRISIS IN THE CATHOLIC CHURCH

The driving force behind the moves towards a united Christendom is the alarm at the decline of religion and a desire to reverse the process of secularization by making a new appeal in harmony with the outlook of a scientific age. Inevitably this gives rise to its opposite—a cleavage between liberal and traditionalist factions. The divisions in the Roman Catholic Church became apparent when Pope John opened the floodgates by reviving the ecumenical Council of 1870. Differences and discontents that had smouldered behind a seemingly monolithic façade were suddenly exposed to an astonished world. It would be rash to predict what the final outcome will be.

Despite its enormous paper strength, Catholicism, like Protestantism, has suffered from a massive erosion. The Church claims 590,000,000 members, basing the figure on estimates of baptism and the principle that 'once a Catholic always a Catholic'. However, at the fourth session of Vatican Council II, Father Peter Arrupe, Superior General of the Jesuits, gave the figure as 480,000,000. He admitted a recent decline: 'In 1961 Catholics formed 18 per cent of the world's population; today they form 16 per cent.'

Considerable allowance must be made in assessing these figures for those who have left the Church or are purely nominal adherents. Although Latin America claims one third of the Catholics in the world it has only one priest for 5,000 members. The illiteracy rate is matched by illegitimacy—some 60 per cent. The number of priests even in Italy has fallen 70 per cent in the past hundred years although the population has nearly doubled. If real membership is judged by Easter Communion—obligatory under pain of sin—only a quarter of French Catholics and still fewer Italian Catholics can be counted. Thus despite its outward pomp and wealth the Catholic Church has also suffered severely from the modern drift from religion.

To repair these ravages the Vatican Council was reopened. Its main task was to remedy internal weaknesses and improve relations with other Christian bodies. Unfortunately for both objectives the worst crisis since the Reformation was provoked by what, to some dismayed ecclesiastics, must have seemed a side-issue: birth control. What began as a quarrel between theologians ended as a big scale revolt of the laity, and for this the Church was ill-prepared. The Church was faced by a challenge to its authority almost as severe as in the sixteenth century. To understand how it came about we must examine the way in which traditionally the Roman Church imposed a tight discipline on the thoughts and actions of its members.

PAPAL INFALLIBILITY

The Infallibility of the Pope is a distinguishing characteristic of Roman Catholic dogma. It is based on a passage in the sixteenth chapter of Matthew which reads, in an English translation of the Catholic Vulgate: 'And I say unto thee: Thou art Peter; and upon this rock I will build my church, and the gates of hell shall not prevail against it. And I will give to thee the keys of the kingdom of heaven. And whatsoever thou shalt bind upon earth, it shall be bound also in heaven; and whatsoever thou shalt loose on earth, it shall be loosed also in heaven.'

Neither the Eastern Orthodox Churches, nor of course, the Protestants of the west, accept the interpretation that this text implied the perpetual primacy of the Bishop of Rome. The metaphors are ambiguous and are not repeated in the other gospels.

With the collapse of the Roman Empire and the split with Byzantine Christianity, it was inevitable that Western Christendom should find a focal point of unity in Rome during the early and late Middle Ages. Although it was many centuries before Infallibility was formally defined, it was generally accepted in practice. Yet, even the formal definition had a curious vagueness. It pronounced the Pope to be infallibly guided by the Holy Ghost when he spoke *ex cathedra* (ie from the chair of Peter) on a question of faith or morals.

How many Papal pronouncements comply with this condition? No authoritative list has ever been drawn up. Clearly the dogma of the Immaculate Conception of the Virgin Mary comes under this heading, though it was defined sixteen years before the definition of Infallibility and had long been disputed by eminent theologians; so does the doctrine of the Assumption of the Virgin Mary, promulgated by Pius XII in 1950. But the bulk of Catholic doctrine, 'the deposit of faith', has not required formal reinforcement, and doubters have been dealt with by disciplinary action. The Holy Office, in practice, used its delegated authority to denounce heresy, silence rebellious priests and ban dangerous books.

The teaching authority of the Church (*the magisterium*) is communicated by the Pope through Encyclicals (circular letters); Bulls, which deal with particular local issues; Briefs, which are short letters; and *Motu Proprio* ('of his own motion') which is a form of address or statement on a special occasion. Although none of these have the absolutely binding force of an *ex cathedra* utterance, they do not normally leave much scope for private judgement. They are not 'irreformable', nevertheless it is considered 'temerarious' to disagree.

Catholics are supposed to obey their teaching whether they are infallible or not. As Pius XII said in *Humani Generis,* 'If Popes expressly pronounce in encyclical letters on matters previously debated, it is obvious to all that the question—according to the mind and intention of those Popes—can no longer be regarded as open to free discussion among theologians.'

For such an ecclesiastical machine to operate smoothly there must be outward obedience, at least, even if there are secret misgivings and mental reservations by individuals. The point is made with candour by a learned contemporary theologian who disagreed with the official teaching on con-

traception and was obliged to publish his views under a
pseudonym without obtaining an *imprimatur*: 'Humani
Generis has condemned the idea of dividing papal pronouncements into those which we must obey (because they
are infallible) and the rest (to which we need not submit).
But to say that non-infallible statements must be obeyed is
not to say they are infallible. Obedience, silence, belief, in-
ward and outward submission—all these may be demanded
by and given to papal declarations, whether infallible or not.
They are no more equivalent to the truth guaranteed by
infallibility than our certitude, persuasion, assuredness and
peace of mind when we assert the statement A is equivalent
to A/s being the case. It is logically possible, though not
usual, to have to correct that of which we are completely
certain; it is logically impossible to have to correct what is
true.' (*Birth Regulation and Catholic Belief* G. Egner p
162)

THE CONTRACEPTION CONTROVERSY

Until recently the discipline worked. For example, Teilhard de Chardin's writings were placed on the Index and he
was forbidden as a Jesuit to publish any more doubtfully
orthodox views during his lifetime. Unlike the Jesuit
Modernist, Father Tyrrell, he submitted and suffered in
silence, though handsome amends were made after his
death, which shows how the atmosphere had changed.
Since then, however, the Index has been abolished and the
Holy Office stripped of much of its power.

It is doubtless easier to submit on dogmas like the
Assumption, remote from everyday affairs, than on a question of morals which touches the lives of millions of ordinary people. Birth control is not an abstract, esoteric question of faith; it is a moral dilemma which, as every priest
knows, is tormenting the more conscientious laity and
causing many others to lapse. But it was also a dilemma
for the Pope, since the official teaching had been that contraception is absolutely forbidden. Pronouncement after

pronouncement had repeated that contraception is 'contrary to the laws of God'.

Although none of these were indisputably infallible, according to G. Egner: 'The obvious candidate for an infallible pronouncement is Pius XI's encyclical on marriage, for the tone of language used seems to commit the Pope to a full exercise of his magisterial power: "The Catholic Church, to whom God gave the task of teaching and defending moral honesty and virtue, placed as she is amid this decay of morality, preserves the chastity of the nuptial bond from this foul corruption, by raising aloud her voice through our mouth as a sign of her divine mission and proclaiming yet again: any use of marriage at all in which the act is deprived by human effort of its natural procreative force, offends the law of God and of nature, and those who so behave are guilty of grave sin."' (*Op cit* p 161)

Pius XII supported the ruling of Pius XI in his address to midwives in October 1951; and a month before his death in 1958 he condemned the contraceptive pill as 'a matter of direct sterilization'. He restricted the use of the rhythm method to those having 'serious economic, medical or eugenic motives'.

Pope John appointed a six man commission on population problems as part of his policy of *aggiornamento* (bringing the Church up to date). Later the terms of reference were widened and the group was expanded to eighteen. After the death of John the first report of the commission was given to his successor in June 1964 and the secret findings were leaked. It was apparent that the experts were divided, though Pope Paul bewildered everyone by declaring that the matter was both undecided and not in doubt.

Subsequent events suggest that what he meant was that *he* was not in doubt. He increased the Commission to sixty-four, including theologians, doctors, psychiatrists, sociologists and economists. The history of the commission has yet to be written, but it was devious and complicated by the manoeuvres of progressives and liberals to gain a majority verdict.

The final report did not go directly to the Pope but to a committee of Bishops created in April 1966. A majority of the Bishops advocated various forms of change from the traditional position which dated back to Aquinas and Augustine. After brooding on the result of this protracted investigation for another two years the Pope issued his encyclical *Humanae Vitae*. It burst on the Catholic world like a bombshell and revealed even more startling divisions than anyone had suspected

'HUMANAE VITAE'

The Pope began by reminding the rebels where authority lay: 'No believer will wish to deny that the teaching authority of the Church is competent to interpret even the natural moral law.' He then condemned, as might be expected, both abortion and sterilization and went on to reaffirm the current teaching that the only permissible method of birth control was the rhythm method. All other methods, including the pill, were rejected as sinful on grounds that baffled many Catholic gynaecologists: 'The Church, calling men back to the observance of the norms of the natural law, as interpreted by her constant doctrine, teaches that each and every marriage act must remain open to the transmission of life.'

He then went on to warn against measures taken by the State to encourage or even enforce 'anti-conceptive practices'. He seemed to be urging the Catholic bloc in the United Nations to renew their opposition to the efforts of the World Health Organization to start clinics in underdeveloped countries. He had taken this line in his first Christmas broadcast in 1963, and repeated it at the United Nations in 1965: 'You must strive to multiply bread,' he told the delegates when he spoke in New York, 'so that it suffices for the tables of mankind, and not rather favour artificial control of birth, which would be irrational, in order to diminish the number of guests at the banquet of life.'

It was evident that the time when a controversy could be closed with the solemn words, 'Rome has spoken' were long over. Rome had indeed spoken, but the Catholic world was in a turmoil. The Progressives numbered bishops high up in the hierarchy—Cardinal Doepfner of Munich, Cardinal Suenens of Belgium, Cardinal Koenig of Vienna. In England Archbishop Roberts was no longer seen as fighting a lone battle. A leading theologian, Charles Davis, left the Church in disgust. A significant number of parish priests either refused to obey the directive or treated the matter so lightly in confession that to admit the use of contraceptives was felt to be merely a venial sin. Whereas formerly absolution might have been refused, the laity were now urged to use the sacraments even though they continued through human weakness to 'sin'. If the Church had insisted on the old hard line there might well have been a mass exodus.

But the harm had been done. Catholicism, like Communism, could no longer show an impregnable, united front. As recently as 1959, the American hierarchy had opposed any public assistance, at home or abroad, to promote birth control. Yet President Kennedy, himself a Catholic, authorized United States support in 1962 for a United Nations proposal to provide birth control assistance to any needy country that requested it. President Johnson did the same. But the American bishops maintained their opposition during the Vatican Council, and so did Cardinal Gracias, the only Cardinal from India, where over-population has such tragic consequences.

THE REVOLT OF THE LAITY

Nevertheless the decline in the authority of the Church is clearly demonstrated by the refusal of the laity to be intimidated. The increase in the sale of contraceptive pills in Catholic countries is an indication of the trend. Drug company figures for the year 1966–7 show the following increases: Australia, 87·6 per cent; France, 122·7 per cent; Italy, 45·3 per cent; Belgium, 34·5 per cent; Spain, 98·8 per cent; Portugal, 87·3 per cent; Brazil, 33·4 per cent. The slower rise in Belgium is due to the market having neared saturation. More Belgian than British women now use the pill.

In Italy both the pill and condoms are either obtained on medical prescription—nominally not as a contraceptive —or on the black market. The Italian birth rate is only one point in a thousand above the British, and criminal abortions number a million a year. In Holland, market research shows that 40 per cent of Dutch Catholics use some form of contraceptive, as against 47 per cent of the population as a whole. The Dutch Church is as liberal as the Irish Catholics are conservative. But even in Ireland the pill is used surreptitiously and can be obtained on prescription from Protestant, if not from Catholic, doctors.

Compared with this upheaval the cautious concessions on liturgical and doctrinal matters following Vatican Council II are trivial. Pope Paul had evidently set himself the difficult task of applying the brakes to a rate of change that threatened the very structure of the Church. The demand for a less centralized administration might have destroyed the whole concept of Papal supremacy unless checked. So, too, the forced admission that 'error has its rights', is a retraction of the historic mission to crush heresy by any means available. Now that the laity are told that in the matter of the pill they must follow their own conscience, the Church comes perilously near ceasing to be distinctively Roman Catholic and to accepting the Protestant principle of private judgment. For that was what the Reformation was essentially about.

The main cause of the revolt is probably that the laity are now more educated—often far better educated than the priests. They are asking questions that never occurred to them before. If the Pope is to be taken seriously as a divinely inspired guide on morals, they ask, why doesn't he

make a ruling *ex cathedra* instead of through a non-infallible encyclical? And what authority is now to be attached
to the elaborate code of casuistry employed in the Confessional? If it is right to follow one's own conscience, why do
we need priests and popes?

The disarray of what was once the most disciplined and
coherent body of Christian doctrine is a further symptom
of the decline of religion throughout the world. The
malaise that has weakened the Protestant Churches has
now infected the Roman Church. It remains to be seen how
far it will spread, and whether Vatican Council II will repeat the success of the Council of Trent in saving the
Church from breaking up. It is hard to see how another
Pope could reverse the ban on contraception without further disastrous damage to its authority; yet unless the ban
is reversed it is even more difficult to see how what remains
of its authority can be salvaged.

The gravity of the situation can be judged by Pope Paul's
anguished appeal for Roman Catholic unity on Maundy
Thursday 1969:

'How can the Church be authentic and enduring if the
spiritual and social bond uniting it suffers such attacks from
opposition to, or neglect of, its hierarchical structure? How
can it be a church; that is, a united people, when a ferment
practically of schism divides and subdivides it, breaks it into
groups attached more than anything else to arbitrary and
basically selfish autonomy disguised as Christian pluralism
or freedom of conscience?'

ELEVEN

CHRISTIANITY IN HISTORY

RELIGION is sometimes regarded, even by sceptics, as a necessary cement holding society together. Without a body of common beliefs and values, it is argued, society would disintegrate. Did not this nearly happen with the collapse of the Roman Empire, and was not civilization saved by the adoption of Christianity? Whether a particular religious system is true is another matter; it could still serve a valuable purpose even if it were false.

This attitude is, of course, very old, though for obvious reasons it was rarely explicitly stated. It was first expressed, somewhat cynically, in a drama by the oligarch, Critias, a disciple of Socrates and relative of Plato. He contended that the gods were invented in order to frighten men into obeying the laws by threats of punishment. It followed that atheism was subversive and must be treated as such.

Plato by no means regarded the gods as a useful fiction, but he was so conscious of atheism as a danger to social order that he proposed what would have been, in effect, the first Inquisition. Heretics and atheists were to be brought before the Nocturnal Council, which was empowered to sentence a first offender to five years' imprisonment, and if he still proved recalcitrant the punishment was death.

The Romans, as is well-known, classed the Christians with atheists. They were charged, not without some justification, with subverting the established order—the charge brought in our time by the Committee of Un-American Activities against the Communists. Equally, the Stalinist trials in Soviet Russia, and the persecution of religious sects were based on the fear that to challenge the basic assumptions of the State could be disruptive.

John Locke, for all his liberal views on toleration, excluded atheists. The very name excited a peculiar horror which has still not entirely disappeared. One reason given by John Foster Dulles for not trusting the Russians was that they were atheists and therefore had no reason to keep promises.

Charles Bradlaugh won the right to affirm, instead of taking a religious oath, but even today the privilege can still arouse prejudice. At the back of this persistent attitude is the feeling that a society without any belief in God lacks a foundation for morality. Hitler and Stalin are held up as dire warnings of where such a road may lead. The fact that individual unbelievers often lead lives of unquestioned rectitude is admitted, but explained as 'living on Christian capital'.

In a sense, of course, it is impossible not to be influenced by the culture into which we are born, Many values inherited from a Christian past would be preserved by the Humanist because of their intrinsic worth. Few atheists would follow Nietzsche and demand a 'transvaluation of all values'. He extolled the qualities of the warrior, the ruthlessness of the tyrant, contempt for the masses, He turned Christianity upside down; but it was a paper exercise and he would have been shocked by the travesty Hitler made of his doctrine of the Superman.

Humanism is a great deal more than atheism. It is a positive affirmation of moral values many of which are common to all the great world-religions, though some are not. What is rejected is the bland assumption that the appearance of Christianity two thousand years ago was like a sudden light bursting upon darkness, and that the life of the good pagan is only a pale reflection of a superior ideal. Yet it is extravagant to say with Gibbon that the rise of the Christian Church was the triumph of barbarism over civilization. Perhaps it is nearer the truth to say that the Church, when it emerged under Constantine as the Establishment, was the triumph of paganism over Christianity.

THE SOCIAL RECORD OF THE CHURCH

The social record of the Church has so many black pages that today the usual line of its apologists is to admit their existence but to suggest it is rather tasteless to refer to them. But if the Christian way of life is superior to any other, surely the history of what it meant in practice cannot be ignored.

The glib plea that 'Christianity has not failed, it has never been tried' will not do. A religion that has lasted for two thousand years without ever having been tried is a curious phenomenon. Either it is too difficult to carry out, in which case it is not of much use, or its message has been misunderstood, in which case God cannot have made his intentions clear.

The humility which some Christians affect when attention is drawn to the past is counter-balanced by the arrogant assumption that even a bad Christian is better than a good pagan. This comes out clearly in Graham Greene's novel about a whisky-priest, *The Power and the Glory*. The same note is struck in the novels of Evelyn Waugh. The Christian, sinner though he may be, is said to have a mysterious 'something more' than 'mere morality'.

Christianity has a long history and it cannot all be irrelevant. It has inspired lives of selfless devotion to suffering humanity and it has given its blessing to appalling cruelty. The fact is that the cruelty and bloodshed have not been lapses from grace owing to human weakness; they have been justified over long periods on purely doctrinal grounds.

When we say 'it', the implication is that we can speak of Christianity as though it were a single, well-defined system of beliefs embodied in a single, unified institution called the Church. This is misleading. We have to deal with a number of Churches, often bitterly opposed to one another. There are, however, certain common factors. They all believe they have a special revelation from God, and in their strange blindness in the past to social justice, in practice if not in theory, and in their intolerance and persecuting zeal.

there was little to choose between Catholic and Reformer. So far from being the unchanging custodian of a divine revelation they have continually changed and are still doing so.

THE LOST UNITY

The traditional view of the Christian Church is that despite its divisions it is essentially a unity. The ecumenical movement today is an attempt to recover as much as possible of what was lost by fragmentation; to go back to the original vision of the Church as a new covenant superseding the earlier Jewish one. The idea of a Church would then replace the Jewish concept of an 'elect race' (Deut x, 15; Isaiah xliii, 20), because Gentiles would be included. Baptism, not circumcision, would be the sign of membership.

Such a Church, composed both of those still living and the souls of the departed, is described metaphorically as the Body of Christ. For a member to be cut off from it would be even more dreadful than for a Jew to be 'cut off from the soul of Israel'. Long after the Middle Ages a literal meaning was given to the famous saying, *extra ecclesiam nulla salus*, there is no salvation outside the Church. All unbaptized persons—infants included—were damned.

This harsh doctrine of St Augustine and the Council of Florence was gradually softened, and was virtually discarded by Vatican II. The first step was taken when Aquinas invented an intermediate state, limbo, to accommodate unbaptized infants and virtuous pagans. More recently the novel idea was added of 'the baptism of desire'—meaning that the wish to be baptized is sufficient if the physical opportunity is absent. It now seems that the desire can be unconscious, so that even agnostic Humanists, if they lead good lives, can be saved.

The Church, therefore, no longer regards itself as the exclusive possessor of the keys of heaven and hell, but it still claims to be unique. One would expect, if the claim were true, that such an organization could be distinguished quite easily by the unbeliever from secular organizations by the superior virtue of its members. Indeed, Catholics do not regard such a picture as too idealized.

A favourite argument is that the Roman Catholic Church can be singled out from its rivals by the conspicuous marks of unity, holiness and miraculous powers. And if we were to rely for our history on Catholic historians we should be struck by the way in which the Roman Church differs from all others. We should learn that it has never added one iota to the revelation made by Christ to the Apostles, that it has never failed to detect incipient heresy, that its Councils and Popes have obviously been guided in their careful deliberations by the Holy Ghost and have never contradicted previous, divinely-inspired pronouncements.

The appearance of change is explained on the lines of Newman's Doctrine of Development. This is to the effect that new dogmas—eg the Assumption of the Virgin Mary, etc—were always implicit in the original deposit of faith, and they were made explicit in course of time. Equally, although some members, even Popes, led scandalous lives, to the discerning eye the mark of holiness in the institution as a whole was always present.

Protestants do not make quite such bold claims. Nevertheless, the semi-official *Doctrine in the Church of England* declares that 'the Church has traditionally been affirmed to be characterized by the "notes" of Unity, Holiness, Catholicity and Apostolicity'. But it goes on to admit that unity has never been actually achieved:

'The divisions among Christians, as a result of which Christendom is split up into a number of competing and rival "denominations" and "communions", are not the least grievous among the scandals that arise from moral imperfection. It is plain that at no time did all Christians, corporately or individually, so fully respond to their position as to exhibit entire sanctification.'

Let us look at the facts of history and endeavour to make due allowance for the bias of those who have collated them. Is there anything in the historical record of the Churches to bear out the claim that they are essentially different from other social groups? Apart from extreme sanctity, are they even conspicuously more humane than secular organizations? Does the way the Church dogma grew suggest the slightest sign of supernatural guidance, or can it be just as well explained by ordinary means? In short, what is the real debt of the world to Christianity, and in what way (if any) is the Christian Church (if we can think of it as unity) a wholly exceptional institution?

THE PRIMITIVE CHURCH

In the first chapters of Acts, the Apostles are plainly regarded as the rulers of the Church, and this is what orthodox theory would lead us to expect. But they abruptly vanish from the scene, and there is no strong tradition about any of them until the third century. A belief grew up that they mostly went to the East, presumably to the Jews of the Dispersion.

Peter is said to have gone to the Asiatic provinces; and there is no overwhelming evidence in support of the other tradition that he founded the Church in Rome. Nor is there much support for the tradition that Thomas went as a slave to the court of King Gundophorus, though there existed a Parthian King of that name in North-west India.

The truth is that we know nothing certain of the fate of the Apostles, and very little about Apostolic Christianity. The document called *The Teaching of the Twelve Apostles*, discovered in 1883, is probably a Christianized version of a Jewish manual of instruction known as *The Two Ways*.

We have already seen that there were opposed schools of thought at the time of Paul. Broadly speaking, these represented on the one hand a Jewish interpretation of Christianity, dominated by the belief that the world was about to end, and on the other a Greek or Gnostic interpretation.

These opposing currents can be detected in Paul's quarrel with the Church of Jerusalem, where naturally the more Jewish construction prevailed.

To the Romans, Judaism was a religion permitted by law (*Religio licita*); and Christianity appeared at first to be a mere variant of it. Indeed, the Jews themselves regarded the earliest Christians as Jewish heretics.

The movement must have seemed to the Jews on a level with the sect started by John the Baptist, which preserved its independence of Christianity. Attention has recently been focused on the sacred books of the Mandæans, a sect which existed in Babylonia and Persia. They practised baptism by immersion and venerated John the Baptist; and although the documents date from no earlier than the seventh century, it is thought that Mandæanism may have originated from Palestine.

Mandæanism came to nothing, however, but Christianity prospered after it had effected a satisfactory fusion between the Jewish and Gnostic elements. The Christian Church broke with the Synagogue when the burning question of observance of the Law was settled. Paul played a decisive part in this controversy, and his arguments are set forth in the Epistle to the Galatians and 2 Corinthians. His efforts were probably less successful in the East than in the West, though even in Rome, if we may judge from the catacombs, the Jewish character of the new religion was strongly emphasized, in the early days.

Some allowance must be made, of course, for pious deception; in the reign of Nero, Christians were outlawed, and to safeguard their tombs they tried to make them look as much as possible like Jewish burial-places. But it seems established that, in the earliest period of the Church, the Eucharist was a sacred domestic meal, partaken in the houses of the faithful after a familiar Jewish pattern.

The picture that finally emerges is not of an Apostolic unity of belief and practice that was subsequently shattered, but of a primitive diversity (one might almost say confusion) which gradually acquired some sort of order. The first three centuries of Christianity show a painful struggle to achieve standardization.

CHURCH IN THE MAKING

It was no supernatural guidance, but a political event, the fall of Jerusalem in AD 70, that finally ended the primacy of the Church of Jerusalem. Orthodox Jews were then at pains to dissociate themselves from a seditious sect that proclaimed the imminent downfall of the Empire, and this fact also strengthened the Gentile and Hellenizing influences.

Another social factor was the existence in the Empire of Collegia, which may be likened in some respects to modern Friendly Societies and Burial Clubs. Some of them may be compared with Masonic Lodges, with appropriate initiations, rituals and periodic celebrations.

Membership was open to slaves, and within the lodge there was no distinction of race or social standing. Under such a guise Christians could meet together in comparative safety in one another's houses. Thus there was a Church in the making before there were church buildings, and it is noteworthy that the term 'priest' was not applied to officiating ministers until late in the second century.

Baptism was at first administered by the Bishop, and at Easter. Even today, for example, no parish church in such a town as Pisa has a font of its own. The Bishops were secretaries and presidents of guilds, responsible for the admission of new members and for the celebration of the sacred meal, during which originally they sat with the elders in imitation of Christ and the Apostles. Professor Garstang, who has excavated the Roman catacombs, comments:

'When it (the Eucharist) was once centralized under the Bishop the danger of publicity had become so great from the number of partakers and the conspicuousness of the work of preparing and serving the meal, that the original procedure, and with it the resemblance to the Jewish rite, necessarily came to an end.'

The Christian ministers were, to outward appearances, the officers of a benevolent society, and gradually a more centralized organization grew up. The Bishop of Rome naturally took charge of the burial clubs that used the Roman catacombs and he appointed deacons to manage the accounts. The importance of Rome as centre of the Empire, rather than the alleged appointment of Peter by Christ as head of the Church, was responsible for later developments.

THE BLOOD OF THE MARTYRS

Reports of the earliest waves of persecution of the Christians have been somewhat exaggerated. As a Christian historian, C. H. Dodd, writes:

'All the evidence goes to show that the Christian problem was a real embarrassment to the Government. It maintained the principle that the religion was illegal, and punished its adherents for obstinacy in not abandoning it at command. Yet the Emperors and their representatives often seemed genuinely anxious to protect Christians from the consequences of their folly and their neighbour's malice. How many actually saved their lives during this period by recantation under judicial pressure, we do not know. The number of those who suffered is not large. Origen, early in the third century, could still say: "There have been but a few now and again, easily counted, who have died for the Christian religion!"' (*Christianity in the Light of Modern Knowledge*)

However bitter and savage repression may have become locally, reaching its climax under Diocletian (AD 303), there was hysteria also on the other side. Gibbon has been abused for directing his irony to the fanatical frenzy with which many Christians deliberately sought the crown of martyrdom, but the facts he gives cannot be disputed. And when Christians were restrained from religious suicide they often turned on one another.

Not a few of the martyrs were slain by their fellow

Christians because of some doctrinal quibble which to the twentieth-century mind is almost incomprehensible. All this was part of the straining of a divided Church towards a unity that it had yet to win. The turning-point was, perhaps, the Edict of Milan, promulgated by Constantine in the winter of AD 312–13. It laid down 'that liberty of worship shall not be denied to any, but that the mind and will of every individual shall be free to manage divine affairs according to his own choice'. All restrictive statues were abrogated, and it was enacted 'that every person who cherishes the desire to observe the Christian religion shall freely and un-conditionally proceed to observe the same without let or hindrance'. Professor Dodd remarks:

'His (Constantine's) idea was to confer upon a single definite body, the *corpus Christianorum*, those powers, liberties and privileges which were to give Christianity its status within the Empire. Unfortunately there was no single body including within it all persons professing Christianity. After vain attempts to secure unity by agreement, Con-stantine standardized Christianity for legal purposes by re-cognizing as the only Christian body before the law that Church which, though in some provinces it might be over-shadowed by other bodies, yet represented throughout the Empire the majority of Christians. In the year after the Council of Nicaea had failed to realize the Emperor's hopes of Christian unity, an edict was issued expressly confining all clerical privileges to "observers of the catholic law" and excepting all "heretics and schismatics".' (*Op cit*)

The policy of toleration proved abortive before the ink was dry. Toleration and organized Christianity were in-compatibles, and the years between the Edict of Milan and Theodosius (313–95) were fraught with strife between ortho-doxy and heresy. The Roman Empire was in the throes of collapse and the balance of power was shifting to the East; but heedless of these mighty historical issues, Christian fought Christian about metaphysical subtleties with a ruth-lessness and violence that today seem almost incredible.

Arius, a presbyter of Alexandria, had declared that 'the Son is totally and essentially distinct from the Father'. The alternative view that the Son and the Father are of the same essence (*homoousios*), though distinct persons, was upheld by the Council of Nicaea by a majority vote. As Selden remarked 'They talk, but blasphemously enough, that the Holy Spirit is president of their General Councils, when the truth is, the odd man is still the Holy Ghost.'

CHRISTIAN TOTALITARIANISM

Once the Church ceased to be an underground movement and seized power, every conceivable resource was employed to liquidate heretics and pagans, although together they formed the majority of the population of the Empire. 'Soon after the accession of Theodosius,' wrote Fleury, in his *History of Christianity*, 'the pagans, particularly in the East, saw the storm gathering on the horizon. The monks, with perfect impunity, traversed the rural districts, demolishing all the unprotected edifices.'

And as Gibbon stated:

'In almost every province of the Roman world, an army of fanatics, without authority and without discipline, invaded the peaceful inhabitants; and the ruin of the fairest structures of antiquity still displays the ravages of those barbarians, who alone had time and inclination to execute such laborious destruction.'

Christianity was imposed on the Empire from above by legal enactments; and its success was ensured by the common informer and even by mob-violence. According to Milman:

'So severe an inquisition was instituted into the possession of magical books, that, in order to justify the sanguinary proceedings, vast heaps of manuscripts relating to law and general literature were publicly burned, as if they contained unlawful matter. Many men of letters throughout the East, in their terror, destroyed their whole libraries, lest some innocent or unsuspected work should be seized by the

ignorant or malicious informer, and bring them unknow-
ingly within the relentless penalties of the law.' (*A History
of Latin Christianity*)

Headed by an Archbishop, a fanatical mob destroyed the
temple of Serapis in Alexandria and proceeded to pillage
the great library, with its priceless manuscripts. In Alexandria, too, the pagan philosopher Hypatia was lynched:

'On a fatal day, in the holy season of Lent, Hypatia was
torn from her chariot, stripped naked, dragged to the
church, and inhumanly butchered by the hands of Peter the
Reader and a troop of savage and merciless fanatics: her
flesh was scraped from her bones with sharp oyster-shells,
and her quivering limbs were delivered to the flames.' (Gibbon: *Decline and Fall*)

Not content with suppressing and destroying classical
learning the zealots perpetrated a series of forgeries to bol-
ster up their claims. Mosheim speaks of 'the base audacity
of those who did not blush to palm their own spurious
productions on the great men of former times, and even on
Christ himself and his apostles, so that they might be able,
in the councils and in their books, to oppose names against
names and authorities against authorities. The whole Christian Church was, in this century, overwhelmed with these
disgraceful fictions.' (*Commentaries on the affairs of the
Christians before the time of Constantine the Great*)

The Sybilline books were a convenient vehicle:

'The prophecies forged by the Christians, and attributed
by them to the heathen sybils, were accepted as genuine by
the entire Church, and were continually appealed to as
among the most powerful evidences of the faith.'

One of the most famous of all such forgeries was produced some centuries later by a cleric who assumed the
name of Isidore Mercator.

These False Decretals, as they are usually called, were
compiled about the middle of the ninth century. They
claimed to consist of letters written by early Bishops of
Rome between the first and the end of the third centuries;

letters of Popes beginning with Sylvester and ending with Gregory the Great; decrees of various councils from that of Nicaea to that of Seville (619); and a copy of the canons passed by Gregory II (731) at a council held in Rome. The crucial point in these fabrications was that it is unlawful to hold a council without permission of the Pope. The sole power of judging and translating bishops and establishing new sees was also vested in the Pope.

For hundreds of years part of the evidence offered by the Church of Rome in defence of its claims to supremacy was these very decretals written by the pseudo-Isidore, together with various earlier forgeries such as the Donation of Constantine. Catholic Historians now admit that this 'evidence' of Papal supremacy was faked, but they do so with bad grace. The apology put forward amounts to saying that although the documents are spurious in form they are true in substance. One writer absolves the pseudo-Isidore from blame because his laudable object was 'to provide for the use of the faithful generally a store of authoritative statements on matters affecting Christian life within the Church'. (*Catholic Dictionary* Addis and Arnold)

Newman became very angry when Kingsley accused Catholics of having a very peculiar view of historical truth; just how peculiar it is may be judged from the following defence of the False Decretals:

'Suppose someone in the twelfth century had anticipated the labour of the moderns, and announced the spuriousness of a great part of the decretals; what then? The feeling would have been: What Fabian, Cornelius, Sylvester, etc, are made to say is true and useful; if they did not actually write it, they might have written it; if these are not genuine letters, then the genuine letters which they did write, and which would have been to much the same effect as those, have been lost; finally, if the Pope of the third century did not command all this the Popes of the twelfth century are ready to command it, because it is true, wholesome and highly necessary to be observed.' (*Ibid*)

STANDARDIZED RELIGION

Looking back from the Middle Ages to the time of the Apostles what broad impression do we receive? What evidence is there that any real unity prevailed in the primitive Church? Unless we deliberately shut our eyes we see—what we might have expected—the nucleus of an organization that develops like a biological cell by polar opposites and repeated fission. What seem to have been the original oral traditions contain the seeds of every future conflict.

Gnosticism and Messianism repel one another and then reach a compromise. The theory that Jesus was 'very God' won acceptance only gradually, and it was decreed as orthodox by a majority vote. All opposition was blotted out by the repressive machinery of the State.

The splitting of Christendom into East and West corresponded to the political division of the Empire. The disgraceful scenes in the Councils, the lobbying and abuse, the rioting and lynching that occurred, do not show the marks of unity and holiness that are supposed to enable us to single out an institution that was guided in its deliberations by the Holy Ghost.

Those who lament contemporary violence and intolerance and anti-Semitism, and blame their prevalence on the absence of Christianity, show a strange indifference to the history of Christianity itself. So far from preserving classical culture, many of the early Christians did their utmost to destroy the learning and art of the best periods of Greece and Rome; and although it is true that a protest was made against the tide of licentiousness that swept over the Roman Empire in its decline, the moderate counsels of the pagan philosophers were rejected and the Church, like many Oriental mystery cults from Orphism onwards, encouraged asceticism, with its invariable accompaniment of cruelty.

The practices of early monasticism and the austerities of the solitaries were no different from the self-torture practised by fakirs in India. In face of such masochism we may echo the sentiments of Lecky, in a famous passage referring to St Simeon:

'A hideous, sordid and emaciated maniac, without knowledge, without patriotism, without natural affection, passing his life in a long routine of useless and atrocious self-torture, and qualing before the ghastly phantoms of his delirious brain, had become the ideal of the nations which had known the writings of Plato and Cicero and the lives of Socrates and Cato.' (*History of European Morals*)

CHRISTIANITY AND SEX

But, as the proverb goes, if you expel the Devil with a pitchfork he will return. Very few pagans, after all, knew the writings of Plato and Cicero, and the average peasant or member of the town proletariat could not attain the ascetic ideal. The letters of Jerome show what a distorted form the Christian view even of normal marriage could take:

'I do not write to tell you of the inconveniences of marriage (he wrote to a young virgin), the swelling of the belly, the wailing of infants, the heart-burning caused by your husband's mistress, the cares of the household, and all the other supposed good things which, in any case, cease at death, but to enjoin you when you fly from Sodom to remember the fate of Lot's wife.

'For my part I say that mature girls must not bathe at all, because they ought to blush to see themselves naked.'

The Church, Bertrand Russell once remarked, never really liked marriage but had to allow it, and so tried to make it as disagreeable as possible. Although marriage came to be dignified as a sacrament, the attitude of priesthood was well reflected in a letter sent by Pope Gregory to Augustine while the latter was a missionary in Britain in AD 597.

Augustine was uncertain whether or not a pregnant woman ought to be baptized. Gregory generously answered in the affirmative, and also agreed that she should be permitted to enter the church after delivery in order to give thanks. This is to be allowed because 'the pleasure of the flesh is in fault, and not the pain; but the pleasure is in the copulation of the flesh, whereas there is pain in bringing forth a child'. (Bede's *Chronicles*) How long such an attitude poisoned the relationship of the sexes is shown by the prudery of the last century, and the continued prohibition of contraceptives.

According to Gregory:

'Lawful commerce must be for the sake of the children not of pleasure.... But when, not the love of getting children, but of pleasure prevails, the pair have cause to lament their deed. For this the holy preaching allows them, and yet fills the mind with dread of the very allowance.' (*Ibid*)

Even if we disregard the extravagances of early monasticism and dismiss the self-castration of Origen as untypical, the Christian attitude to marriage was utterly at variance with the rational view. Some protest against the sensuality of Roman decadence was needed, but by allowing the pendulum to swing to the opposite extreme the attempt to check the abuses was abortive. The Church failed to raise the general standard of morality; indeed, it became hopelessly infected with the very evils it tried to expel.

Today the Roman Church adopts a somewhat more tolerant attitude towards sex despite—and in a sense because of—its condemnation of any act which 'deprives the generative action of its natural procreative force'. (Pius XI) This obscure phrase precludes contraception and *coitus interruptus*, but not—strange to say—*coitus reservatus*, intercourse during pregnancy or with a sterile wife; and not during the so-called safe period.

It is conceded that there is another quality of conjugal love besides its biological aim. Even Pope Paul, in *Humanae Vitae*, said: 'These acts by which husband and wife are united in chaste intimacy, and by means of which human life is transmitted, are, as the Council recalled, "noble and worthy", and they do not cease to be lawful if, for causes independent of the will of the husband and wife, they are foreseen to be infecund, since they always remain ordained towards expressing and consolidating their union.'

THE PROTESTANT ATTITUDE

The Protestant Churches, partly because of their rejection of Mariolatry and the conventual life, made no special virtue of celibacy. They strongly emphasized chastity, by which they meant that sexual relationships must be confined to marriage. Even so, they were in no hurry, after the break with Rome, to permit a married priesthood—at least not in England.

Henry VIII was no prude, but he frowned upon clerical marriages, and Cranmer had to conceal his wife from public gaze. Luther regarded marriage as God's gift to mankind. He urged Wolfgang Reissenbusch, who hesitated to marry, to brush aside his scruples. 'Why should you delay? It must, should and will happen in any case. Stop thinking about it and go to it right merrily. Your body demands it. God wills it and drives you to it. There is nothing you can do about it.' On the other hand he was so influenced by Pauline theology that he defended marriage elsewhere as a prophylactic against fornication. But although marriage was a medicine it must not be made 'a pigsty in which the lecherous and sensual can wallow'.

The more liberal attitude which developed in the Church of England on divorce and contraception is shown by successive Lambeth Conferences since 1908. It was first declared that all artificial methods of family limitation were an evil which jeopardized the purity of family life. In 1920 'the spread of theories and practices hostile to the family' was also denounced, but a loophole was admitted for 'abnormal cases'. In 1930, however, by a majority of 193 to 67, the bishops acknowledged that when 'a clearly-felt moral obligation to limit or avoid parenthood' was felt, contraception might be justified. The bishops admitted that coitus has 'a value of its own' in marriage, though the primary purpose must be procreation.

The Lambeth Conference of 1958 went much further and denied the absolute primacy of procreation. Contraception by methods 'admissible to the Christian conscience' was approved. The extent of Anglican rethinking can be judged from the following quotation from a pamphlet *The Family in Contemporary Society* (SPCK 1958):

'Those relational acts of coitus between husband and wife which cement and deepen their love, relieve their physical and psychological sexual tensions and contribute to their personal fulfilment and integration, have an effect which naturally overflows the bounds of one flesh, so that such coitus is beneficial to the whole family. It cannot too strongly be stressed that the well-being of the family depends to a greater extent than perhaps has been realized hitherto, on the well-being of one flesh—and to that well-being coitus makes a profound contribution.'

Some radical Christians went even further. Thus Dr J. A. T. Robinson, then Bishop of Woolwich, appeared for the defence in the prosecution of the publishers of *Lady Chatterley's Lover*, a novel justifying adultery. He gave a generous interpretation to Augustine's dictum, 'Love and then do what you will'. In his controversial book *Honest to God* he wrote: 'For nothing can of itself always be labelled as "wrong". One cannot, for instance, start from the position "sex relations before marriage" or "divorce" are wrong or sinful in themselves. They may be in 99 cases or even 100 cases out of 100, but they are not intrinsically so, for the only intrinsic evil is lack of love.' (p 118)

THE REVOLUTION IN ETHICS

Radical Christians were moving towards 'situational ethics' as opposed to legalistic ethics. According to the latter the existence of the moral law entails a positive system of prohibitions. Since the moral law is a revelation of God's will—supplemented by what human reason can deduce from natural law—it must be unalterable. Consequences are therefore irrelevant. Hard cases must be endured. The change is rightly described by Dr Robinson as 'the revolution in Ethics'.

He writes, 'There is no need to prove that a revolution is required in morals. It has long since broken out; and it is no "reluctant revolution". The wind of change here is a gale.' (p 105)

The wind was felt in the Vatican Council, though the Roman Church still maintained the doctrine of the absolute indissolubility of marriage. To escape from the logical rigidity of this position, however, casuists fastened on the distinction between a sacramental and secular marriage, and emphasis was laid on the right intention of the contracting parties.

For example, if they did not intend it to be permanent, or if they were resolved never to have children, the marriage was invalid. So, too, a marriage that is not consummated is not a real marriage and can be annulled. If one of the partners had been previously divorced—assuming the first marriage was valid—the second marriage is null.

Oddly enough, lacking these humane quibbles, the Anglican Church took a more rigorous view until recently when the Archbishop of Canterbury, Dr Ramsey, agreed to divorce on the sole ground that a marriage could be proved to have broken down beyond any hope of repair.

Rationalist critics of the Church are often accused of unfairness in drawing attention to its past record. All this, it is urged, happened a long while ago: which invited the rejoinder that it took an unconscionable long time before the Church mended its ways. No doubt the Dark Ages might have been still more barbarous without the influence of Christianity, just as the paganism of classical Greece and Rome received a humanitarian influx from the new religion.

Thus, an ancient Greek who brought a law suit could state, as though it were the most natural thing in the world, that his motive was revenge. Certainly revenge was not eliminated by Christianity, but at least it was condemned.

But a religious intolerance, unknown in the classical world, weighed heavily on the debit side and has only just begun to die down.

The puzzle of why the precepts of Christianity made such a slight difference in practice cannot be explained as being due to some natural bias towards evil. If that were so we should still have to explain why, within the past 100 years, the social conscience has become much more sensitive. Part of the reason must be that Christianity had become the ideology of the Establishment, and it operated to uphold and justify the existing social order. Seen from this point of view there was little difference between the Catholic and the Reformed Churches.

THE DISPOSSESSED

There can be no doubt that many gross abuses were ended by the Reformers, though it is also true that during the counter-Reformation the Roman Church made some attempt to put its house in order. The moral corruption of many monastic orders was ended by their suppression; but the motives which led, for example, to the confiscation of Church property under Henry VIII give Protestants little cause for pride. Dr Tawney writes:

'In England, as in Germany and Switzerland, men had dreamed of a Reformation which would reform the State and society as well as the Church.... the disillusionment was crushing. Was it surprising that the Reformers should ask what had become of the devout imaginations of social righteousness, which were to have been realized as the result of a godly Reformation? The end of Popery, the curtailment of ecclesiastical privileges, six new bishoprics, lectureships in Greek and Latin in place of the disloyal subject of the canon law, the reform of doctrine and ritual—side by side with these good things had come some less edifying changes, the ruin of much education, the cessation of much charity, a raid on corporate property which provoked protests even in the House of Commons, and for ten years a

sinister hum, as of the floating of an immense land syndi-
cate, with favourable terms for all sufficiently rich, or influential, or mean, to get in on the ground floor. The men
who had invested in the Reformation when it was still a
gambling stock naturally nursed the security, and
denounced the revolting peasants as communists, with the
mystical reverence for the rights of property which is
characteristic of all ages of the *nouveaux riches.*' (*Religion
and the Rise of Capitalism* R. H. Tawney p 136)

The English peasant's lot under feudalism is described by
G. G. Coulton in *The Medieval Village*:

'The serf was worse off at Magna Carta than at the
Conquest, and much more than half the population were
serfs in 1324 (when the slave had become non-existent in
England). In strict law the serfs scarcely had any right
against their dominus—lord and master. In the courts in
which he pleaded, custom and arbitrary will ruled. He was
bound to the soil and his "brood" could be bought, sold or
given with land. On the tenant's decease the lord claimed as
heriot the dead man's best beast or best movable possession,
and the priest took the second best as a *mortuary,* thus
arraying clerical interests against the serf. It was a medieval
tenet that class divisions were of God's making.

'The serf or villein was therefore half slave in many respects, though he held some land of his own which he was
permitted to till at certain times. His labour was not hired
but given to the lord of the manor for a specified number of
days in the year. The serf could neither emigrate nor
strike; but neither could he be evicted nor have his rent
raised. If he ran away it was not easy for him to settle
elsewhere; on the other hand, it was extremely difficult for
the lord to replace him.'

Such a system probably worked better in practice than
might be expected—thanks to the fact that a willing serf is
more profitable than an unwilling slave—but it hardly deserves the rhapsodies of those to whom Medieval Europe
was a Golden Age. Professor G. M. Trevelyan describes it as

charitably as possible in his *History of England*, but he does not depict the medieval peasant as a product of which Christian civilization can be proud:

'The serf was what poverty and submission made him: shifty, fearful, ignorant, full of superstitions, Christian and pagan, trusting to charms and strange traditions of a folk-lore of immemorial antiquity, cheating and sometimes murdering the lord or his officers; incompetent and fatalistic in presence of scarcity and plague in the village and murrian among ill-kept beasts. The soil was undrained and sodden to a degree we can now hardly conceive. The jungle kept rushing in, weeds overspreading the ploughland, as bailiffs complained. Under the open field system, with its unscientific farming, the soil after centuries of use became less fertile, and the yield per acre was reduced.'

Peasant revolts date from as early as 821. There were serious outbreaks in Normandy in 1000 and 1250; in Languedoc and Flanders nearly a hundred years later, and in England in 1381. They were put down by massacre, and agitators were treated as heretics. Nor did the Reformation bring any relief to the lot of the lowest level of society. The Peasants' Revolt in Germany, in 1524, was suppressed with appalling bloodshed, to the hearty satisfaction of Luther.

The German peasants merely demanded that villeinage should end because 'Christ has delivered and redeemed us all, the lowly as well as the great, without exception, by the shedding of his precious blood.' Luther indignantly declared that such a proposition 'would make all men equal and so change the spiritual kingdom of Christ into an external worldly one. Impossible! An earthly kingdom cannot exist without inequality of persons. Some must be free, other serfs, some rulers, others subjects.' In the most fiery language Luther urged on the princes to greater ferocity. 'No one need think that the world can be ruled without blood. The civil sword shall and must be red and bloody.'

CHURCH AND STATE

Such in practice was the new version of Christianity. The refusal of Lutheran Churches to take sides on questions of social justice was maintained until the time of Hitler. As A. E. Garvie wrote in the *Hibbert Journal* (January 1941):

'The dualism of Lutheran theology, which separated the realm of grace from the social order, and held each to be autonomous under God as Redeemer and as Creator, has made it possible for Christians in Germany to acquiesce in policies, which the Christian conscience would otherwise condemn.'

Another Christian writer, H. D. Lewis, points out more frankly that the Confessional Church in Germany protested against Hitlerism only when it touched matters of Church doctrine and worship. It was unmoved by acts of brutality and terrorism that so shocked the rest of the world:

'But this is less strange when we turn to the actual teaching of the leaders of the Confessional Church in regard to the relation of Church and State. Witness the fulsome, almost blasphemous, reverence of the State in a celebrated pamphlet on *Church and State* by Barth. The author is loth to withhold the aura of a divine sanction even from the vilest acts of the State. An annoying allusiveness of style does not obscure the conviction that "the State cannot lose the honour that is due. For that very reason the New Testament ordains that in all circumstances honour must be shown to its representatives."' (*Morals and the New Theology*)

Barth has been hailed as the greatest of living theologians, and his influence is immense both on the Continent and in America. Canon Alan Richardson ranks Barth's *Church Dogmatics* with Schleiermacher's *Christian Faith* and the *Institutes* of Calvin as one of the most influential works to which Protestant theology can point. And yet Barthianism paralysed the action of the Confessional Church in Germany at a crucial period in history.

Calvin's 'Reign of Saints' in Geneva seems remote from

current controversies, but again it is pertinent to ask to what extent this version of Christianity, any more than that of Luther or Aquinas, has in fact promoted what is usually meant by 'Christian values'? The rules drawn up by Calvin had a simple object—to enable 'each man to understand the duties of his position'. Dr Tawney writes:

'It is sad to reflect that the attainment of so laudable an end involved the systematic use of torture, the beheading of a child for striking its parents, and the burning of a hundred and fifty heretics in sixty years.' (*Religion and the Rise of Capitalism*)

It is neither possible nor necessary for our present purpose to go more deeply into the social phenomena which pass under the general term, Christianity. When its critics use the word they are referring to a fact of history, not to an idealized conception that has never existed except on paper. The double sense in which the word 'Christianity' is used is a constant source of confusion. In the many arguments to the effect that civilization owes a profound debt to 'Christianity' the word is used to denote an ideal rather than a concrete fact. And so the discussion appears to be about what the Church has accomplished, but in reality it is about what some members of the Church have said ought to be done. Wycliffe and the rebelling German peasants said that according to Christianity no man ought to be a chattel; but the Roman Church in supporting serfdom, and the Lutheran Church in condemning the rebellious peasants, took the opposite line in practice.

One favourite line of argument attributes all that is good in history to Christianity and all that is bad to the lack of it. It runs as follows:

Nationalism owes to Christianity its high and almost mystical conception of the nation as a spiritual unity—a sacred community for which the individual will gladly sacrifice his life; yet divorced from Christianity this conception becomes a principle of hatred and destruction. Liberalism and democracy owe to Christianity their humanitarian idealism and their faith in progress; yet this idealization of humanity has become a substitute for the Christian faith in a divine order, and has made it possible to regard secular civilization as man's final end. The consequences are all too plain.

The Oration of Pericles, however, shows that men were ready to die for the community, and that they believed in some of the essentials of democracy, long before Christianity either as a noble ideal or a concrete fact, appeared on the human scene. It is true that Athenian democracy rested on slavery; but when did the Christian Churches condemn slavery?

A wholly false idea is spread that the gradual easing of the lot of common man has been due to the influence of Christian ideas. This unhistorical notion is so prevalent that we may conclude our brief survey of the record of the Churches by noting their attitude until fairly modern times towards a barbarity that everyone will nowadays condemn, whatever his religious views.

CHRISTIANITY AND SLAVERY

According to G. G. Coulton, slavery was never prohibited by the primitive Church, but the Eastern Church forbade monastic slavery in the eighth century. Early in the eleventh century Benedict VIII would not permit the children of priests to be slaves, but Clement V condemned the whole population of rebel Venice to slavery in 1309; and Paul III decreed slavery for all Englishmen who supported Henry VIII against those princes whom in 1535 he called on to invade England.

Innocent X bought slaves to use in his army, and Alexander VII dealt in slaves in the seventeenth century. Indeed, in the eighteenth century slaves were commonly used in Italy as household servants, and in 1760 the Russian clergy possessed one million slaves.

There were protests against the inhumanity of slavery in Mexico and South America, and individual ecclesiastics were sometimes courageously outspoken. But papal licences were granted to the Kings of Portugal in the fifteenth century to conquer heathen countries and reduce the inhabitants to 'everlasting slavery'. Although the enslavement of Indians was sometimes condemned, the horrible sea-traffic in Negroes was not merely approved, but encouraged. Nor is this surprising in view of the toleration of slavery in the New Testament writings. (Gal. iii, 28; Cor. iii, 17; 1 Cor. vii, 22; Phil. vi, 5–9). It was natural enough for Methodist ministers in the Southern States during the American Civil War to defend slavery in the plantations by Scriptural texts.

Slavery was finally abolished by this country in 1833. The efforts of Wilberforce were magnificent, but it can be argued that they were unscriptural. So, too, the statement by Gregory XVI in 1839 that slavery was unchristian entailed a condemnation of the precept and practice of very many Popes who had gone before him. The truth is not so much that slavery was formerly unchristian as that it was out of date. Slavery, as the main foundation of social economy, faded from Europe after the anarchic eighth century. But it was not the pleading of Christian Churchmen or the anathemas of Roman Pontiffs that turned slave into serf. No such appeals or condemnation can be traced. Classical slavery was inordinately wasteful, and we need not look further than economic causes to discover the reason for the transition to feudalism.

When feudalism had outlived its usefulness, capitalism needed neither slaves nor serfs except in outlying areas. That individual Christians were painfully conscious of new evils, arising out of the Industrial Revolution, is unquestionable; but although Wilberforce condemned slavery he opposed the rise of Trade Unions.

THE RECORD OF HUMANISM

Throughout the nineteenth century those individual Christians who, to their great credit, agitated for the reform of factory laws and the amelioration of the plight of the

poor, received scant encouragement from official spokes-
men. The first moves which culminated in the twentieth
century in the concept of social security and the Welfare
State were made by such agnostics as Jeremy Bentham,
Robert Owen and John Stuart Mill.

The emancipation of women owed little or nothing to a
religious impulse. It is impossible to isolate a single cause,
but it seems significant that the spread of education, and
the advances in science and technology, were followed by a
widening of the area of concern for suffering. It is not to
denigrate the work of medical missionaries in Africa and
elsewhere to point out that they were in fact, if not in intention, the agents of the old colonial order—and that is how
the newly independent countries now seem to regard
them. The original task of saving souls has yielded priority
to the task of saving lives, and the most effective instruments today are the secular agencies of the United Nations
—ie the World Health Organization, and the Food and
Agricultural Organization.

It is difficult for anyone who has been brought up in the
Western tradition to regard Christianity as objectively as,
say, a Jew, a Moslem or a Buddhist. Yet how is it possible,
when we look back on the long record of the Churches to
contend that idealism and social progress owe their very
existence to Christianity, and that disbelief must ultimately
bring a relapse into barbarism and inhumanity? The argument still persists and the following is typical:

'The Church has been in existence for nearly two thousand years. It is not to be denied that its ministers have
often blundered and often sinned. But it has retained its
fundamental doctrine and its historic character. Its claims
have been justified not only by the deaths of martyrs and
the lives of the saints and by the inspiration that it has
given craftsmen, artists and poets, but even more by the
happiness and solace that it has afforded to countless millions of the simple. To the Catholic Church we owe all that
is seemly and just in our Western civilization.' (*Religion in*

the England of Tomorrow Sidney Dark)

Such a picture does not correspond to any historical reality. There is no need, of course, to dwell unfairly on the historical side, but although today we can no longer echo Voltaire's famous outburst, *Ecrasez l'infame*, there were many centuries when it would have been justified.

The ideal of loving humanity and pitying the weak and suffering is not exclusively Christian. When we inquire what difference Christianity made we must surely turn to those features that were absent from other religions and philosophies and which, for that reason, may be presumed to be the marks of a special divine favour. We then see that among the specific Christian virtues were a spirit of intolerance and persecution, and a hostility towards secular knowledge that were both alien to paganism. So far from giving us 'all that is seemly and just in our Western civilization', the rise of Christianity was accompanied by many of those detestable things with which we have lately become familiar again—forgery as a tool of propaganda, torture as an instrument of policy, mass-killings, forced conversions, oppression of minorities, the burning of books and organized anti-Semitism.

If these are said to be due to merely human frailty, then we may again agree. What we fail to find in the record of the Church is something so superhuman that its presence can be explained only by a supernatural cause. Instead of ending 'the martyrdom of man', the totalitarian version of Christianity prolonged it by struggling against the emancipation of the serfs even while its theologians defended an abstract justice, or by ignoring the brutalities of the Industrial Revolution on the Lutheran principle that the concern of the Church must be exclusively with men's souls.

In the great crises of the modern world the respective Churches aligned themselves on a purely national basis, German Churches supporting Germany, English and American Churches supporting Britain and America, as slavishly as the Shinto sect supported Japan. The Vatican, the sole international Church, quite obviously refused to commit itself until it was certain which side would win. Surely something better than this might have been expected from an institution which claims to be the mouthpiece of God.

TWELVE

VARIETIES OF HUMANISM

HUMANISM, in contemporary usage, is a generic term, a family of ideas issuing from a common tradition that antedates Christianity and had its origin in ancient China and Greece. As an organized movement it was sufficiently advanced in 1952 for the many different societies in all parts of the world to meet in Amsterdam and form the International Humanist and Ethical Union under the aegis of Sir Julian Huxley.

The various groups wore different labels, partly owing to their respective historical origins—Secularists, Ethical Humanists, Scientific Humanists and Rationalists. The impulse which brought them together is paralleled by the ecumenical spirit which underlies the attempt of the Churches to find common ground.

It cannot be said that they merely wished to close their ranks in face of a common enemy. Their ranks were not divided on points of doctrine. There was nothing corresponding to a creed, nor did they present a single, coherent philosophical system. What united them was a common purpose and set of values. They were rationalist, in the sense that they put their trust in reason as a means of discovering truth and of settling disputes. They accept the discipline of using reason to explore the world—submitting all judgements of fact to the test of evidence—as advocated by T. H. Huxley, when he coined the term 'agnostic', and as it is used in the normal course of scientific inquiry.

Kant had led the way by proving that reason could discover nothing about the dogmas of religion. But he held that for practical purposes of morality the existence of God and the immortality of the soul must be postulated. And this, of course, was precisely what the Victorian Rationalists objected to. Some of them, therefore, seemed to be left with the 'Unknowable' on their hands. Reality seemed to be wider than experience, but they preferred to keep silent rather than to guess about those regions into which the scientist had not yet succeeded in penetrating. Huxley wrote:

'When I reached intellectual maturity and began to ask myself whether I was an Atheist, a Theist or a Pantheist; a Materialist or an Idealist; a Christian or a Freethinker; I found that the more I learned and reflected, the less ready was the answer, until, at last, I came to the conclusion that I had neither art nor part with any of these denominations, except the last. The one thing which most of these good people were agreed upon was the one thing in which I differed from them. They were quite sure that they had attained a certain "gnosis'—had, more or less successfully, solved the problem of existence; while I was sure I had not, and had a pretty strong conviction that the problem was insoluble. So I took thought, and invented what I conceived to be the appropriate title of "Agnostic". It came into my head as suggestively antithetic to the "Gnostic" of Church history, who professed to know so much about the very things of which I was ignorant.

'Agnosticism, in fact, is not a creed, but a method, the essence of which lies in the rigorous application of a single principle. Positively, the principle may be expressed: In matters of the intellect, follow your reason as far as it will take you, without regard to any other consideration. And negatively: In matters of the intellect do not pretend that conclusions are certain which are not demonstrated or demonstrable. That I take to be the agnostic faith, which if a man keeps whole and undefiled, he shall not be ashamed to look the universe in the face, whatever the future may have in store for him.' (*Science and the Christian Tradition*)

There is nothing essentially new in this principle itself. It is part of the technique of scientific investigation. An

hypothesis is accepted or rejected—in either case only pro-
visionally—after being tested. The first distinguishing
characteristic of scientific thinking, to quote Dewey is 'facing
the facts—inquiry, minute and extensive scrutinizing, observation'. This requires an attitude of mind utterly incom-
patible with blind trust in revelation:

'The experimental attitude substitutes detailed analysis
for wholesale assertions, specific inquiries for temperamen-
tal convictions, small facts for opinions whose size is in
precise ratio to their vagueness.'

Agnosticism, then, as Huxley conceived it, was not
merely concerned with the existence of God, not a soft
alternative to atheism. It was an attempt to lay the foundations of a general scientific outlook and to turn man's
attention from unanswerable questions.

How far this can succeed is partly a psychological problem.

CONSEQUENCES OF AGNOSTICISM

Neither Mill nor Huxley—and certainly not Karl Pear-
son—were mechanical materialists. Neither were they
atheists of the type of Marx and Engels. It was not the
cosmos of science, but the religious framework, that was
undermined by subsequent developments.

How completely it was undermined is brilliantly illustrated by Walter Lippman, in his *Preface to Morals*. He
compares the story of the Fall and Redemption to a play
which the world has been watching for centuries:

'Into this marvellous story the whole of human history
and of human knowledge could be fitted, and only in
accordance with it could they be understood. This was the
key to existence, the answer to doubt, the solace for pain
and the guarantee of happiness. But to many who were in
the audience it is now evident that they have seen a play, a
magnificent play, one of the most sublime ever created by
the human imagination, but nevertheless a play, and not a
literal account of human destiny. They know it was a play.

They have lingered long enough to see the scene-shifters at work. The painted drop is half rolled up; some of the turrets of the celestial city can still be seen, part of the choir of angels. But behind them, plainly visible, are the struts and gears which held in place what under a gentler light looked like boundaries of the universe. They are only human fears and human hopes, and bits of antique science and half-forgotten history, and symbols here and there of experiences through which some in each generation pass.'

He continues, more pensively, to describe the position of those for whom the old beliefs have vanished: 'Among those who no longer believe in the religion of their fathers, some are proudly defiant, and many are indifferent. But there are also a few, perhaps an increasing number, who feel that there is a vacancy in their lives.' They cannot organize their lives on the basis of a scientific dogma, Lippmann points out, because there is no such dogma available. The scientific attitude is *necessarily* undogmatic— which does not mean that individual scientists are never guilty of making dogmatic statements.

The nineteenth century Rationalists were limited by the knowledge and the terminology then available. Twentieth-century Rationalists stand on the shoulders of the pioneers of the movement. They have reaped the harvest of a subsequent revolution in thought, due to the extraordinarily rapid advance of psychology and physics. But they certainly do not regard their position as being weakened by the fact that science has not stood still. Why should they, indeed? The object of Rationalism is to speed the development of science and use the new knowledge to lessen the material miseries of man.

The statement sometimes made that 'the Uniformity of Nature' is among the discarded doctrines of science shows a misunderstanding of the philosophical speculations of those physicists who have toyed wth the idea that Nature itself may be irrational. If that were literally the case there could be no science; there could be no miracles, either; no meaning in saying that Christianity is concerned with historical happenings, and no human responsibility or divine retribution.

To pursue this question would take us into a metaphysical discussion of great complexity. It is sufficient, perhaps, to recall Bertrand Russell's dry comment that we are at least able to construct nautical almanacs that work, and that what is as important for science as the Uniformity of Nature is the fortunate fact that its laws are simple enough for us to understand.

MAN'S PLACE IN NATURE

Darwin knew nothing about genetics. That is a new branch of biology that has sprung up since his day. But even apart from genetics, it would be very surprising if a theory worked out ninety years ago needed no revision. No modern biologist has any doubt about the fact of evolution itself; and it was not because of a clash of evidence, but because man was inserted into the scientific picture, that evolution aroused such a theological storm.

We must take care not to be confused by irrelevant details. The early Rationalists placed man in the scientific scheme and therefore concluded that the sacred writings which purported to explain man's origin were merely human documents. This led them to deny the doctrines of Special Creation and Special Revelation. What 'discovery' has since been made that demands the slightest retreat from such a position? We have yet to be told.

The American Pragmatist, John Dewey, has done as much as any man to show the philosophical significance of Darwin's achievement, and his *Infuence of Darwin on Philosophy* should be read in this connection. Again, as Lancelot L. Whyte states in *The Next Development in Man*:

'To Kepler it was enough that God linked man to nature; to Bruno, his contemporary, it was not. For him, as for many thinkers, from Aristotle and Lucretius to Darwin,

Marx and Freud, the integrity of thought required that man must be understood as a part of nature.'

This is what the traditional theologian must deny and what the scientist must affirm. Sir Charles Sherrington, whose researches into the nervous system won for him a pre-eminent place, could not be charged with 'wallowing in discredited science'. In *Mind and Nature* he wrote:

'Evolution speaks to us in the same breath of body and of mind. Our bodily life carries with it its own evidence that its origin is terrestrial. Its chemical elements are among those commonest on our planet. Its whole is redolent of Earth where it was dug. Even likewise with finite mind. Its ways affirm it to be so. Our stock is the vertebrate stock; our body is the vertebrate body; our mind is the vertebrate mind. If the vertebrates be the product of the planet, our mind is a product of the planet.... Our mind is part and parcel of terrestrial nature, in which it is immersed and there and only there can it meet with requitals and fulfilments.'

What possible justification, then, is there for continuing to say—or, what is worse, to hint—that in the last sixty years science has undermined the conclusion that the early Rationalists drew from the Theory of Evolution—namely, that man is one with the earth and the rest of Nature. Rationalism, however, did more than deny the supernatural itself, as indeed it must always do if no frontiers are to be set to scientific investigation.

THE FLIGHT FROM REASON

'Faith in the Supernatural is a desperate wager made by man at the lowest ebb of his fortunes; it is as far as possible from being the source of that normal vitality which subsequently, if his fortunes mend, he may gradually recover.'

In this oft-quoted passage from Santayana, faith is not regarded as a good but a bad thing. More recently, Professor Sidney Hook has deplored the resurgence in some quarters of 'blind faith in the supernatural':

'The new failure of nerve in Western civilization at bottom betrays the same flight from responsibility, both on the plane of action and on the plane of belief, that drove the ancient world into the shelters of pagan and Christian supernaturalism.' (*Partisan Review* January 1949)

He opposed Rationalism (or 'Naturalism') to this recrudescence of superstition.

'The philosophy of Naturalism, which wholeheartedly accepts scientific methods as the only reliable way of reaching truths about man, society, and nature, does not decree what may or may not exist. It does not rule out on *a priori* grounds the existence of supernatural entities and forces. The existence of God, immortality, disembodied souls or spirits, cosmic purpose or design, as these have customarily been interpreted by the great institutional religions, are denied by naturalists for the same generic reasons that they deny the existence of fairies, elves, leprechauns and an invisible satellite revolving between the earth and moon. There is no plausible evidence to warrant belief in them or to justify a probable inference on the basis of partial evidence.' (*Ibid*)

The demand for evidence to support a belief is chiefly responsible for the historic cleavage between Reason and Revelation, or between Science and Religion. When Rationalists speak of 'the supremacy of reason' in matters of belief they do not mean the supremacy of deduction—which the phrase would have meant in the seventeenth century—but trust in evidence rather than in unsupported intuition or supposed revelation.

'It is wrong, always, everywhere, and for anyone, to believe anything upon insufficient evidence,' wrote W. K. Clifford (1845–79). And Huxley never tired of emphasizing the point: 'Scepticism is the highest of duties, and blind faith the one unpardonable sin.'

Such language may seem somewhat extravagant. It disturbed William James, and he invented an alternative which tampered with the idea of Truth by allowing its adherents to believe in anything that was found useful in practice—anything that 'works'. To the early Rationalists this seemed a very dangerous doctrine. Their attitude is summed up by Lord Annan as follows:

'Let us never forget the moral and intellectual work of the Victorian Rationalists. We should remember that they were opposing the bigotry and uncritical prejudice of their times. To all criticisms they would have replied that we must always form our beliefs on the best evidence available and that merely to believe what we want to believe and to appeal to the 'heart' or to 'intuition' is to give in to a temptation and acquire a frame of mind which may be very dangerous when applied, say, to politics. (*Strands of Unbelief* BBC Talk)

Against this we can set the dismay of T. S. Eliot:

'The world is trying the experiment of attempting to form a civilized but non-Christian mentality. The experiment will fail; but we must be very patient in awaiting its collapse; meanwhile redeeming the time so that the Faith may be preserved alive in the dark ages before us; to renew and rebuild civilization and save the world from suicide.'

What seemed in the last century an unhappy experiment made by a few intellectuals has now become a world-phenomenon. The disasters that have overtaken us and those that still seem to threaten the world are blamed on irreligion, just as in Nero's day the fire of Rome was blamed on 'atheists' and 'enemies of mankind', as the Christians were then, somewhat ironically, called.

It would be fairer to blame our troubles on using reason too little than too much. The appeal to the sword, and even the stake, has been made often enough in the name of religion. But when have intolerance and massacre been defended by Rationalists? It is important to remember in this connection that a Rationalist is not merely a man who rejects the religious account of the universe. He is a man who dislikes interfering with anyone's beliefs, who holds that people should be encouraged to think for themselves.

To become a Rationalist it is not enough to give up a set of irrational beliefs; it is necessary to stop behaving irrationally. Dr K. R. Popper writes:

'I am a rationalist because I see in the attitude of reasonableness the only alternative to violence. When two men disagree, they do so either because their opinions differ, or because their interests differ, or both.... To reach a decision may be a necessity. How can such a decision be reached? A rationalist, as I use the word, is a man who attempts to reach decisions by argument, and, perhaps, in certain cases, by compromise, rather than by violence.... It will be realized that what I call the attitude of reasonableness or the rationalist attitude is an attitude which presupposes a certain amount of intellectual humility. It is an attitude which perhaps only those can take up who are aware of the fact that they are sometimes in the wrong, and who do not habitually forget their mistakes....' (*The Hibbert Journal* January 1948)

EVOLUTIONARY HUMANISM

The moral values without which a merely scientific outlook would be as dangerous as blind led many people to prefer to call themselves scientific or ethical Humanists. Some, like Sir Julian Huxley, preached 'Religion without Revelation'; others, like Margaret Knight, saw Humanism as 'Morality without Religion'. Whether or not Humanism is a religion is a question of how the word 'religion' is used, and whether it is felt that a 'secular religion' is a useful or confusing mode of speech. For Sir Julian Huxley Scientific Humanism can best be described as a religion for modern man—for man, in Bonhoeffer's phrase, who has 'come of age'. He bases it firmly on the concept of evolution:

'The most significant contribution of science in this vital field is the discovery of man's position and role in evolution.... Man is that part of reality in which and through which the cosmic process has become conscious and has begun to comprehend itself. His supreme task is to increase that conscious comprehension and to apply it as fully as possible to guide the course of events. In other words, his role is to discover his destiny as agent of the evolutionary process, in order to fulfil it more adequately.' (*Religion without Revelation* p 236)

Evolutionary Humanism has a certain affinity with the Emergent Evolution (Alexander) and Creative Evolution (Bergson) philosophies which attracted attention fifty years ago, though they have since somewhat fallen out of favour. Samuel Alexander constructed a metaphysical system according to which the universe has evolved from bare space-time. At each successive stage of development new qualities 'emerged' which could not be deduced from the most complete knowledge of the previous level. The final quality, the goal to which the whole cosmic process was tending, is 'deity'.

The theory of the 'unborn God' was novel, and was, of course, teleological in that it postulated a Final Cause. To the question, 'What is the purpose of it all?' Alexander would reply that the purpose is the emergence of the quality of deity, intimations of which are our human strivings for moral goodness and heightened sensibility.

A Christian variant of Evolutionary Humanism is provided by the Jesuit scientist Teilhard de Chardin. His book *The Phenomenon of Man* was condemned by the ecclesiastical authorities and he was forbidden to publish further speculations in his lifetime. After his death, however, he became the object of a cult among some of his co-religionists, though others regarded his ideas—with some justification—as heretical.

The fact that Huxley wrote an introduction to *The Phenomenon of Man*, praising it with some qualifications, was hardly reassuring to the orthodox. In a devastating review of the English translation in *Mind* (January 1961) Sir Peter Medawar dismissed it as 'philosophy fiction'.

Briefly, Teilhard set out to establish that evolution had a direction, namely towards increasing 'cerebralization'.

The emergence of higher consciousness in the primates he called 'noogenesis', and the new level thus created, the 'noosphere'. This process culminates in the 'Omega-point', a kind of collective super-consciousness which, as far as one can gather from the obscure language, is awareness of, or union with, the Divine consciousness.

There is a certain likeness to strands in both eastern and western mysticism in the idea of the soul attaining a state of super-consciousness in which the hard contour of the individual ego dissolves. By trying to reconcile this mystical theory with evolution and theology Teilhard had to imply that every soul would be ultimately redeemed. There was no room for hell in this optimistic fantasy.

Huxley could not follow Teilhard 'all the way in his gallant attempts to reconcile the supernatural elements in Christianity with the facts and implications of evolution'. In more sober language Huxley described the cultural advance of mankind as 'psycho-social evolution'. He contended that whereas biological evolution is outside the control of the species concerned, psycho-social evolution brought to man an understanding of the laws of nature and consequently gave human beings an opportunity, denied to other animals, of guiding the course of future development.

'This brings me back to where I started—the idea of religion as an organ of destiny. It is clear ... that twentieth-century man needs a new organ for dealing with destiny, a new system of beliefs and attitudes adapted to the situation in which he and his societies now have to exist, and thus an organ for the better orientation of the human species as a whole—in other words, a new religion. Like all other new religions and indeed all other new movements or ideas, it will at the outset be expressed and spread by a small minority; but it will in due course of time tend to become universal, not only potentially and in theory, but actually and in practice.' (*Op cit* p 235)

THE NEW MORALITY

It is difficult to see how anyone can doubt that scientific knowledge has given us the power to relieve the frustrations, end much of the disease and raise the material standard of living in all parts of the world. The only chance that the under-nourished millions in Asia, for example, have of averting periodical famines and plagues is in the application of scientific knowledge to the prevention of malaria and similar scourges, to the extermination of locusts and other pests, to improved agricultural methods and to control of the birth-rate. To bring these benefits to ignorant and superstitious millions, thereby forcing a rise in their level of education, is the aim of all humanists, no matter what political differences they may have. At present they lack neither the will nor the technique, but the authority; and those who continually harp on man's sinfulness and the impossibility of improving his lot are placing needless obstacles in the way.

J. D. Bernal very clearly expresses the impatience that the Humanist feels at the obstructionist attitude to the employment of technical knowledge, which is, ironically enough, justified by an appeal to a 'higher' ethic:

'It has seemed to many in the last few years a sad paradox that while man's powers of understanding have everywhere increased, we should find ourselves in a state of want, dissatisfaction and justified apprehension which has not been felt, at least by the upper classes of society, for over a hundred years. To shallow minds which can see only one thing at a time, science is made to be the single cause of our troubles, and it is asserted that man's moral nature is not competent to deal with the vast powers which his intellect has put at his command. They foresee doom, and demand, without either considering it or really expecting it to happen, that we abandon our knowledge and relapse into a pious and mystical ignorance. The alternative to this attitude comes from the realization that we are at this present moment of time at a particularly critical stage of transformation that began some hundreds of years back and may go on for some scores of years into the future.'

The objection that since the secular moralist has no basis for absolute values there can be no rational foundation for his admittedly high ideals has been answered in several ways. In *The Rational Good* L. T. Hobhouse argued that reason is essentially a striving for harmony:

'It is the impulse to develop harmony, on the one hand by extending the control of mind over the conditions of its life, on the other hand by establishing unity of aim within the world of consciousness itself. The measure of harmony so achieved at any given stage is not complete, and its rules accordingly are not necessarily final. But they are to be modified only in the interests of some fuller harmony to which such a change will demonstrably lead.'

Barbara Wootton draws attention to the fact that for every organism there exists a condition of full normal development. The body strives to adjust itself to changes of temperature, it operates to heal a wound, and so on. Self-maintenance, reproduction and physical development are goals the organism pursues without conscious intervention. Similarly when the mind is disturbed, for example by shock or stress, it seeks to redress the lost balance. Unaided, neither the body nor mind may be able to cure themselves; but if intelligence takes over and uses rational knowledge, physical well-being and mental health may be restored. Thus we have a built-in goal of physical and mental health. 'It is as though in the one case (of unconscious processes) Nature had supplied us with a self-maintaining and self-repairing outfit; in the other case she has given us the tools (and exceptionally delicate and complex ones at that) and left us to finish the job.' (*Testament for Social Science* p 142)

She continues: 'A system of moral values, therefore, which identifies the physical and mental self-maintenance, development and reproduction of its members, demands, on the mental side, both that the individual organism should consciously seek that good for itself, and that this organism should live in a good society, correspondingly defined as one which does everything possible to promote this good for all its members. And this in turn, since a society is only a group of individuals acting co-operatively and not an entity over and above them, means that every individual must contribute by his own co-operative action to the making of such a good society.'

Humanists may belong to different political parties and different philosophical schools—as indeed do Christians— but it is clear that they are united in their fundamental values. They make no claim to a formula that will remove the evils of the world at a stroke. They believe that although some causes of unhappiness are beyond control, many of the causes of misery can be eliminated by the use of human reason—which, in practice means the unrestricted application of science. The anti-humanist downgrades science at every opportunity. The belief that man can save himself by the use of purely human resources is denounced as the modern equivalent of the Serpent's lie: 'Ye shall not surely die ... ye shall be as God, knowing good and evil.'

To the question, What is the purpose of life? Humanists reply that the purpose of our lives is the meaning we ourselves give them by choosing a goal to pursue. There is no sense in asking whether the physical universe has a purpose. Only a self-conscious individual can have a purpose.

A HUMANIST MANIFESTO

The goals agreed upon by Humanists are summarized in the manifesto of the first congress of the International Humanist and Ethical Union at Amsterdam in 1952. The fundamentals of modern Humanism were tentatively defined as follows:

1. *It is democratic.* It aims at the fullest possible development of every human being. It holds that this is a matter

of right. The democratic principle can be applied to all human relationships and is not restricted to methods of government.

2. *It seeks to use science creatively, not destructively.* It advocates a world-wide application of scientific method to problems of human welfare. Humanists believe that the tremendous problems with which mankind is faced in this age of transition can be solved. Science gives the means but science itself does not propose ends.

3. *Humanism is ethical. It affirms the dignity of man and the right of the individual to the greatest possible freedom of development compatible with the rights of others.* There is a danger that in seeking to utilize scientific knowledge in a complex society individual freedom may be threatened by the very impersonal machine that has been created to save it. Ethical humanism, therefore, rejects totalitarian attempts to perfect the machine in order to obtain immediate gains at the cost of human values.

4. *It insists that personal liberty is an end that must be combined with social responsibility in order that it shall not be sacrificed to the improvement of material conditions.* Without intellectual liberty, fundamental research, on which progress must in the long run depend, would not be possible. Humanism ventures to build a world on the free person responsible to society. On behalf of individual freedom Humanism is undogmatic, imposing no creed upon its adherents. It is thus committed to education free from indoctrination.

5. *It is a way of life, aiming at the maximum possible fulfilment, through the cultivation of ethical and creative living.* It can be a way of life for everyone everywhere if the individual is capable of the responses required by the changing social order. The primary task of Humanism today is to make men aware in the simplest terms of what it can mean to them and what it commits them to. By utilizing in this context and for purposes of peace the new power which science has given us, Humanists have

confidence that the present crisis can be surmounted. Liberated from fear the energies of man will be available for a self-realization to which it is impossible to foresee the limit.'

Obviously there is much in the above that Christians would approve, though even the most radical Christian cannot agree with the assumption that we must rely *solely* on our human resources. What is misleadingly called the 'God is dead' movement is mainly concerned with the use of the *word* 'God'. It is more a question of semantics than of theology. Similarly, it is hardly possible to regard a man as a Christian who does not believe in some form of survival after death.

The more traditional Christians emphasize the other-worldly aspect of religion. This life is seen not as an end in itself but as a preparation for eternity. Consequently they are much less concerned than Humanists about what happens in this brief prelude to our final destination, except in so far as it decides our ultimate destiny.

Neo-Calvinism washes its hands of the world. Faith and Reason, this world and the next, stand opposed to each other in violent contradiction. We cannot understand it by intellect because there is a warp running through the entire cosmos and infecting our minds. 'The world is a cracked mirror,' said Brunner; and man is totally depraved.

The destruction of false beliefs is a necessary preliminary to the discovery of truth. Not, indeed, that we can ever hope to find absolute, unchanging truths. 'To the scientific mind no theory is ever final or absolute,' as Professor Mac-Murray points out. The cross-purposes at which the Humanist and the Christian often find themselves in discussion is largely due to the inability of the theologically-trained mind to be content with probability. It is the mistake, too, of those, who, like William James, speak as though there were only two alternatives: blind belief or total scepticism.

THE ABUSE OF SCIENCE

The Humanist is not blind to the dangers of the misuse of knowledge, nor is he given to jejune optimism. Before either of the two world wars that have so tragically revealed the destructive use of science, yoked to irrationalism, Dewey wrote:

'Physical science has, for the time being, far outrun psychical. We have mastered the physical mechanism sufficiently to turn out possible goods; we have not gained a knowledge of the conditions through which possible values become actual in life, and so we are still at the mercy of habit, of haphazard, and hence of force.... With tremendous increase in our control of nature, in our ability to utilize nature for human use and satisfaction, we find the actual realization of ends, the enjoyment of values, growing unassured and precarious. At times it seems as though we were caught in a contradiction; the more we multiply means the less certain and general is the use we are able to make of them. No wonder a Carlyle or a Ruskin puts our whole industrial civilization under a ban, while a Tolstoy proclaims a return to the desert. But the only way to see the situation steadily and see it whole is to keep in mind that the entire problem is one of the development of science and its application to life.' (*The Influence of Darwin on Philosophy*)

Apart from obvious enemies, organized science itself—like the Churches and every human institution—tends to develop a conservatism as it becomes more and more organized. It is necessary for the Humanist to be also on his guard against any ossification of theory into dogma, as Professor C. D. Darlington, among others, has repeatedly insisted.

In *The Conflict of Science and Society*, Professor Darlington points out that fundamental scientific discoveries 'always entail the destruction or disintegration of old knowledge before the new can be created. And it is this destruction, or fear of it, which arouses the opposition of the well-

trained and well-established scientist as well as of those outside science whose beliefs the new ideas threaten to disintegrate.'

The danger that a particular world-outlook may become
frozen into a dogma would still remain even in a secularized State. If theology were merely replaced by metaphysics
we might have a false Humanism hostile to innovations
and even persecuting those who challenged its creed. In
effect this would be another religion, though it would repudiate the name. It would protect science, but without
freedom of expression there could be no fundamental
advance. We must be suspicious, however, of those who lay
too much stress on these dangers. Freedom of inquiry belongs to the scientific tradition itself; it is one of those
'Western values' that certainly owes nothing to Christianity.

THE HUMANIST ALTERNATIVE

The scientific tradition emerged in Europe in the sixteenth century, and gradually it eroded the foundations of
the religious tradition. Looking back, it seems to an increasingly large number of people who have been trained to
approach problems scientifically, that the religious beliefs
which were for so long regarded as divinely revealed are no
longer credible. Apart from what seems manifest mythology, the deep contradiction running through the entire
Christian scheme is now exposed. The basic contradiction
was due to the impossible fusion of Jewish and Greek conceptions of God. Yahweh was mingled with Plato's De-
miurge and Aristotle's Unmoved Mover, and for nearly two
thousand years theologians have sought in vain to reconcile
these irreconcilables. As Professor Lovejoy put it:

'Perhaps the most extraordinary triumph of self-contradiction, among many such triumphs in the history of
human thought, was the fusion of this conception of a self-
absorbed, self-contained Perfection—of the Eternal intro-
vert who is the God of Aristotle—at one with the Jewish
conception of a temporal creator and busy interposing

Power making for righteousness through the hurly-burly of history, and with primitive Christianity's conception of a God whose essence is forthgoing love and who shares in all the griefs of his creatures. When applied to the notion of creation—which is the aspect of this syncretism which here concerns us—the doctrine of the self-sufficiency of deity implied that from the divine—that is from the final absolute—point of view, a created world is a groundless superfluity.' (*The Great Chain of Being*)

There was no need for God to create the world, said Augustine; he did so because he chose to do so. But if God arbitrarily chose to create this sort of world, is he not responsible for its imperfections? The tortuous debates engendered by this problem have not yet died down. Those who contended that creation resulted from divine reason had to show that it was reasonable that evil should exist. Even Aquinas was driven to state that 'a universe in which there was no evil would not be so good as the actual universe'.

In the eighteenth century there was a wave of Protestant optimism expressed by such comforting doctrines as 'Whatever is, is right', and this is 'the best of possible worlds'. The contradictions remained, however, and in our time the breakdown of Christian rationalism is reflected by a return to ancient pessimism. The grand design of Nature, at which Pope and Young and Addison marvelled has become 'a cracked mirror'. And since reason has failed 'to justify the ways of God to man' we are enjoined to turn to blind faith.

There is, however, another alternative. If reason has been unable to resolve the inconsistencies of Christianity, and if the amassing of knowledge has intensified them, what is the point of struggling to maintain incompatibles? Let us turn frankly to the scientific and Humanist tradition and endeavour to encourage, not insincerities, but an attitude of mind that is ever responsive to new ideas, opposed to all orthodoxies, prepared to submit every problem to the test of reasoned discussion and evidence.

This does not mean that we disregard non-intellectual elements; but knowledge, in the sense in which we have been using the word, is what is public and communicable. Obviously a great part of our awareness consists of private feelings; we *enjoy* the universe as well as attempt to understand and *describe* it, and this subjective enjoyment gives rise to the highest flights of the creative imagination and passes beyond the limits of language. It cannot therefore be brought within the rational system of knowledge. In the closing words of Wittgenstein's *Tractatus Logico-Philosophicus*: 'Of what we cannot speak we must keep silent.'

SELECTED BIBLIOGRAPHY

CHRISTIANITY: *Theological*

Altizer, T. J. J. *Radical Theology and the Death of God*, 1966
Barth, K. *Commentary on Romans*, 1918
   Church Dogmatics, 1936
Bonhoeffer, D. *Letters and Papers from Prison*, 1953
Braithwaite, R. B. *An Empiricist's view of the Nature of Religious Belief*, 1955
Bultmann, R. *Kerygma and Myth*, 1953
   Eschatology and History, 1957
Buren, P. van, *The Secular Meaning of the Gospel*, 1962
Croxall, T. H. *Kierkegaard Studies*, 1948
   Kierkegaard Commentary, 1956
Dibelius, M. *From Tradition to Gospel*, 1935
Flew, A. G. N., and MacIntyre, A. C. *New Essays in Philosophical Theology*, 1955
Hepburn, R. *Christianity and Paradox*, 1958
Kierkegaard, S. *Philosophical Fragments*, 1936
   Training in Christianity, 1941
   Either/Or, 1944
   The Concept of Dread, 1946
Lewis, C. S. *The Problem of Pain*, 1940
Mackintosh, H. R. *Types of Modern Theology*, 1937
Macquarrie, J. *The Scope of Demythologising*, 1960
   Studies in Christian Existentialism, 1965
Manson, T. W. *The Teaching of Jesus*, 1931
Mascall, E. L. *Christian Theology and Natural Science*, 1956
Newman, J. H. *Essay on the Development of Christian Doctrine*, 1845

Niebuhr, R. *The Nature and Destiny of Man*, 1951
Pascal's *Pensées.—Bilingual Edition*, 1950
Richardson, A. *Christian Apologetics*, 1947
Robinson, J. A. T. *Honest to God*, 1963
  with Edwards, D. L. *The Honest to God Debate*, 1963
Tillich, P. *Systematic Theology*, 1951
    Ultimate Concern, 1965
    The Shaking of the Foundations, 1949

CHRISTIANITY : *Biblical*

Bettenson, H. *Documents of the Christian Church*, 1963
Bultmann, R. *Jesus and the Word*, 1935
Burkitt, F. C. *The Earliest Sources for the Life of Jesus*, 1910
Burrows, M. *The Dead Sea Scrolls*, 1956
Conybeare, F. C. *The Historical Christ*, 1914
Couchoud, P. L. *The Creation of Christ*, 1924
Drews, A. *Witnesses to the Historicity of Jesus*
Dujardin, E. *The Ancient History of the God Jesus*, 1938
Dupont–Somer, A. *The Essene Writings*, 1959
Eisler, R. *The Enigma of the Fourth Gospel*, 1938
Frazer, J. G. *Folklore in the Old Testament* (abridged), 1923
Fritsch, C. T. *The Qumran Community, Its History and
    Scrolls*, 1956
Gardner Smith, P. *The Christ of the Gospels*, 1938
Goguel, M. *The Life of Jesus*, 1932
    Jesus of Nazareth: Myth or History? 1925
Guignebert, C. *Jesus*, 1935
Kenyon, F. C. *The Bible and Modern Scholarship*, 1948
Kirsopp Lake. *An Introduction to the Old Testament*, 1938
Loisy, A. *The Birth of the Christian Religion*, 1948
Richardson, A. *The Bible in the Age of Science*, 1961
Ogden, S. M. *Christ without Myth*, 1962
Schoeps, H. J. *Paul: The Theology of the Apostle in the
    light of Jewish Religious History*, 1961
Schweitzer, A. *The Quest of the Historical Jesus*, 1910

Smith, A. D. H. *Jesus not a myth*, 1942
Streeter, B. H. *The Four Gospels—A Study of Origins*, 1926

CHRISTIANITY: *Historical*

Bailey, D. S. *The Man–Woman Relation in Christian Thought*, 1959
Brandon, S. F. G. *The Fall of Jerusalem and the Christian Church*, 1951
Cohn, N. *The Pursuit of the Millennium*, 1957
Coulton, C. G. *Five Centuries of Religion*, 1923
Dodds, E. R. *Pagan and Christian in an Age of Anxiety*, 1965
Harnack, A. *Mission and Expansion of Christianity*, 1908
Lea, H. C. *History of Sacerdotal Celibacy*, 1907
MacIntyre, A. C. *Secularization and Moral Change*, 1967
McCabe, J. *The Testament of Christian Civilization*, 1946
Mascall, E. L. *The Secularization of Christianity*, 1965
Neill, S. *The Church and Christian Union*, 1968
Robertson, A. *The Origins of Christianity*, 1963
Robertson, J. M. *A Short History of Christianity*, 1902
Runciman, S. *A History of the Crusades*, (Two Vols) 1951–54
Schonfield, H. *The Passover Plot*, 1965
  Those Incredible Christians, 1968
Tawney, R. H. *Religion and the Rise of Capitalism*, 1926
Weber, M. *The Protestant Ethic and the Spirit of Capitalism*, 1930
  The Sociology of Religion, 1963
Wells, G. A. *The Jesus of the Early Christians*, 1971
Yadin, Yiguel. *The Message of the Scrolls*, 1957

CHRISTIANITY: *Roman Catholicism*

Abbott, W. M. *The Documents of Vatican II*
Aquinas, Thomas. *Summa Contra Gentiles*, 1955
  Summa Theologica, 1926

Blanshard, P. *Paul Blanshard on Vatican II*, 1967

Bull, G. *Vatican Politics*, 1966

Copleston, F. C. *Aquinas*, 1955

de Chardin, P. Teilhard. *The Phenomenon of Man*, 1959

Egner, G. *Birth Regulation and Catholic Belief*, 1966

Joyce, E. H. *Principles of Natural Theology*, 1923

Kung, Hans. *The Council Reform and Reunion*, 1961

Mercier, Cardinal. *A Manual of Modern Scholastic Philosophy*, 1921

Rickaby, J. *Moral Philosophy*, 1923

Salmon, G. *The Infallibility of the Church*, 1948

Zahn, G. C. *German Catholics and Hitler's Wars*, 1964

RELIGION: *General*

Argyle, M. *Religious Behaviour*, 1958

Barrett, W. *Irrational Man*, 1961

Cornford, F. M. *From Religion to Philosophy*, 1912

Frazer, J. G. *The Golden Bough* 3rd Ed, 1914

Freud, S. *The Future of an Illusion*, 1928
    Civilization and its Discontents, 1930

Hawkins, D. J. B. *The Essentials of Theism*, 1949

Harrison, Jane. *Themis*, 1903

Hooke, S. H. *Myth and Ritual*, 1933

Hume, David. *Dialogues concerning Natural Religion*, 1935

Huxley, A. *The Perennial Philosophy*, 1946

James, E. O. *The Cult of the Mother Goddess*, 1959
    The Ancient Gods, 1960

James, William. *Varieties of Religious Experience*, 1902

Murray, Gilbert. *Five Stages of Greek Religion*, 1935

Otto, R. *The Idea of the Holy*, 1923

Smith, Elliot G. *In the Beginning*, 1932

Smith, H. W. *Man and His Gods*, 1957

Smith, W. Robertson. *Religion of the Semites* 3rd Ed, 1927

Schmidt, W. *The Origin and Growth of Religion*, 1931

ETHICS

Breasted, J. H. *The Dawn of Conscience*, 1912
Broad, C. D. *Five Types of Ethical Theory*, 1930
   Ethics and the History of Philosophy, 1952
Edwards, P. *The Logic of Moral Discourse*, 1955
Hick, J. *Evil and the God of Love*, 1966
Hobbes, T. *Leviathan*, Ed by W. Molesworth, 1939
Kant, Immanuel. *The Critique of Pure Reason*, Trs by N. Kemp Smith, 1934
   The Groundwork of the Metaphysic of Morals, Trs with notes by H. J. Paton, 1948
Moore, G. E. *Principia Ethica*, 1903
Popper, Karl. *The Open Society and its Enemies*, 1945
Pritchard, H. A. *Moral Obligation*, 1949
Ramsey, I. T. *Christian Ethics and Contemporary Philosophy*, 1966
Robinson, R. *An Atheist's Values*, 1964
Ross, W. D. *The Foundation of Ethics*, 1939
Russell, Bertrand. *Human Society in Ethics and Politics*, 1954
Smith, P. Nowell. *Ethics*, 1954
Stevenson, C. L. *Ethics and Language*, 1943
Toulmin, S. E. *An Examination of the Place of Reason in Ethics*, 1950
Warnock, G. J. *Contemporary Moral Philosophy*, 1966
Warnock, M. *Ethics since 1900*, 1966
Wootton, Barbara. *Testament for Social Science*, 1950
Westermarck, E. *Ethical Relativity*, 1932

PHILOSOPHICAL

Ayer, A. J. *Language, Truth and Logic*, 2nd Ed, 1946
Blackham, H. J. *Six Existentialist Thinkers*, 1951
Eddington, A. *The Nature of the Physical World*, 1928
Einstein, A. *Out of My Later Years*, 1950
Farrer, A. *The Freedom of the Will*

Flew, A. G. N. *God and Philosophy,* 1966

Gellner, E. *Words and Things,* 1959.

Gilson, E. *History of Christian Philosophy in the Middle Ages,* 1955

Hutten, E. H. *The Origins of Science*

Kaufmann, W. *Critique of Religion and Philosophy,* 1958

Lovejoy, A. O. *The Great Chain of Being,* 1936

Ogden, C. K., and Richards, I. A. *The Meaning of Meaning,* 1923

Russell, Bertrand. *A History of Western Philosophy,* 1946

Ryle, G. *The Concept of Mind,* 1949

Sartre, J–P. *Being and Nothingness,* 1957

Schroedinger, E. *What is Life?* 1944
   My View of the World, 1964

Sherrington, C. *Man on His Nature,* 1939

Stace, W. T. *Mysticism and Philosophy,* 1960

Taylor, A. E., *Does God Exist?* 1945

Waismann, F. *How I See Philosophy,* 1968

Whitehead, A. N. *Science and the Modern World,* 1926
   Process and Reality, 1933

Whyte, L. L. *The Next Development in Man,* 1944

Wittgenstein, L. *Philosophical Investigation,* 1953

HUMANISM

Ayer, A. J. Ed. *The Humanist Outlook,* 1968

Bury, J. B. *A History of Freedom of Thought,* 1913

Blackham, H. J. *Humanism,* 1968

Cassirer, E. *An Essay on Man,* 1944

Frankel, C. *The Case for Modern Man,* 1957

Hawton, H. *The Humanist Revolution,* 1963

Huxley, Julian. *Religion without Revelation,* 1927
   Ed *The Humanist Frame,* 1961

Knight, Margaret. *A Humanist Anthology,* 1961

Lamont, C. *The Philosophy of Humanism,* 2nd Ed, 1965

Lecky, W. E. H. *A History of Rationalism in Europe,* 1865

Lippmann, W. *A Preface to Morals,* 1929

Mouat, Kit. *What Humanism is about,* 1963
Tribe, D. *A Hundred Years of Freethought,* 1968
Robertson, J. M. *A Short History of Freethought,* 1916
Sartre, J–P. *Existentialism and Humanism,* 1948
Stebbing, Susan. *Ideals and Illusions,* 1941

INDEX